Grandfather's House

Clive Doucet

Copyright © 2018, Clive Doucet

All rights reserved. No part of this book may be reproduced, stored in a retrieval system or transmitted in any form or by any means without the prior written permission from the publisher, or, in the case of photocopying or other reprographic copying, permission from Access Copyright, 1 Yonge Street, Suite 1900, Toronto, Ontario M5E 1E5.

Nimbus Publishing Limited
3660 Strawberry Hill Street, Halifax, NS, B3K 5A9
(902) 455-4286 nimbus.ca

Printed and bound in Canada
NB1434
Cover art: *Seaside, Cape Breton*. Painting by Andrea Doughtie, andreasart.doughtie.com
Design: Jenn Embree

Library and Archives Canada Cataloguing in Publication

Doucet, Clive, author
Grandfather's house : returning to Cape Breton / Clive Doucet.
ISBN 978-1-77108-710-0 (softcover)

1. Doucet, Clive—Family. 2. Doucette family. 3. Authors, Canadian (English)—20th century—Biography.
4. Grandfathers—Nova Scotia—Cape Breton Island—Biography.
5. Grand Étang (N.S.)—Biography. 6. Cape Breton Island (N.S.)—Biography. 7. Autobiographies. I. Title.

PS8557.O787Z46 2018   C813'.54   C2018-905827-7

Nimbus Publishing acknowledges the financial support for its publishing activities from the Government of Canada, the Canada Council for the Arts, and from the Province of Nova Scotia. We are pleased to work in partnership with the Province of Nova Scotia to develop and promote our creative industries for the benefit of all Nova Scotians.

Thinking of my parents, Katherine (Kay) Oliver (September 28, 1921–September 26, 2009) and Fernand (Fern) Doucet (May 28, 1923–December 29, 2009)

Contents

Preface 1
Introduction 3
1 Being a Grandfather 6
2 The Job Year 9
3 Rowing with Clea 13
4 Highland Trails 25
5 Interview at the Harbour 36
6 Netsuke and Fiddles 48
7 Great-Great-Grandparents 56
8 What Superpower Would You Choose? 66
9 Lost Landscapes and Safe Harbours 70
10 Fundraiser for Fort Mac—Tonight 81
11 Never an Issue to Our Happiness 88
12 Flora MacDonald and "The Gaelic Ship" 100
13 Myles from Nowhere 119
14 The Undertow 130
15 Wars and the Family Forest 134
16 The Nerf Wars 145
17 "Harry the Whale" and the GAMS Cooperative 148
18 In the Shadow of Évangéline 154
19 Goodbye Grandchildren 166
20 Russell Daigle, His Farm, and "The Bishop's Candlesticks" 168
21 The Kitchens of Grand Étang and "Moving Ice" 182
22 Burying Mother 196
23 Ronald Caplan, *Cape Breton Magazine*, *and "Philibert the Sheep"* .. 205
24 St. Maximin la Sainte-Baume 222
25 The World Acadian Congress, Barbara LeBlanc,
   and "The Scholarship" 228
26 Father DeCoste Goes to Heaven 250
27 On Hope 256
28 A Safe Harbour 259
   Epilogue 265

Preface

I am playing cards with my granddaughter Clea in a coffee shop. She is on crutches and taking a day off school. Clea is drinking a hot chocolate with lots of whipped cream, and I'm on my second large *caffe latte*. In spite of the crutches, it's a very pleasant grandfather/granddaughter afternoon. Clea beats me consistently at cards, being way faster on the draw than I am. She is pleased and I, never liking to lose at anything, complain that I'm getting bad cards.

In the comfort of the relationship, it's no different than the connection I had with my own grandfather. But in the details, it's a world apart. My grandfather never drank a coffee in his life. It was tea drinking in Cape Breton, and the idea of spending fifteen dollars on a couple of very expensive beverages and a couple of biscuits, he couldn't even imagine. Twenty dollars could get a horse shod.

There was no restaurant in the village. People entertained in the kitchen; that's where tea and biscuits came from. Both were very good and cost nothing but the promise of return hospitality. It was a different universe. My granddaughter cannot imagine clip-clopping down to the harbour in a buggy with her grandfather—everyone has cars. But for me, it was normal—that's how we travelled. Grandfather didn't know how to drive and had no car.

Today, children go to summer camps where they learn sports and skills. I learned no sports, no improving skills. I wasn't connected to the world with the internet or to home via mobile phone. We had one phone in the house and it rang very rarely. During the summer, I cannot recall a single phone call from my parents, who remained in Ottawa. Long-distance telephoning was regarded as too expensive.

In Grand Étang, the great outing was to drive down to the harbour and visit the Co-op with the sea and cliffs on the left, houses, barns, and fields on the right, the sky arcing above. It felt like the village was at the centre of the universe, not the edge. It was there as a young boy I conceived of the idea that one day, I might build my own house by the sea. I could not imagine when or where this might be.

It was an inchoate feeling that had no beginning or end, but no matter how far I was from Cape Breton, hidden away at the back of my mind was this feeling that one day I would be like my grandfather and live in a house by the sea, a feeling that to a small boy felt as eternal as the night sky.

Introduction

When I think of my two grandfathers today—one English and one French—I realize that I had no idea of who they really were beyond being a grandfather. My English grandfather, George Oliver, had been in the trenches for four years during the Great War. He was one of very few soldiers in his regiment who signed up in 1914 who survived until 1918. On the Acadian side, Grandfather Doucet was born the year Louis Riel was hung as a traitor for defending Metis rights. These events had seminal effects on each grandfather, but neither would register on my consciousness until long after they were both gone. As a child, there was just too much time, too many experiences separating us. Perhaps that's the attraction between grandparent and grandchild. Grandfather sits on one side of the buggy driving the mare with a casual flick of his wrist, and I am on the other. We are so close that our shoulders and hips touch. It is enough to simply be.

When I was spending summers at my Acadian grandfather's farm, he had already been a widow for several years; my grandmother, Marie Hache, died at seventy-two, not much older than I am now. There were just three of us in the old house: grandfather, Aunt Germaine, and myself, a boy. My aunt was a prickly character, rail thin, tense, headachy, and very, very bright. My father often said Germaine was the smartest of them all. She spoke French at machine-gun speed.

The words hurling out of her with great force, splattering around the kitchen, often had to do with the futility of life. Neither Grandfather nor I knew what would trigger Germaine's wrath, so we would escape to the barn and the fields, rarely venturing back to the house once the day had started.

It was an intimate time. I would wake around six o'clock to the sound of kindling crackling in the wood stove downstairs. Grandfather and I would eat breakfast quietly then go out to the barn to milk the cows by hand. The sun would be just coming up behind the mountains. It was very quiet in the barn. Just the sound of songbirds in the loft and the swishing of cows' tails. I remember how proud I was the first time I was able to fill an entire silver-sided bucket with milk.

We spent the summer days in each other's company from sun up to sun down, separating the cream from the milk for sale to the dairy, feeding the calves, splitting small wood for the stove at the start of each day. I followed along behind Grandfather doing as he did. In this way, I learned the rhythm of a small farm, the feel of the land, and as my parents hoped when they sent me from Ottawa for the summer, began to apprentice myself to the French language.

It must have occurred to me that my aunt was just lonely, but in such a vague way it hardly registered. Did I think Grandfather had concerns beyond the company of a noisy grandson? I don't think I did. Grandfathers were magical creatures, much like unicorns, and just as unicorns were always unicorns, grandfathers were always grandfathers. The idea that they had once been children themselves or had lived both moments of passionate disappointment and exhilarating triumph didn't seem possible. A child sees the world with limpid vision. Everything is in the foreground, very bright and clear.

After my grandmother died, Grandfather received a letter from a woman he had known as a boy. Her husband had passed away, and she wanted to know if "William" would like to share her house with her, which she found too large and lonely.

I couldn't imagine Grandfather accepting such an offer to leave the place where he and Grandmother had raised my father and all my uncles and aunts. When my father was a boy, there had been seventeen people in the house, and the barn was filled to bursting with cattle and fine horses, among them breeding stallions and powerful bulls. At the same time, Grandfather ran a sawmill with his oldest son. He was busy all the day long, running from sunrise to sunset. Now, he had one grown child left, one mare, one young colt, and eight cows, hardly anything at all.

In spite of his many skills, Grandfather never learned to read. Grandmother read all the letters that came to the house and kept the farm's accounts in good order. Now that she was gone, it was Aunt Germaine who read the letters, and when she read the letter from Grandfather's childhood friend she quietly burned it in the kitchen stove. She didn't think her father should be gallivanting off to live with someone else. No doubt I would have thought so too. Grandfathers were supposed to be settled in their own place and time. It was best he stay in the old house. But I didn't understand my grandfather, and my aunt was wrong to interfere.

Nor did I really understand what the most important thing about being a grandfather really is. It's not about having a house by the sea or a little farm. The only important thing about being a grandfather is that you adore your grandchildren and they adore you back...and that you tell them stories. *Grandfather's House* is not so much about a house but about my stories.

CHAPTER 1
Being a Grandfather

Aboriginal wisdom divides life into four stages. Infancy is for joy. Childhood is for learning. The adult years are for work. The elder years are for teaching. It makes sense to me, although it strikes me that there's considerable overlap. At three, six, and eight, my grandchildren certainly have a foot in both the joy and the learning camps.

At three, Évangéline is confidently in the joy camp. Certain that the purpose of life is to have her every need met. If she doesn't like the service, she tells you and demands adjustments. If there's no snow on the sidewalk and you're out with the sleigh, no problem. Pull it, Grandpa! At six and eight, Clea and Felix are busy in the learning stage; learning how to swim and skate and do their homework, but they also have a lot of time left for joy of all sorts. From the adventures of Harry Potter to the adventures of making sure that they get the first pancake in the morning, and more importantly, that someone else doesn't.

I find it quite comforting to hear Clea and Felix battling away over who gets the first pancake. It puts the ejection of Russia from the G8 into the kind of place that I think it should be. But to my surprise, in spite of my age, I'm not sure that I've quite reached the teaching stage yet. Perhaps I should be worrying about this, because I seem to be sliding backwards toward the earlier joy/learning stages of life.

One thing I've disovered from being a grandfather is that you learn as much from the children as they do from you. For example, Felix tells me that although it's not widely known, unicorns can change shape. That's why they are so hard to spot, which I am sure is correct. There is a magic to both unicorns and grandfathers.

There are little differences between a horse and a unicorn; without the horn you would never be able to tell a unicorn from a horse. Just like a grandfather can look exactly like a grandfather with grey hair and more years than he wants, but in fact, he's not a grandfather. He's a little boy, not much older than grandson Felix. At the same time that I was Felix's grandfather, I was also a child saying goodbye to my own parents during their final days. At that time, my father had what my mother described as a little memory problem. The rest of the world describes it as Alzheimer's.

My father had been a pretty good guitarist all his life, and during his last days, I discovered that even with a little memory problem he could still sing the songs that he had sung to us when we were children. So I took his guitar to his apartment in the hopes he might be tempted to play. He refused to, saying his fingers hurt when he played now. Not knowing what else to do, I started to play one of the tunes he used to play for us when we were small. He remembered the words and immediately sang along. At the same time I was singing to my father, I was singing the same songs to my grandchildren. There is a magic in that for which I am grateful.

I don't find myself drawn to teaching much. Perhaps it is because my adult years were mostly about teaching, not in a school but always trying to advance the idea that we needed to build cities in more sustainable ways. These days anything with the adjective sustainable attached to it has a certain currency, but I always found the idea of the sustainable city was little understood in practice.

Sustainability for most people is about polar bears sitting stranded on melting ice or maybe even a Cape Breton storm.

For me it was always about how we humans lived, not how polar bears did. I figured our best present to the polar bear was figuring out how our own species might live in a more sustainable way. In cities, for example, sustainable buildings should be no taller than a tall tree—about six storeys. In this way streets and dwellings can be shaded by trees in the summer and the buildings are small enough to blend into the landscape instead of hanging over it, creating wind tunnels and shadowed canyons. During my years as a city councillor in Ottawa, I would often give talks about these ideas in all kinds of places and situations.

In Ottawa, I would recall for people that the most intensively populated city in the world is Paris, a city of low-rise buildings, no more than six storeys. The most intensive communities in Ottawa are the older neighborhoods like the Glebe and Sandy Hill, which until recently had few high-rises. The least populous is Centretown, which is composed of streets of twenty-storey buildings that are used for ten hours a day, five days a week and the rest of the time just sit there being heated and cooled.

Fortunately, my grandchildren are not interested in learning about urban sustainability, and I am not inclined to try teaching them either. I'm inclined to sing. A favourite of Évangéline's is "Have you seen the muffin man, the muffin man, the muffin man? Have you seen the muffin man, who lives in Drury Lane," which she has decided needs better verses. So we have invented some: "Have you seen the librarian, the librarian, the librarian, who lives in the library." I like her new verses and change them up as she wishes. Then there's the "Harry the Whale" song, which we invented to sing about whales. No one has ever heard these songs except my grandchildren and no one is likely to, and that is the principle delight of being a grandfather—it's a complete world. *Grandfather's House* is about trying to share a little of that world for you and for my grandchildren, when I have become mythical like a unicorn.

CHAPTER 2

The Job Year

My parents died in 2009. In that same year, my wife, Patty, was diagnosed with a terrifying cancer. The same day she received the diagnosis, she lost her job. On top of all this, after four terms as a city councillor, expecting a comfortable run into retirement, I was instead caught in a vicious struggle with a group of developers who wanted to convert an old park in my ward into a mall.

It didn't seem possible, for there was nothing in the city quite like Lansdowne Park, cradled in a broad curve of the Rideau Canal. In winter, visitors skated by the park and in summer it was a mecca for cyclists, canoeists, and runners. The centrepiece of the old park was a nineteenth-century exhibition barn built when farming was king and dominated by a great silver dome that soared spectacularly over the whole park. The history of the park was the history of the city. It had hosted just about every major event that the city had ever celebrated, from the first Stanley Cup, to Ringling Brothers circuses, to the solemn mustering of troops for war.

In spite of Lansdowne's history and extraordinary location, this grand old place had fallen on hard times; big sections had been paved over by the city. There hadn't been a nickel invested in it for decades. Sensing the property's vulnerability, three of the city's most powerful land developers began to circle Lansdowne like vultures with roadkill in view. Forty acres a few kilometres from Parliament Hill was indeed a treasure.

By chance, the park was at the centre of the ward I represented on city council, and a very long battle began to try and save it. It would last years. It wasn't just about forty acres of greenspace. In the final analysis, Lansdowne was about who was running the city, the developers or the elected representatives. If the developers could convince council to privatize a public legacy, the gift of a group of farmers that dated back to 1868, they could do anything. I saw the destiny of the park as an axial moment in the city's history.

The cycle of family life and the destiny of the park consumed me. My mind was a very long way from Cape Breton. It took my mother's death to bring the island back into my thoughts.

The last time I saw my mother was a gorgeous September morning in 2009 with a gentle mist rising along the Ottawa River and the city's trees bursting with autumn colours, but the day didn't impress her. Mother was in full lamentation mode. Her mind had gone to the past, where it fixated on Gabarus Bay and a summer home she and Dad had rebuilt there. When they moved to Ottawa, Dad sold their summer home there without her consent, giving it away for nothing more than the cost of the materials he had put into fixing it up.

The house had been a vast but creaky old saltbox right on the bay. At night, you could hear the waves gently moving the beach stones as the surf rolled in. My parents had restored the house board by board from a crumbling wreck into a bright, warm place at the sea's edge. They had lived very happily there and entertained widely until Dad was appointed by the federal government to be the next chair of the Canadian Freshwater Fish Corporation in Ottawa.

We weren't alone in leaving the island for distant places. When Grandfather died, his home and farm were all sold for not much more than taxes. Like so many Atlantic families, the Doucets had dispersed across the country in search of employment. The harsh reality is you can't live on scenery. You need work, and that opportunity was elsewhere.

The more I listened to Mother's lament, the less it seemed about losing her house on Gabarus Bay and the more it seemed about wanting her youth back, to return to the day when she could jump in the car with Dad and be off to the bay. She hadn't agreed to growing old or to selling bits and pieces of her life to strangers. Time had betrayed her.

Wanting only to comfort her, I said, "What if I built a house in the village? A big house by the sea like Grandfather used to have. Then you could come down and visit, whenever you wanted."

Mother hesitated for a moment and then her face brightened. "That would be nice," she said, allowing herself a small smile.

If I had known this was to be our last conversation, I would not have talked of building a house, I would have just said, "I love you, Mum." But my mind was already sailing toward other things. Another election was looming, with the front-runners being the incumbent mayor and a former mayor. Although they gave the public the impression that there was a clear choice between them, it was just optics. Both had been in bed with developers for so long that they scarcely noticed the company. Both were keen to privatize the park.

In the spring of 2010, there was some good news. Patty was now cancer-free. Nonetheless, the chemotherapy and radiation had been very hard. She was exhausted and understandably wasn't keen on the stress of me entering the fray for mayor. Four elections were enough. She was right, but I could not face leaving the city to the old mayors. It would have felt like running away. I knew I had to at least give it a try.

My candidacy was not without hope. In 2004, I had been voted Canada's greenest councillor and in 2010 surprised everyone including myself by being chosen in a public poll as Ottawa's Man of the Year. Nonetheless, the harsh reality was not encouraging. Only one mayor in 150 years had been elected without developer funding, and both Tweedledum and Tweedledee (the former mayors) were sitting happily in that comfortable seat. Money was no problem for them. Their signs and smiling faces were everywhere.

Nothing ventured, nothing gained. I was determined to prevail in spite of the odds. Building a house in Cape Breton would have to wait. My burning ambition was to be the mayor of a different kind of city, one where parks were preserved and rail projects were not changed to serve developer condos. This was where my heart was. My campaign team rented an empty storefront in Hintonburg and we started to campaign with energy and confidence.

CHAPTER 3

Rowing with Clea

To be ignorant of what occurred before you were born is to remain always a child. For what is the worth of human life unless it is woven into the life of our ancestors by the record of history.
—Marcus Tullius Cicero, 106–43 BC

Cicero was right about this as well as many other things. The human adventure is a collective one, but it is a longer and more complicated one than he could have imagined. Human history is about more than one family, one city, or one nation. The human story takes us all right back to the people who chipped stone tools, to the women who first crooned and soothed their babies with song. What we are today is linked to all those who have learned and created before us and will be to those who come after. We can choose to be a strong or a weak link, but we have no choice about the link itself.

To my eternal delight, one of my links is a little girl called Clea with flaxen pigtails, no front teeth, and an irrepressible spirit. Her grandfather, Clive, has no buggy, no horse, and no farm, but I have rented a lovely summer house at the Grand Étang harbour for the family to stay in for the summer after the election. It's a wonderful, old place with large, beautiful windows and a wraparound veranda, but I still find myself wanting my own house. I'm supposed to be in the downsize generation, but I have no desire to downsize into anything. I like working with my hands. The idea of taking care of a house and a garden is pleasing.

In politics, you have no time to worry about the future. You're too busy taking care of the present, but since losing the race for mayor, the question of exactly how I am going to live has become more pointed. As a city councillor I had every day and every week organized before me as steady and sure as a row of railroad ties. Now all I have is this vague image of a house with a view of the sea with some land around it. The inside should be large enough to welcome family and friends. There should be art on the walls and music.

This kind of place cannot be bought. It must grow from the ground in an organic way with tentacles reaching out from the corners of your life. I want to find or build a place that can grow with me in my elder years and welcome grandchildren as they grow. There must be enough land so that the house is not pressed in by neighbours nor set upon the land like a carbuncle but cradled in a natural way. These are the muddled thoughts I am thinking as we tour around looking at houses and gazing at landscapes.

I can't seem to talk much about it because I am only just sorting out in my own mind exactly what I want to do, and there is much to sort out. It can't be a farm like my grandfather had. Sixty acres facing on the sea today would cost more than I could ever afford even if I could find it, and a real farm with a big barn and work sheds, surrounded by carefully tended pastures and field crops, takes a lifetime of effort. I cannot hope to replicate that. Yet I would want my place to have the same comfortable feeling of connection to the land as Grandfather's farm did. Those connections would have to be on a much smaller scale, but I'd like the same harmony his farm had, with a vegetable garden at the side of the house, some flowers in front, and a small meadow running down to the sea where in the spring wildflowers grow and bees hum.

My children wonder a little nervously why I am often quiet. They are used to me being more talkative. They think I am getting old. I am. I am always seeing things that others cannot. I am walking with Clea along the harbour road to the boat launch. Clea is chattering to me about swimming, and have I remembered her beach shoes? I have. Our feet make a crunching sound on the gravel. The waves lap softly against the rocks. It seems like a long walk but it isn't. The boat launch is not far. My father is on the other side of us. He is very young and very thin, striding down this very same lane. With him is the taller, greater bulk of Father Moses Coady, his cassock billowing about him. They are arguing about big fishing boats versus smaller boats. My father is vigorously defending the idea of bigger boats and bigger catches, the priest less so. He worries that if the boats become too big, they will start to be bought up by corporations like National Sea Products, and the small fishermen will all be squeezed out.

They are having a wonderful time arguing, my father with youthful vigour, the priest in a big voice with a grave delivery. Moses Coady must be six foot four, and Dad is over six feet. They seem like giants to me. Seeing his little son falling behind, my father scoops me up like a feather, holding me high on his shoulder. "This is my son," he says, and I can see as he can, far and wide.

Then they are gone, fading into a beam of sunlight, and I am left looking at Clea with the sun shining on the water of the harbour. Our old rowboat is waiting for us. Clea looks at me and asks, "Is there something wrong, Grandpa? You look sad." I shake my head and smile back. I can't explain to her that I am sometimes a little melancholy but it doesn't have anything to do with her. It's about the brevity of life and memories of two men now gone.

Clea nods, taking me at my word, and is already trying to get in the rowboat. "I can do it by myself!" This is a theme with Clea. She doesn't like anyone doing anything for her. When she was a baby she insisted on feeding herself long before her hand-eye coordination was up to navigating the spoon to the mouth, but helping her was impossible. She was going to do it by herself! Her little sister, Évangéline, is following along in her footsteps. She is going to be an "I can it do it myself" girl too. I have learned that it's easier to let them spread the food around the high chair until it looks like a compost heap; somewhere in constructing their personal composts, the babies manage to feed themselves. But getting into the boat "by myself" is proving more difficult. The gunwale is up to Clea's head, and after some eccentric attempts to jump up, she allows me to quickly hoist her inside. This help is ignored as if it was a kind of accident, not worth noticing.

My daughter, Emma, waves to us from the veranda, checking to see if I'm putting the life jacket on Clea. It's not that she doesn't trust me, it's just that she doesn't trust me. She has good reason, knowing that I used to swim across an Ottawa Valley lake to a beach on the other side with her on my back. It never occurred to me anyone should wear a life jacket. It was summer, I could swim, and Emma could ride on my shoulders. Different times.

Happily, Emma survived her dangerous childhood and grew into a tall, strong, beautiful woman. She smiles. I smile and make sure Clea has her life jacket smartly snapped around her. I throw my own life jacket into the bottom of the boat. I find it encumbering and irritating. Some things don't change.

Clea chatters gaily at me about mermaids and her best friends. She doesn't seem to notice my lack of volubility. This is how I was with my grandfather. Mostly I chattered. Children are busy being brand new. Grandfathers aren't so new. I row toward the small bridge at the end of the harbour, under which is the passage to a large pond. The oars always feel welcome in my hands and I put my back into the strokes, lifting the bow as we run with the tide toward the bridge. The boat begins to move crisply, setting up a little bow wave, and Clea bounces up and down with excitement as the little skiff surges forward. My muscles begin to burn pleasantly with the effort, and the air feels sharp in my lungs.

It's not that I want to become silent, but sometimes it feels as if I cannot help it, as if the past is becoming too complicated even to recall to myself, that too much has happened. My son writes edgy French TV shows featuring women who smoke, pole dance, and talk to the Virgin Mary. He is a thoroughly modern man. He doesn't like it when I reflect on the state of the world today in terms of the past. It sounds too much like disappointed-old-guy stuff. You don't have to dwell in the past, but I don't see how the present can be separated from it any more than a flower can be separated from the earth. The present grows out of the past.

This thought doesn't please him. It seems like I'm not moving with the times.

"Let the past go, Dad. It's gone. Look to the future," says my son.

He's not alone with this thought, and no doubt the old do start to look wistfully into the rear-view mirror, because the transient nature of the view becomes more vivid as you age. Nonetheless, that doesn't make you senile. Curiously, while the past does become more alive as you age, it also becomes more disposable. The old are often ready to let things go in a more brutal way than the young. In the kitchen of the house we have rented I found a copy of Edmund de Waal's brilliant biography of his mother's Viennese family, *The Hare with Amber Eyes*. In it he recounts how his grandmother Elizabeth burned thirty years of correspondence with her own grandmother Evelina and refused to talk about her mother, Emmy, at all, probably because of her love affairs.

Trying to understand this, de Waal reflects, "Why should everything be made clear and brought into the light? Why archive your intimacies?...Just because you have it does not mean you have to pass it on. Losing things can sometimes gain you a space to live. 'I don't miss Vienna,' Elizabeth would say, a lightness in her voice, it was claustrophobic. It was very dark.'"

As the years accumulate I empathize with de Waal's grandmother, for like her, the world where my memories were formed is no longer. The old life of the village has been buried by global capitalism. Grand Étang is now at the end of the same global supply lines that stretch from the sweatshops of Asia to the super stores and mega malls of Toronto. The world is now divided into where the resources come from and where they are consumed. In Cape Breton, we have neither. The great resource, the fishery, is gone, and we do not have the population to be a mecca for consumers. To expatriate has become the principal option for the young, for the money is elsewhere.

Then I remember Cicero's thought that it is via the connections between generations that meaning in life is created. For Cicero, both the present and the future are fictions without considering the past. For how can you create meaning if the present is nothing more than a momentary effusion of immediate sensations? But this is the way the internet seems to be moving people. The American president sets global foreign policy through Twitter phrases: Immigrants are dangerous. A wall is necessary. Yes or no? Do you agree or not?

Even the use of language, in both French and English, is changing to accommodate the centrality of the yes/no world. Values that impede the smooth flow of immediate response/gratification are not appreciated. People are constantly connected through their portable screens. Immediacy is everything. Communicate now! This manner of living conforms with Jean-Paul Sartre's existential thought, that meaning comes from choosing. "I choose therefore I am." Choosing has never been easier. Press a button and choose.

I am often caught between two contradictory impulses. The first is to be like de Waal's grandmother and sink into a private ocean that no one else can enter, a place where I can slide into a sunbeam and become like eel grass moving in the clear water of the harbour. The other is to join the yes/no world of constant chatter. The comfort of the eel grass is real, but so is the comfort of my granddaughter in the boat, talking, bright as a new penny and beautiful as the day is long. I'm not ready for eel grass yet. Some talk still seems required, and I tell Clea about my father, her great-grandfather, as we row along.

He was as proud of his little village as my mother was of the great city of London. He would remind people that in 1915 the people of his village organized the first Fisherman's Marketing Co-operative for the sale of fish in all the Americas from Tierra del Fuego to Baffin Bay. He was stretching the truth slightly, for it wasn't Grand Étang. It was our larger neighbour, Chéticamp, where the first co-op was founded, but he was making a point, not giving a history lesson. Ordinary people had taken care of the fishery for a long time, and they had done it well enough that each spring the fish populations were renewed.

Clea's great-grandfather, my father, had a very distinguished career. He was appointed chair of the Canadian Freshwater Fish Corporation, became a close advisor of a powerful Fisheries minister, Roméo LeBlanc, and ended his career working for the United Nations. He was sent all over the world to study fish populations. He used to ask the UN folks in Rome not to send him to an underdeveloped country because he had grown up in one, but his pleading did no good. He was sent most often to Africa, Sri Lanka, Latin America. Apparently, they didn't need fisheries economists in Paris and Rome.

The measure of my father's life is best summarized by the history of the Canadian fishery written by Joseph Gough, *Managing Canada's Fisheries*. It is the story of how Canadians have tried to protect the fisheries from British Columbia to Newfoundland and from the forty-ninth parallel to the Arctic. The story takes the reader from the indigenous fishery right up to the twenty-first century. It covers a lot of complex territory, for each fish species lives in its own biological universe. The fishery on Great Slave Lake in the Northwest Territories is a long way from the great runs of Pacific salmon or Bay of Fundy herring. On the final page, the author mentions three people: Roméo LeBlanc, a federal minister of Fisheries and Oceans; Derrick Iles, a biologist; and Fern Doucet, an economist whom he thought exemplified Canada's many battles to preserve the fisheries for future generations. Dad must have known this, but he never mentioned it to me. I found it by accident, after he was gone.

His great interest was in sustainable fisheries. I know this because I had the good fortune to ask him in the last weeks of his life whether there was anything he regretted. I had no idea what he might reply, because although he remained clear thinking, he could not remember the recent past. He would forget it almost as soon as it happened. I thought he might reply that he regretted not becoming the Deputy Minister of Fisheries and Oceans, which he had designs on at one time. But he didn't. He said, "I would have liked to have been asked to study a fish population that wasn't in crisis." The clarity of his answer astonished me. Because of the dementia he suffered from, he could remember only the things that were buried very deep in his mind, like songs and memories from his youth. To speak this thought so quickly and clearly, it must have been with him for a very long time, and yet if I hadn't asked him the question so directly, I never would have known. He didn't like to talk about his own hopes and ambitions.

In his elder years, Fern was in demand all over the world, although he would say his studies weren't complicated. He would use a simple regression model, the research of biologists, and interviews with fishermen to determine what a yearly, sustainable catch of a fish population might be. When the study was all done, he would go to the oldest fisherman he could find and ask what he thought of my father's numbers for a yearly, sustainable catch. Were they too high? Too low? About right?

Governments don't always like what scientists tell them. The government of Morocco suppressed my father's report on their fishery, and it was pirated around that country's back rooms. Difficult to believe a fishing report could become X-rated material, but his work sometimes did because people rarely like to be told they must take fewer fish from the sea. My father was right, though. The sea was being fished dry. A few years after he retired, the unthinkable began to happen: Canada's vast shoals of cod disappeared.

For at least a thousand years, fishermen had been fishing cod from the coastlines of Atlantic Canada. These vast fish populations had always moved like clouds in the water. Five hundred years ago, Basque fishermen had summer fishing camps on Cape Breton Island and at Port aux Basques in Newfoundland. Their fishing camps were dotted here and there, all along the coast. They didn't stay for the winter. Each autumn, the Basques returned to Europe with their boats loaded down with rich cargoes. They kept the sources of their fishing wealth secret for centuries.

The cod were dominant, but every layer of the sea's living spaces, from ocean floor to the waving surface, abounded with life. There were fat, surging halibut chasing bright clouds of darting silver capelin; flat-faced flounder cruising like paddles; banks of haddock, smaller cousin to the mighty cod, that finned calmly in uncountable numbers across vast tracts of the ocean; and just under the surface were great shoals of flashing herring and glinting mackerel.

While on the ocean floor, crabs crept about in a carpet so thick that they were cursed for tangling fishing nets. Above the crabs, troops of armoured lobsters floated up and dove down in impressive, silent cavalry charges, jousting like underwater knights, their largest claw held out like a spear ready to dismount opponents. Seals, whales, swordfish played about on the surface, while cruising in the sky above were puffins, terns, cormorants, seagulls, hawks, and eagles drifting with the wind like leaves with wings.

The harbours of Cape Breton used to be so crowded with inshore boats that a small boy could walk across the harbour jumping from one boat to another without getting wet, entirely innocent of how hard his elders worked or how little they earned. Everything was hauled hand over hand into and out of the sea. To us, fishermen were gods of all they surveyed. To be a fisherman was a very great thing.

When farmers like my grandfather awoke at six o'clock, the sea was already dotted with the floats of fishing nets announcing that fishermen had been hard at work. The outlines of their nets would appear and disappear into the shimmer of a thousand reflections as the sunlight played with the surface of the ocean, and in the early morning light the fishing boats changed to silvery shadows skittering across the ocean surface.

By the time the cows had been milked and the farmers had sent them back to their pastures, fishermen were already hauling their nets and preparing to return to the harbour. In this way, a shimmering river of silver fish flowed from the ocean into the fishermen's boats, then to the harbour and the fish plant, only stopping when the river eddied to a halt in the kitchens of far-off cities. Fish were life.

In 1989, 15 million pounds of fish were purchased by the Chéticamp Fisherman's Co-op. Four years later, it was 1.2 million pounds, and in 2004, the oldest Co-op in the Americas stopped purchasing fish entirely. These aren't cold statistics to me. They're connected to powerful memories of people and place. Oil is all very fine. I like my little car and the convenience it brings, but I can't help but wonder why we have let oil become more important than fish or clean water or anything else you can eat or drink. Can you drink oil? Can you eat it?

As Clea and I row along, our boat skips happily onwards. The water is crystal clear. You can see right down to the bottom. If there are mermaids around, we will find them. The gentleness of a maritime summer is everywhere. It is a great thing to be here with my granddaughter. Clea can't imagine this, but to me she is a greater amazement than mermaids. Time spins in her voice and reflects life back to me as a glass of wine captures light, bending it, changing it, enhancing it.

We pass under the bridge. Clea hangs over the gunwale, watching the water flow by, eyes peeled for mermaids. The pond, after which the village is named, is a tidal inlet and a little shallow for mermaids, but you never know. Better to be a mermaid than any fish unfortunate enough to remain in the shallow waters, for it makes them easy targets for the great ospreys that float calmly above, watching for fish as carefully as Clea does for mermaids.

"Grandpa! Grandpa!" Clea cries and points ahead. Then I see it too. A fishing eagle circles lower and lower in the sky, flat and powerful like a dark flag against the blue. "I am therefore I am," the eagle announces without the slightest equivocation in the harsh cry of his species. The eagle voice has as much confidence as Descartes's pen ever did when he wrote, "I think therefore I am" or Jean-Paul Sartre's with his, "I choose therefore I am."

I look at Clea and think to myself, "I am connected, therefore I am." For surely, like the eagle our own soul's voyage toward eternity is a collective, not a solitary one. No one gets to heaven alone.

I turn the boat and begin to row back to the house where Clea's mother, Emma, is waiting. Clea hitches her legs up onto to the gunwale, leans back, and watches clouds.

CHAPTER 4

Highland Trails

The morning sun rises
like a rose spear
over the hills,
a spear into the heart
announcing the world
is beginning again,
that we have another chance.

There are many beautiful hiking trails in Cape Breton Highlands National Park. People come from all over the world to enjoy their tranquility, their vistas, their peaceful sense of time and space. The park's walking trails were built in the 1930s at the height of the Great Depression as part of a federal makework project for Acadian farmers and fishermen. These were very hard times when a good fall herring run could be the difference between enough food and not enough.

The trails were constructed with nothing but hand tools and sweat. William Doucet was one of two foremen on the west side of the park who, with his crew, began to cut walking trails up from the sea into the mountains. If you were a visitor from outer space, you would want to visit Cape Breton's Skyline Trail. On the Skyline Trail, you are standing at

Mother Earth's front door where the earth, the sky, and the sea are on magical display.

The Skyline Trail is used to sell Nova Scotia all over the world. Nor are the photographs exaggerated. The forest path becomes a boardwalk perched along a mountain crest with nothing but a vertiginous view of the mountains, coast, and sea. Below, the cliff face plunges to a crystal ocean where whales dance, all framed by the changing bowl of the mountains and sky. It is a scene that announces you are standing on the edge of eternity. The soul can find ease here.

Nonetheless, my first choice for a highland hike would not be the Skyline Trail. My first choice would be the humbler Rivière à Lazare (Corney Brook) Trail. This trail is near the entrance of the park and hidden away in the forest. It follows a broad, strong-flowing mountain brook that springs from high up on the escarpment and has carved a narrow gorge that plunges from the top of the mountains to a beautiful cove below. Within the gorge there is a benign microclimate where the trees grow tall and strong. Walking beside the mountain stream after which the hike is named with the summer sunlight shafting through the tall trees, the sound of the sparkling water bubbling and rushing by has a dense, comforting feeling as if, like the trees, you are protected from life's vicissitudes.

The Scots call this kind of place an intervale. When it's a big intervale, the cascading mountain water has been large and strong enough to have cut a small valley from the steepness of the mountains and there are small mountain meadows to farm and live by. These are lovely, sheltered places. But when the stream is smaller, it cuts only a narrow gorge from the mountain. There are no mountain pastures. Here the intervale remains narrow and wild, and it becomes a good place to camp, hunt, and fish, but not to settle.

Walking up Rivière à Lazare, the gradient of the trail is so firm and steady that you are rarely aware of how steep the climb is, but the incline never relents. At the start, the trail clings directly to the edge of a steep gorge and you can still find the traces of the old cart tracks made by my grandfather's crew. Here, the gorge cuts into the mountain like a knife and the view becomes perilous. Once you are higher, the trail turns away from the gorge and begins to meander back and forth through the tall, leafy forest, criss-crossing smaller mountain streams that are feeding the larger one.

Small vistas open. Round a corner and a river of giant rocks appears, hanging above the trail like a stone avalanche forever poised to descend. I never see this mountain scree without wondering how it is possible to create such a thing. There is an obdurateness to this view that defies every human vanity. It gives a visual reality to the famous Biblical dictum of the mountains being levelled to the plains.

Then the trail bends back toward the main brook before wandering off across wooden bridges to follow a smaller watercourse. How did Grandfather's crew pick this route? And I wonder if they did. Perhaps they just widened a Mi'kmaw hunting trail, for the intervale is alive with deer and small animals. Above, the forest canopy is so thick and high that walking beneath it is cool and pleasant even on the hottest day in midsummer.

The walking continues to be easy, and you are surrounded by noble forest vistas. It stays that way until you get very near the top. Here, the trees begin to pack more closely together as if they are already preparing themselves for the harsh winds that fly across the mountaintops. As you near the summit, there is an at first indistinct then stronger sound of water falling, but it is difficult to locate. You come around a bend in the trail and suddenly it appears directly in front of you, white foaming water tumbling down a steep rock face. But the falling water is so shrouded by overhanging tree branches that the water seems to be springing directly from the roots of the trees themselves.

This dancing, singing water, the rustle of small animals, the soft air in the green bower from whence the water springs have the magical quality of elves and the planet's secret places.

I often think of my grandfather (Clea's great-great-grandfather) when I walk this trail. He liked recounting stories of building the hiking trails. It wasn't easy work. One of the psychological tricks William Doucet used to keep the men enthusiastic through the long day and hard work, was mapping out at the beginning of each week exactly how far he wanted to drive the trail by Friday. Then he promised that when they arrived at that spot, no matter what time it was, they would lay down tools, leave the camp, and return to their homes. It didn't matter if it was noon on Friday, he would tell the timekeeper to log his crew out as if it was five o'clock so that the men would not be penalized for working hard. All that mattered was where they finished the week's work. No one gave him permission to do this, he just did it.

His crew accomplished so much so quickly that the park superintendent wanted to put Grandfather in charge of all the crews, but he refused, figuring that someone in that position should be able to read and write. Undeterred by my grandfather's refusal, the superintendent promised to find him an assistant who would do the paperwork as long as he ran the crews, but Grandfather still refused.

Whenever I walk the trails, I think of those skinny men working in patched, worn clothes in the depths of the Depression, building trails to lookouts in the mountains for reasons that they could not discern. In the 1930s, tourists in northern Cape Breton were more an idea than a reality. The island was too isolated, too difficult to get to, and the idea of creating a park to preserve the wilderness at its northern extremity seemed at best foolish. The wilderness didn't need preserving. People did. Yet the men took their jobs seriously, and they carefully built the trails as if one day people would magically arrive and be interested in wasting their time walking. They built them so well that the old trails remain unchanged, still following the same paths with the same buttressing and culverts. Only basic maintenance has been necessary.

It is a good thing that they built them so well because people now come from all over the world to walk in the park. There is even a very active village hiking club. The village is filled with visitors every summer and well into the fall. I tell my grandchildren how their great-great-grandfather was foreman of a crew that built some of the hiking trails. I tell them stories that he told me: about the horse who was blind in one eye; about the man who could run faster with one leg than anyone else could on two; about his father, Arsène Doucet, who was lost at sea in his schooner, *Richmond Queen*.

If my life has had any direction it begins here, for it is the stories and lives of my parents and grandparents that have given definition and a sense of purpose in my own life. This is where I began to form convictions about what it meant to be a Canadian and what government itself should mean. Long before I had ever heard of Jane Jacobs or had the slightest idea of what a more sustainable city might look like, it was the stories of building hiking trails in the national park and the importance of being a good steward of the sea that formed the foundation from which everything else would one day flow.

The decision of the government to hire poor men to build mountain trails imbued in me from the youngest age the conviction that government was a good thing. I still feel that way every time the garbage truck shows up at my front door to whisk away my weekly household debris or I open the sink tap and receive cold, clean water from the city's filtration plant. How wonderful are these things! Government is rarely as magical as waterfalls, but it does do necessary, important things—

creates health care for all, builds universities, dredges harbours, paves roads, funds pensions for the elderly, builds theatres and concert halls. Each of these things is magical because it connects us in so many important ways.

I did not grow up with the idea that government was controlled by corporate lobbies working diligently in the service of their own private interests. No doubt, I was wrong about this, for the manipulation of the government agenda in the service of greed has been around for as long as government itself has. There has never been an age without theft. Nonetheless, I grew up confident that in its essence, the Government of Canada belonged to the people of Canada and that it worked for us, not for some faceless hedge fund in New York.

I was equally confident that each person's vote was an essential dimension to being Canadian. I remember very clearly the first time I was old enough to vote. I was an archaeology student working at Fortress Louisbourg on the east side of the island, peeling back layers of soil to reveal the buildings and living patterns of the past. Our voting station was in a decommissioned clapboard church by the harbour, not far from the entrance to the fortress.

The election was on a warm summer day. The sun was shining brightly. Bobbing flowers dotted the long grass in the field around the old church. It was a fine day in every regard, and I was very pleased to finally be old enough to vote. I felt very grown up. If you had told me that one day, not so far off, a man would tell me with obvious pride, "I never vote" when I campaigned myself, it would have seemed utterly bizarre. It would have seemed like the man wanted to remain a child. Even stranger, I have come to understand and sympathize with the "I never vote" attitude. When mayors of great cities are for sale to land developers, and presidents are purchased like so much cheese by the corporatized wealthy, the question does become, what's the point of voting?

When the trails in Cape Breton Highlands National Park were being built, most everyone in the village thought that they cost a great deal of money for not very much, but it turned out to be very little for a great deal. For the price of sending a couple of soldiers to Afghanistan, those Highland paths have brought millions of people great joy. For in the mountains, the innate, immutable connection to the life of Earth is revealed. Walking a Highland trail, it is impossible not to recognize that the natural world is where our species began and where our future will always be anchored. This thought is essential.

Forests, oceans, fields, villages, cities are all connected. Farmers need cities and cities need farmers, and they both need to be sustainable. An environment that renews itself with water, animals, and plants is a principle upon which the life of our species depends. No species, no animal can survive well in a degraded and hostile environment. This very simple thought has been the motor of much of my life. In this way, the meaning of life was never very complicated for me. To defend my city was to defend myself. I never learned to think of myself separately from the world around me. It's what drove me to fight against the privatization of Lansdowne Park and work for a return to light rail transit in Ottawa. The national park, trails, and marine life of coastal Cape Breton need to be defended for the same reasons as sustainable cities do, because they also connect us in many good ways to the continuing life of the planet.

The search for meaning to life isn't a new voyage. It has occupied people for as long as people have looked up and beheld the night sky or drawn images on cave walls. How can you not be amazed at such a magnificent, imponderable vision cast before us each night? But grand as it is, the night sky—like the forbidding rock face of a mountain scree, like the idea of eternity itself—is too remote to be of much use at the breakfast table.

For my grandfather, meaning in life came from tending a small farm, feeding a large family, and building walking trails in the mountains. My father's professional life was about safeguarding the fisheries. Concern for the sustainability of the fisheries was the last coherent thought I heard him utter just a week before he died. My father grew up in a traditional fishing village. He related to the world through the idea of stewardship. It's a very Acadian way of being. At the end of the day, marsh dykes, the fishery, the land, the forest have to work for everyone, not just the most successful. I am sure I was imbued with this idea also. Fighting for a more sustainable city came as naturally to me as advocating for sustainable fisheries came to my father.

After losing the run for mayor, I began to wonder if I was suffering some version of post-traumatic stress. Like a record with a scratch in it, my memory kept flicking back to Ottawa, the election, and the long fight to save the old park. In body I may have returned to Cape Breton, but I wasn't really there. No one places their name on the public ballot to lose, and I had come third behind the two former mayors.

I never had much sympathy for defeated politicians. Just get on with it was my attitude, but it turned out just getting on with it when your entire waking and sleeping life has been devoted to something that you are now excluded from wasn't that easy. The mind tends to dwell on things, to go around in destructive circles. I have found that anger and grief make ugly partners. Suddenly everything seems to hurt more. Anger is often a way of avoiding tears.

When Cicero's only daughter died in childbirth, he abandoned the senate, his fight to save the republic, and retired to a cottage he owned south of Pompeii. This most public man became the most private. He stayed away from Rome for a year. At times he felt such anguish, he wrote of rolling around on the ground in the woods howling like a dog in pain. Eventually, he wrote a book called *On Grief*. It was his most popular book and continued to be read well into the Middle Ages, when it disappeared, leaving behind only the book's title.

I'm persuaded *On Grief* must have been about him finding a way to rediscover hope. At the end of a year of mourning for his daughter, now a man in his sixties, Cicero returned to Rome to begin his final, vigorous defence of the republic. He came very close to winning the day and re-establishing the republic. The judgment of history is that if he had had just a little bit of Caesar's magnificent military luck, he would have prevailed over Caesar's young nephew, Octavian.

One thing I am sure of is that anger is not a good response to grief. People who like power feed profitably on the divisions that anger generates, because divisions can be manipulated. You can control a city if you control people's anger. You can control a nation the same way if you are able to divide people through anger and then manipulate that anger to the advantage of the group you support.

I grew up in a city that had been built around streetcar lines. Today people grow up in a city organized around cars. They are two different cities with two different narratives. How do you reconcile them? How you prevent one group from being angry with another whom they see as not understanding them? That is the question, not how does one vision or one narrative beat up another.

I will always feel some grief about the loss of the north–south rail line and Lansdowne Park. It's a personal grief. I can't help it because I feel that it was not just about the city being diminished by the loss of these projects—I was also. Like a wave in a pool ricocheting off the pool edge, when connections between people change, everything gets touched. No one escapes.

I never mention the names of the three developers involved in the park's privatization because their names aren't important. If it hadn't been this particular group, it would have been another. What matters is having a vision of the city that preserves parks. If that vision had been in place, the park would never have been turned into a mall. Safeguarding public spaces and building city surface rail are less about city projects and more about having a different vision of how a more sustainable life in a city can be composed.

That summer after the election, I took long bicycle trips along the Cabot Trail, balanced along the bluffs from the village to Margaree Harbour before turning up the valley toward the Dancing Goat Cafe. It was a beautiful ride and it helped. On these trips, one of the things I noticed was the For Sale signs that decorated the edge of the Cabot Trail. I regarded them closely, for in a village, a real estate sign isn't just about the house or a bit of land. It's about the history of the village. It's about who lived in that house, what they did, how many children they had. Why are they selling? Where have they gone? Who might buy it?

The For Sale signs were frequent enough to make it look like the whole village was on the auction block, but these little signs are deceiving. The land with the fine views, reasonable prices, and solid homes rarely had a For Sale sign decorating a fenceline. My grandfather's farm hasn't changed hands since Aunt Germaine passed it on to a neighbour more than fifty years ago, and there it has remained ever since. Many houses have been in the same family since they were built. Good properties rarely get to the real estate office. It was the ones that didn't work that constantly rotated on and off the market.

As the summer wore on, I kept looking for something that might be suitable for a family house until I finally admitted to myself that it was much harder than I had ever realized. What had seemed like a fairly simple matter wasn't. In northern

Cape Breton, Mother Nature ruled. Climate change was giving an entirely new dimension to life in the village. Each winter, weather changes are driving hurricane-force winds up the eastern coast of North America. Their end point is often Nova Scotia. In the village people have begun building new houses very carefully, sometimes creating their own earthen berms on the windward side of the house. Building a house here would be no simple task.

CHAPTER 5

Interview at the Harbour

*The arms of the Milky Way
hold the planet safely
in the arms of its own desires.*

I used to have strong opinions about a great deal, today not so much. More and more, I find myself unwilling to explain anything. There is something immensely reassuring in simply walking along the beach and hearing the steady roll of the ocean beside you. If eternity has a voice, it must be something close to the sound of waves breaking rhythmically, endlessly against the shore.

The sea always brings surprises. It took my great-grandfather Arsène, his schooner, and his crew. Nothing tangible of his life remained. But one day a fisherman showed up at my door with a bill of sale for my great-grandfather's little schooner, *Richmond Queen*. I didn't even know such a document existed. The fisherman had found it in an old trunk in the attic of his house. The trunk had once belonged to my grandfather.

He said, "I thought you should have this," and he put a long, worn, brown envelope into my hand. I opened it carefully. The envelope was thick and the document inside was on brown paper and torn along one of the creases. Seeing the straight, black ink script, the red seal, and my great-grandfather's name, Arsène Doucet, affixed therein was a powerful moment, as if the past had suddenly reached out to nudge me.

This morning I have something I used to have every day but now rarely do—a formal appointment. I'm late and leave the house quickly without saying goodbye. I must walk across the bridge to the Co-op side of the harbour. It's a grand summer day. The sun is bouncing off everything it touches, glinting off the green waves of the mountains and sparkling off the ocean. Two academics from France have arrived in the village, video camera in hand, to talk to the locals. They are investigating isolated French-speaking populations in North America. I'm not sure why they want to speak to me. Apparently, someone has recommended that they should.

It turns out to be an awkward conversation. I am used to being able to frame answers to questions quickly in front of a camera, but those interviews have always been about cities, not villages like Grand Étang. Instead of answering smoothly and easily I stagger clumsily from question to question without any confidence in my responses. Yes, my family is French speaking, but it is also English speaking. My grandchildren go to French schools and speak French with their dad, but they also speak English with their mother and live in the city. They see themselves as Canadian, not Acadian. My explanations feel lame, as if I'm trying to avoid really talking. The truth is I don't know how to answer their questions. I don't know what the future holds for our little village or if the French language will survive here.

"The Doucet family has lived here a long time," I hear myself say, searching to anchor the conversation in something in which I have some confidence, but the uncomfortable truth is that the family returns to the village for funerals, but that's about it. I have only one first cousin, Robert, left here, in the neighbouring village of Chéticamp, and I have twenty-seven first cousins. I can find more cousins in Maine, Alberta, Boston, Halifax, Ottawa, or Montreal than in Grand Étang, and the family has no land here at all. It's all gone either back to the coyotes and bush or to others.

Nor do I have any sophisticated history to recount as Edmund de Waal did with his Viennese banking family and the vestiges of their past lives after the family was murdered and dispersed by the Nazis. The Doucets of Grand Étang, like the Ephrussi family of de Waal's recounting, have disappeared from the world where they once shone. The farms, sawmill, fields, cattle, sheep, tractors, and trucks are all gone. Unlike the Ephrussi, there are no grand palaces to mark our passing.

I am the only Doucet in our family that has returned with the idea of finding or building a house in the village. Most of my relatives think I'm crazy or that I have more money than I know what to do with. The first may be true. The second isn't. The long and the short of it is there are all kinds of uncomfortable truths that I don't want to talk about. If I had won the election for mayor, I wouldn't be standing on a Grand Étang dock staring into a video camera.

The two academics, a woman and a man, are very gracious, but it seems like we're conversing through this translucent screen. Neither they nor I are in focus. She is asking me something about building a house in some other place. Wouldn't a house closer to Ottawa or Montreal make more sense for me and my family? Perhaps something in the Laurentians or the Eastern Townships? No doubt she is right, it would make more sense.

All I can think to do is talk about Arsène Doucet, who sailed a small schooner out of this harbour to the French islands of St. Pierre and Miquelon, where he traded fresh produce for spirits. Arsène was my grandfather's father and the son of Magloire who was a storekeeper but who is not remembered for his store. He is remembered for refusing to attend church, which was considered to be a very strange thing. But that didn't stop him from succeeding. His store did well and his eldest son, Moise, became the first Acadian member of the Nova Scotia legislature. Moise's passing is marked by a tall and impressive gravestone in the St. Joseph du Moine church cemetery. Of course, there is nothing in the graveyard to celebrate Magloire, as he was an atheist. He is simply gone.

Nor is there anything to mark his younger son Arsène's death at sea. We have no photographs of Arsène or his schooner. All that I have in his memory is this torn brown bill of sale, which says *Richmond Queen* weighs 36.98 tons, has two masts, and was built in Little River, Richmond County, Cape Breton. In April of 1895, when the Ephrussi family was collecting Impressionist paintings in Paris, Arsène bought *Richmond Queen* for $260.

The bill of sale is a large, official-looking, brown paper document with a red royal seal pressed in wax on the lower right-hand corner. The seal is affixed next to the *X* that marks the signature of the seller, Anselm Fougere. The Registrar of Shipping has entered the details of *Richmond Queen*'s construction with the bold, black ink strokes of a straight pen. There can be no confusion about what is being bought here. You could build another *Richmond Queen* based on the description in the bill of sale. In spite of the detail about the schooner's size and shape, it's not clear that Nova Scotia's Shipping Registrar has the same understanding of Canada as people do today. For under the box marked "British or foreign built" is written "British." Yet, in another box, it clearly records *Richmond Queen* being built in Little River, Richmond County, Cape Breton. In 1895, it seems Cape Breton is not quite Canada yet.

In spite of *Richmond Queen*'s grand name, it is nothing more than one of those ragged, two-masted pickup trucks that have been traipsing up and down coastlines for millennia. She had a crew of three, including the captain. On his last voyage,

Arsène was caught in a storm somewhere between the French islands of St. Pierre and Miquelon and Cape Breton. If Arsène had been in the food for booze business twenty years later when the American Congress decided to criminalize alcohol, family lore is confident that the Grand Étang Doucets would now be as rich as the Montreal Bronfmans. I have my doubts, but it makes a nice "what if?" story.

Today, boats the size of *Richmond Queen* are equipped with powerful diesel engines, capable of driving the boat directly into thundering seas, and the captain's wheelhouse looks more like a computer station. Boats equipped only with sails stay in the gentle waters of the Bras d'Or lakes. They don't risk sailing the open seas of the gulf as Arsène Doucet routinely did. The ocean is too unpredictable, the seas too big, and possibilities of disaster too present with only sails to power the boat.

No one knows if *Richmond Queen* was just over the horizon or far away when she disappeared beneath the waves, and no one ever will. There was no way to communicate with a ship at sea. Lost at sea was not just an expression.

Sometimes absences have greater impact than presences do, and so it was with Arsène's death. His only son, William (my grandfather), was twenty years old when *Richmond Queen* vanished. Until that moment, the last thing on young William's mind was to stay in Grand Étang. He had been saving money since he was twelve years old with the intention of moving out west to homestead, and at twenty, he was ready. He had a young man's energy and a thousand dollars saved to begin his farm. When news came about the loss of his father and the crew of *Richmond Queen*, William was already on his way to Inverness with a chum from the village to catch the train west. Their moment had come.

The coal town of Inverness in northern Cape Breton was where the transcontinental train line ended. As planned, William's friend caught the train west. He would return once as a mature man to see relatives and friends and show them photographs of his western farm, but William never did catch the train west. He had to stay. His own mother had died and his father, Arsène, had remarried a much younger woman scarcely out of her teens herself. While Arsène had been at sea, she had given birth to an infant daughter, Rose.

The idea of suddenly being solely responsible for a new infant and her husband's two teenage daughters was overwhelming. The young woman fell into such a depression that she was unable to care for her baby. The infant was taken in by the Lelièvre family in Chéticamp, and the young mother disappeared from the village as completely as her husband did when he vanished beneath the waves. Where she went or what happened to her is a complete mystery; not even the memory of her name has been conserved.

Grandfather moved into Arsène's old house to take care of his teenage sisters. There was a great deal to do. Sailors don't have time to till the land and worry about the thousands of things a farmer must. Arsène had some chickens scratching around the house with a horse and a cow in a tumbledown shed, that was it. It's no wonder his young wife could not cope with an infant and such little circumstance. Young William went to work with a ferocious energy. He organized a barn-raising and remarkably quickly pegged together a very impressive barn. The hay mow on the north side was three storeys high and is still one of the largest in the village. At the same time, he started to convert the thin soil of the farm into something rich and complex enough to actually bear crops. He worked every day but Sunday from sunrise to moonrise. His denim shirts were always stained with sweat.

When I think of William changing a few acres of rocky land into a prosperous farm with a big, red barn housing two fine stallions, a handsome breeding bull, mares, dairy and beef cattle, it still strikes me as amazing. Anyone can farm land that has metres of thick, rich topsoil, but thin, stony land takes a miracle. William had dozens of tricks to make his sixty acres work. He spread seaweed harvested from the beach on his fields and in the fall used white limestone dust to reduce the soil's natural acidity. Beside the barn, he built a long compost bed that ran the entire length of the night pasture. He was soon spreading compost on his fields to increase the organic content, and his thin acres began to grow abundant crops of hay, oats, potatoes, and turnips.

When one drives by the farm on the main road, William's fields glow with a deep, emerald green. Even to someone who knows nothing about farming his fields looked prosperous. If the apocalypse comes, I would want to be with someone like William, who with a few simple tools could fill a house with warmth and food.

Grandfather worked alone, taking care of his sisters until they were happily married to boys from the village. It was at the marriage of his youngest sister, the woman I would know as Tante Juliette, that he noticed a distant and very beautiful cousin named Marie-Anne. Even in the faded photographs that we have of her, she has an ethereal beauty that reaches out from the picture. Together they had two beautiful boys, but Marie-Anne was not long for the world. She died in childbirth after delivering her second son.

William was alone again but this time with two babies to care for and a farm that had to be worked. A long grieving period was not a luxury he could afford.

William proposed to Marie Hache, a woman of his own age who at thirty would have been considered *une vieille fille*, an old spinster. Marie Hache was a different kettle of fish from the ethereal Marie-Anne Doucet. She was strong-willed, tall, and more imposing than beautiful. She also had something William didn't have—an excellent school education. She had earned a high school matriculation and spoke with the calm authority the discipline of a convent school education imparts. Her Bescherelle was not forgotten, and she made sure her children wrote well. A devout Catholic, she quickly brought eight children into the world and raised Marie-Anne's sons as her own.

Marie Hache and William Doucet made a good team. Their whole lives unfolded on the western shore of Cape Breton. Besides enlarging his farm with a horse stud and cattle breeding service, William built a sawmill at the head of the pond, which provided cut lumber for the community. Later he was hired to be a foreman on one of the crews, cutting hiking trails in the new park. His crews quickly developed a reputation for hard work, and William was recommended to head the team that would build what would become the famous Highland Links golf course at Ingonish on the other side of the island.

Grandfather had no idea what a golf course looked like, so the designers took him to Sydney where he got the chance to walk around one. He found the idea of grown men chasing a white ball that they hit ahead of them using a thin stick very strange, but he kept these thoughts to himself. The pay was excellent and he was glad to take the job.

These are some of the memories that crowd around inside my head when the French academics are asking me their questions, but I keep these thoughts to myself. I look around the harbour past their video camera, which remains focused on my face, conscious that I am sounding lame. What would Edmund de Waal say if he were in my shoes? His family is as spread out as mine. His favourite great-uncle lives in Tokyo. He has relatives in Mexico, New York, London, everywhere but Vienna. Mine is the same. We are everywhere but the place we came from, Grand Étang.

The mountains and the sea are still magnificent, but the population of the island is diminishing, not growing. Schools are being closed, not built. The size of families has plummeted.

So why am I here? Why am I building a house? The academics pose sensible questions. Why not choose some peaceful little Quebec village? Somewhere with a ski hill close by where you could mingle with the smart people from Montreal who come for weekend skiing? These are all reasonable questions, but I don't have answers for them. Their disappointed expressions speak for themselves. I have been through five city elections and am accustomed to confidently articulating my thoughts in front of a camera. I've done it many times, so I am surprised to find myself so inarticulate.

When I was a child people here were confident in our use of the French language, even though it sounded different from French-French. Sometimes, at a kitchen party, Grandfather would mimic the Paris accent, which he called "mouton French" because to him it sounded like sheep looking for pasture. It sent everyone laughing. Not that he would have ever done this in the presence of a French-French person. It would have been deeply offensive to their conviction that there was only one way to speak French—their way. The world may have been going global, but the Académie Française still ruled the French part.

Now, I'm not so sure if even the Académie Française has the same place in the world. French society is heaving under the pressure of migrations of people from the south, and I notice a subtle but real shift in the national attitude. The two French academics talk enthusiastically about Chéticamp's little community radio station CKJM. They are knowledgeable about our little corner of the world and don't seem patronizing at all. There is no colonial vision here. They are just genuinely curious about our village's destiny.

I had been expecting them to say something like "your French is good," which is the ultimate French put-down, as if it is amazing that someone in Grand Étang knows how to hitch a verb to a noun with the proper liaison, but they don't. They just want to know why I want to build a house here.

My son would say that my memories are a conversation with the dead. There is no future to it. You don't build a house in a remote village because of a bill of sale in a sock drawer and some old stories about hiking trails. There must be a better reason.

I have no answer. In spite of our family history here, I grew up in the Ottawa Valley, not Grand Étang. A boat for me is a canoe, riding the rapid, little rivers that flow into the Ottawa River. Winter in the Ottawa Valley is long and cold and made for skating, which I have always loved. The spring is short, beautiful, and effervescent as a tulip blooming. The harsh turning of the Ottawa Valley seasons I wear carelessly like a second skin.

Ottawa is the city where my parents are buried. Where I raised my children, wrote most of my books, and battled on city council. Home is where you go to the funerals, and I go to the funerals in Ottawa. My Uncle Philias used to say, "You can take a boy out of the country but you can't take the country out of a boy." If I belong to Cape Breton, it is the belonging of a boy.

While my hair is now grey and I have four wonderful grandchildren, I'm not my grandfather. My hands do not hang from my arms like great spades from a lifetime of manual labour. I can't take an axe and chip a perfect surface from a rough-cut log. I can't read the land and tell you exactly what will grow where or how land needs to be ditched. I am a writer and reader. My house is filled with books. Words are my seeds. If I plant potatoes it won't be because I must do it to feed a large household but because it is something I wish to do for the joy of watching things grow.

The interview grinds to a halt. I smile hesitantly. They smile more genuinely. I do like them. They don't seem imperial or falsely interested at all, and I am genuinely sorry I have been so little use to them. We shake hands and part amiably, but no one in France is going to care about Magloire the atheist or

Arsène and his little schooner. They want to know about the future. What is the future for our little village? They don't say it but the unstated idea is that because I am building a house here I must know. No one builds a house without some idea of his future in it and of those around him, but the truth is I don't know. I wish the French academics well and hope they can find someone more authentic than I.

Unsettled, I walk around the harbour and keep going until I get to the house we have rented. The children are tumbling and rolling down the grassy hill like small bear cubs. Their mother not far away, watching. I keep on going past the house until I round the bend at the end of the harbour where the road starts to climb up to the top of the bluff. I follow the road, just wanting to shake my legs, as I have done many times, just walking and watching the eagles.

It's easy to marvel at Paris, the City of Light, with its magnificent buildings, boulevards, and history, but for me the most moving place in the world is the height of land that runs from Margaree Harbour to Grand Étang where the road winds along the bluffs above the sea. I never travel it without a catch in my throat. The road climbs up a long incline, dips, climbs again to the crest of another ridge, curves, and swoops behind a headland before you come upon the houses and farms of the little valley of Le Moine and then finally to the harbour of Grand Étang.

It is along these bluffs, along the Old Cabot Trail, not far from where we are renting that I notice a small, bent Land for Sale sign. The field with the For Sale sign has no buildings, no fencelines, nothing to distinguish it. It is just grass and wildflowers running from the cliff to a small ridge buckled across the height of land. Nonetheless, it feels familiar. I could imagine my grandfather cutting hay here with his team of horses. I jump the ditch and walk up into the field, up to the highest point. From here you can see the coastline stretch toward the spire of St. Pierre in Chéticamp, and in the other direction, to the southwest, the ocean flows unimpeded to the horizon line that lines the planet's edge.

The For Sale sign is scarcely visible from any direction. It's as if someone planted it at the edge of the field and then forgot they had done it. It flutters slightly in the breeze, buried in the tall grass, curled around the stick. I stand there for a long time, thinking.

CHAPTER 6

Netsuke and Fiddles

*I was wondering
when you would come back.
I was wondering when
you would come paddling
over the water,
the canoe balanced
like a dry leaf
on the clear membrane
of the lake.*

To be young is to confront life as it appears. The sun rises on the present, not the past, but for a grandfather, everywhere you look there are biographies. Even the roughest landscape is invested with history. Sometimes, I bend down and just lay the palm of my hand on the earth. It has its own feeling, its own heartbeat. In Grand Étang, it is red and clay-like and sticks to everything. Good land for potatoes.

The orange-red cliffs rising from the sea look grand, but they are soft and tumble easily before the ocean's might. Erosion has long since tumbled the site of Magloire's store into the sea. It was a general store with a little bit of everything. He even had a few books for sale, which he ordered mostly for himself then tried to sell as unread. It didn't work very well because there were only two people in the village who read books, the priest and the doctor. The nuns in Chéticamp read, but they rarely came to Magloire's store.

I grew up in a reading household. My mother, especially, loved to read and from her I picked up the habit of reading everything that was within reach. In this way, books become like people you meet by chance on a street corner. You strike up a conversation and perhaps even a brief friendship and then they move on, leaving the perfume of the acquaintanceship that is remembered long after you have forgotten the face. In the book that has surfaced in the house we are renting, *The Hare with Amber Eyes*, prior to the Second World War the very rich, cosmopolitan Ephrussi family ran in the same circles as Austrian dukes and duchesses and bankers like the Rothschilds. A family of Vienna banking princes couldn't be more different from the Doucets of Grand Étang, but such is the magic of reading that you can get to know them without ever traversing the ocean. For a reading moment, they can become your friends as if they had been right in the room with you, conversing as you turned the pages of the book.

The author, Edmund de Waal, was the son of an Anglican minister who grew up in an English rectory with three noisy brothers; his mother was a granddaughter of the Ephrussi banking family. I find de Waal and his family history easy to relate to because just as he is the product of a cultural and religious tangle, I am the son of a very Catholic, very French Acadian father and a very English, very Anglican mother.

The Doucets of Grand Étang were never rich and were very far from being cosmopolitan as de Waal's mother's family had been, but like the European Jewish community, the Acadians were also connected to a world war that shattered their families and decimated their population. A third of the Acadian population would die between 1755 and 1763 as they were dispersed across the planet by the British navy. Nothing quite compares to the industrial deaths of the Holocaust, but just as the European Jewish community never recovered from those terrible years, neither did the Acadians from their deportation from Nova Scotia. To this day, Acadian history is divided into before and after the 1755–63 deportation, and this will always be. As long as there are Acadians, there will be two historical realities for them. The first settlers of Grand Étang are all refugees from the deportation.

Paul-Marie Doucet, the first Doucet to arrive in Chéticamp, would be the only one in our family to escape. He was eight years old when the deportation began in Beaubassin, near where Sackville, New Brunswick, sits now. Family tradition has it that he fled to a Mi'kmaw camp where he lived until making his way to the new Acadian fishing communities along the Baie de Chaleurs. Paul-Marie's parents and grandparents would die on ships or in refugee camps or disappear into the bayous of the Mississippi Delta.

Nor is there any sophisticated *objet d'art* that might serve as a metaphor for the Acadian story the way the Ephrussi family's collection of netsuke, tiny Japanese carvings, mirror the travels, successes, and travails of de Waal's family. The miniature carvings are the only things to survive when the Ephrussi home was ransacked by the Nazis. A maid quietly decided to save the little carvings by carrying them in her apron pockets and hiding them under her bedroom mattress. After the war, these button-sized sculptures found their way back to Japan, where they came to rest in the apartment of de Waal's favourite great-uncle, who had settled there with his partner. When this uncle and his partner died, the netsuke were inherited by de Waal and the collection travelled once more to Europe, where it was settled into the quiet harbour of de Waal's London house. The peregrinations of the sculptures paralleled the loves, the culture, success, tragedy, and continuity of the Ephrussi family itself.

With the deportation of the Acadians, there was nothing physical to be saved. When the settlers were brought in to take over their farms, they found handmade wheelbarrows on the shore filled with small, rotting household objects. Everything else had been appropriated and moved or burned. The only remnants of past lives that have floated up onto the shores of my life are my grandmother's treadle sewing machine, a carpenter's tool box, and a bill of sale for a boat. The carpenter's box is made of wood. It's long and heavy, made to carry hand tools—some saws, a mitre box, a level, hammer, nails, and so on. Grandfather would add or subtract tools in his carpenter's box depending on the job. For fixing fence posts, the finer tools would be left in the workshop. Then it was pliers and a clincher for taking out old staples, a hammer to set the new staples, an axe to trim the new post, and a heavy mallet to drive the posts into the ground. Grandfather always carried three saws with different teeth settings and a needle file to sharpen the teeth when they dulled.

Today, carpenters use a circular saw or skill saws that can rip through an eight-foot piece of plywood end to end in sixty seconds. The blades are changed right on the saw. Chain saws and hydraulic splitters have replaced axes. Even the modest hammer has been replaced by pneumatic guns that drive in nails like bullets at the pull of a trigger. Old hand-powered tools have become rusty curiosities. I keep Grandfather's carpenter box in a shed and use it to store a few old tools.

The Ephrussi palace still stands grandly on Vienna's Ringstrasse, just across from the famous Vienna State Opera House. While the palace's imposing walls and physical position in the city are unchanged, the harbour and landscapes of my childhood in Grand Étang have changed utterly. They are so different that without photographs it's impossible to recall how they looked, let alone to use them as memory portals for a family's life. The village fish plant is long gone. The many quays and waterside sheds are gone. The harbour looks neat and tidy now with just enough activity to remind the viewer that fishing still happens here. The disappearance of the fish has been like the sun fading. Yet I have the impression people better understand the situation of hungry polar bears in the Arctic than what has happened to Atlantic fishing villages.

What could I use as a metaphor to explain my own family's history? The fiddle is central to Acadian cultural life, but a fiddle isn't a precious unchanging *objet d'art*. Fiddles are made to be played. No one keeps them in a glass case. When the Nazis arrived to appropriate the Ephrussi's Vienna home, de Waal's great-grandfather was practising his cello in the library as he liked to do in the afternoon. There were no cellos, nor any home libraries on the Acadian shore, but there sure was a lot of fiddle music.

Acadian society, like Metis society, was a New World invention. It had roots in the Old World but had evolved differently from the European models. When my grandfather William Doucet was born in 1881, Acadian society had no bankers, no lawyers, no accountants, and very few schools or teachers. Acadian villages, like Mi'kmaw reserves, were scattered, remote places of refuge that depended on an intense relationship with the land.

It was an insular world. Grandfather conducted all his business with a handshake. "A man's word is his bond" wasn't a quaint expression; it was the way life was. *Évangéline*, the great poem of the Acadian deportation, was written in English by a Boston poet/Brahmin with a mouthful of a name: Henry Wadsworth Longfellow. It was known among Acadians but rarely read. Grandfather's five eldest sons went to school but only enough to learn to read, yet the three youngest all studied at university. In the span of just one generation, Acadians emerged from their long isolation to become the quintessential Canadians—firm believers in federalism yet still anchored in their own culture, language, and history.

When I think of the Acadian fiddle, it does not have an adjective before it. It is just a fiddle. Fiddles are played until they are worn to the nub or passed on to another player until they are. My cousin Marcel Doucet played at his first dance when he was eight years old. To no one's surprise, he became a professional musician, playing from Whitehorse to Edinburgh. He began by hitchhiking from town to town on Cape Breton Island, his knapsack over one shoulder, his battered violin case over the other.

The recording studio in Chéticamp is named in memory of him, but I have no idea where his violin has gone, and his music went with him. He recorded only one tune of his own. Some friends asked him to fill in the last track of a CD to complete their recording. He obliged them and called the tune "Available Space." In spite of the curious title and last-minute composition, whenever I hear Marcel's tune, I am always surprised at how confident it sounds. It swoops and dives, pauses and rushes. It's as if Marcel had all the time in the world to lay down his musical thoughts. "Available Space" is no more than a couple of minutes long, but it is still played by Maritime musicians.

Marcel's fiddle had purpose and meaning when he played it, and he played a lot—in parish halls, taverns, schools, at summer festivals, even at the National Arts Centre in Ottawa. But the Acadian fiddle belongs to the moment and the dance, and the dance belongs to the community. A fiddle will never find a comfortable home in a display case like the netsuke do.

If I could choose something to represent the Doucet family or the community, it wouldn't be any object, not even a fiddle.

A landscape makes more sense, for everywhere Acadians settled they carved a distinctive shape from the land, whether it was a Mississippi bayou or the Bay of Fundy wetlands, but this wasn't an individual achievement. It took the community to build a dyke or create a bayou town. There were eight boys and two girls in my father's family. Except for their sixth son, all the boys in the Doucet family worked the land from the youngest age, plowing, weeding, and creating that distinctive narrow Acadian farm that runs in a long strip from the seashore to the mountains. On the mountain side, Grandfather had planted a beautiful apple orchard. His mill cut timber into planks and rough wooden blocks for the furnace. Nearer the coast, the land was cleared for cattle pasture, and next to the sea, there were hayfields and gardens.

It sounds romantic and I found it so, but the romance came with immense amounts of work. Apple trees had to be pruned, the apples harvested carefully, and the land around the trees kept clear of weeds and invasive scrub. In winter, timber was cut and sleighed out from mountain woodlots. When houses were heated entirely with wood, this wasn't a trivial task. Animals, hayfields, and gardens constantly needed tending, and when my father, Fern, her sixth son, was born, Grandmother said to her husband, "William, this one doesn't go to the barn."

Grandmother had decided this son would stay in the house to help her. So instead of doing field and farm work, Fern learned how to cook at his mother's apron. Wherever he lived the cooking skills he learned there served him well—and all those lucky enough to sit at his table. When I think of Dad, I often think of the delicious meals he created. He did it all so naturally and quickly that I was scarcely aware of him working at all.

Cooking has proved to be more enduring than the landscape, which has changed again as the conifer tribe has come marching down from the high mountains to gobble up the untended orchards, pastures, and fields that my grandfather's generation wrenched from the soil with so much sweat and toil. On the east coast of the island, the disappearance of small farms is so extensive and the omnipresence of the forest so dense and powerful that the Cabot Trail has turned into this green tunnel in the forest, the fields and ocean views now gone.

Today, the old Acadian landscapes of the marshlands and the coastal fishing villages are remembered more than lived in, so what alchemy can I use to recall five hundred years of history for my grandchildren? What thread can I unwind for them to sew the coat of their family story as de Waal did so well with his netsuke?

CHAPTER 7

Great-Great-Grandparents

*There is a poem
in every moment.
They rise up
from the cracks
in the earth
to put wings on the day.*

My own grandfathers are so vivid in my memory that it's sometimes hard to accept that for my grandchildren they scarcely exist. For them, my grandfathers are their great-great-grandfathers, and who remembers someone so distant? A great-great-grandfather sounds Biblical, like the generations between King David and Abraham, but that's not the way it is for me. Their great-great-grandfathers are still present in my life.

My English grandfather, George Oliver, had a favourite pub beside the Thames. He would drink from a tall mug of golden beer, and I would drink lemonade and eat "crisps." It was from the pub's small terrace just behind the river wall that I saw my first rowing races and like my grandfather conceived a great interest in the sport. Like him, I would join a rowing club and spend many a fine summer morning on the river.

I can still see his figure. He was a tall, strong, well-built man with a ruddy English face and a calm demeanour. Nothing rattled him. He was very different from my Acadian grandfather, who was short and wiry with high cheekbones, all energy and movement.

I understand why a great-great-grandfather seems out of mind, out of time. It is that way for me. My great-great-grandfather takes me back to Magloire, the atheist storekeeper. Magloire, or Magah as he was called, was my grandfather's grandfather. He had two sons, Arsène, a schooner captain, and Moise, a politician—a small family. For the rest, he is as mysterious as the Great Auk, but among Acadians, remembering some small thing of a great-great-grandfather is not uncommon. I am Clive à Fernand (*dit* Fern), à William, à Arsène, à Magloire (*dit* Magah). This is how my father explained who I was before I was sent off to the village for the summer. My cousin Roland was instructed in exactly the same way by his mother for his first day at school. "Remember, you are Roland à Gerard, à William, à Arsène, à Magah," and along with his school books that's what Roland took to school. It was such a small thing, a single line of names, no more than some dots in a helix of DNA.

My English grandfather was a brave redcoat. George Oliver wore the uniform of the Queen's Household Cavalry in the Great War, and if he had been born a century or so earlier, he might have been one of the redcoats assigned to herding Acadians onto the deportation ships at Beaubassin and Grand-Pré. I would want my grandchildren to remember this so that they could also remember that your enemies may not be who you think they are. Their English great-great-grandfather fought in the Great War because that's what patriotic young men did, no matter that the war itself made no sense. In the Second World War, he drove an ambulance and pulled people out of burning buildings, and I'm sure he would have signed up for the Seven Years War.

If your government decides to commit the nation to war it's very hard to reject that call, and for a soldier impossible. This is worth remembering when one is tempted by the cynicism of the thought that voting or governments don't matter. It mattered for my generation that the Canadian government decided the Vietnam War was not for Canada, because I would have gone, just as Canadian boys in this generation have gone to Afghanistan without thinking about it until it was too late.

Part of the reason it is so hard to remember great-great-grandfathers is that their times are so different. My great-great-grandfather Magloire had no car, no running water in the house, no telephone, no radio, no television, no phone, no easy access to a newspaper. My grandson Felix can't imagine such a primitive existence. Felix thinks electricity is like water. You turn on a screen and it blinks to life just as turning on the tap at the sink makes pure, clean water flow. It's a birthright, not an invention. It's part of the natural round.

Charles Ephrussi would understand cellphone screens and virtual reality today because he understood mediated reality in 1895. He was a passionate admirer of how artists were reinterpreting life though painting, writing, sculpture, drawing, and poetry. He understood instinctively that reality was both perceived as well as substantive and used his inherited wealth to forge a career as an art historian, critic, writer, publisher, and editor of the famous *Gazette des Arts* magazine.

As I read de Waal's family biography, I could easily imagine Charles Ephrussi promenading down a famous Paris boulevard with Jules Laforgue, his literary secretary at his side, conversing volubly about the next edition of the magazine. And if you can't, there is a pencil sketch reproduced in the book of Charles and Jules doing exactly that. Long before there were selfies, these men were creating their own with just pencil and paper.

You can see the modern imaginative dimension in its nascent form in the Parisian life of Charles Ephrussi. He was a global citizen before the idea was invented. His private collections of radical Impressionist art and Japanese netsuke were all harbingers of the new global, mediated reality that a century later would launch the internet, international awareness, and the selfie universe.

On the Cape Breton side of the Atlantic, this perceptual revolution was a very long way from being obvious. In the 1890s, the little harbour of Grand Étang was deeply rooted in old-fashioned, direct physical action, not any mediated reality. The day's work needed many hands and immense physical labour. There were no powerful diesel engines to drive a boat effortlessly over the sea, no satellite weather forecasts, no power winches to drop and haul the lobster traps, no sonar to read the sea bottom. No touch of a button or flick of a switch.

Photographs from those days show men lean as wolves, their faces burned dark brown by the sun, their hands thick from constant work, their muscles ropy. The physical work was unrelenting. Body fat burned away from the young men like rainwater shed from a rain slicker. "Wooden ships and iron men" wasn't just an expression. The young men were all wire and fire, the older men strong and solid as oak trees, but there is more than work in the harbour. There is also lightness and music. On Sunday night when the fishermen returned to the harbour from their families and tending their Sunday gardens, inevitably someone pulled out a fiddle and the tunes would sail. There would be dancing. When she was ninety-five, Madame LeBlanc, whose old house we are now renting, admitted with a sigh, "We were poor but we had fun. How we laughed!"

In Grand Étang, no one thought of curating one's life on Facebook or Instagram. Life was just lived. One summer, my English grandmother (my grandchildren's great-great-grandmother) visited from Britain to meet the parents of her daughter's husband. It wasn't every day someone from a great city like London visited Grand Étang, and the occasion was long remembered. After supper, Grandfather would place two comfortable, wooden chairs at the front of the house for Elsie Oliver and Marie Hache to watch the sunset. There they would sit together, side by side, and watch the sun go down behind the sea. Elsie Oliver spoke no French and Marie Hache very little English. Yet they sat together companionably and watched the sun send its rosy fingers across the summer sea.

No one ever thought to take a photograph of that moment and those women from different sides of a vast ocean united by the marriage of their children. The only one that exists is in my head. Nor did Marie Hache-Doucet want one taken. She found cameras intrusive and unpleasant. We have only one photograph of her. She is standing beside the buggy, frozen in the frame, looking uncomfortable and severe. It's Sunday and she is on her way to church with Grandfather. Marie Hache is in her late sixties. She is a tall, imposing woman dressed severely in dark colours. She stares off into the distance, aware that my mother is snapping a quick photograph of her with her little brownie camera. She does not look pleased.

Grandfather is sitting in the buggy, waiting for her to climb into the seat beside him. The driving reins are held loosely in his hands. He is wearing a handsome leather coat over his Sunday suit. I never look at the photograph without feeling some sadness, because not long after the photograph was taken, Marie Hache developed a blood clot in her leg and had to have it amputated. She recovered but died a little later of another one. When I look at her guarded expression in the photograph, I wonder if she already suspected that her life would not be long.

It doesn't seem fair. After ten children, she deserved a longer, easier old age. She died at seventy-two, and Grandfather never remarried but lived many vigorous years without her. In that photograph, I always feel the rough hand of mortality on my grandmother's shoulder pulling her away.

The photograph now hangs in my study. I'm sure my children rarely pause to consider that they are intimately connected to this tall, forbidding woman standing beside the horse-drawn buggy. The photograph seems ancient, as if from a time beyond imagining.

Nor could you imagine a more different place from my grandparents' white clapboard house than the sophisticated Paris apartment of Charles Ephrussi. The most compelling characteristic of the farmhouse was its simplicity. There was nothing in it that was superfluous to function. A large Findley wood stove from Ontario stood on one side of the room and accomplished many things. The fire heated water in a tank beside the stove. The oven baked bread. Pots and pans and food were warmed in a special box above the stove, and the surface was always busy with teakettles and bubbling soups.

Opposite the stove, on the other side of the kitchen, was a long countertop that ran the entire length of the room. Above it were rows of cupboards. At one end of the counter was a sink and at the other end were barrels of flour and oats that were accessed from the top of the counter with a scoop. "Eating oats by the barrel full" wasn't an antique expression. It reflected the reality of big families and rural life.

In the middle of the kitchen was a work table on castors that could be shifted around from one side of the kitchen to the other at a moment's notice. It was used for breakfasts, small meals, and kneading dough. The kitchen floor was covered in gold-coloured linoleum and was always polished immaculately. Such was the kitchen's simplicity that without people to animate the room, it looked spare to the point of being denuded. But with people it changed entirely, for the kitchen was the principal stage upon which the life of the household unfolded, and stages must be kept uncluttered. The set must always be ready to be struck in preparation for the next event, which could be anything from the simple serving of breakfast to the jump and jazz of an evening kitchen party.

Charles Ephrussi's Paris apartment was also a stage but a very different one. It was an intimate, private, densely appointed one with a library and a magnificent collection of Impressionist paintings. The apartment was furnished with elegant furniture and soft carpets where Charles's literary secretary, Jules Laforgue, liked to linger as much as work.

In Grandfather's house, there were no paintings on the walls, not a single one. There was a small crucifix near the kitchen door as there was in every village kitchen, and in the parlour the famous photograph of the Cabot Trail as it snakes up the side of French Mountain. Neither could be described as art. The photograph portrayed exactly what you would see with your own eyes if you stood at the same place the photographer had. The crucifix represented the village church, which could be found if you turned left at the end of the farm lane and clip-clopped along for a couple of kilometres. The cross and the photograph were simple flags of belonging to the community and the land. They were not metaphors standing in for reality but direct representatives of the reality that surrounded people.

Change came faster and easier in Paris. When people saw Renoir's painting of a summer luncheon (with Charles Ephrussi in the background), it wasn't just the size of it or the quality of the painting that impressed. People's interest was also animated by the shock of recognition. This summer scene wasn't an evocation of aristocratic château life or a portrait of a church icon. In its essence, the famous summer boating party was familiar, something that many did.

Today, that sentiment of "I've been there, done that" has broadened from a large oil painting into millions of tiny, instant electronic images of everything from people zip-lining between mountain peaks to the intimacy of a family dinner.

Every man and woman with a phone has become their own recorder of his or her life. The self-absorption of the modern mediated life squeezes distant communities like Grand Étang, pressing it from both sides, leaving it simultaneously both more connected to the wider world and less by presenting reality as it is processed among people in cities but curated—not necessarily how people live.

In spite of the physical distance, history, and cultural gap between the Ephrussi bankers of Vienna and Doucet farmers and fishermen of Grand Étang, de Waal and I have one important thing in common—our reason for writing. De Waal begins his book with the reflection that intimate family memories, like the hours his great-grandmother took to dress for the social battle of the Ringstrasse in Vienna, were becoming the subject of dinner table anecdotes. Even the story of how the tiny netsuke carvings survived the Nazi looting was beginning to sound anecdotal and curious rather a courageous act in a terrifying reality.

Absorbed in his own career and the busy life of his young family, de Waal realized that unless he made a sustained effort to create a coherent narrative around his own family memories, they would all inevitably slip away into stories around the dinner table that would betray their subjects by caricaturizing them.

Like de Waal, I can feel my own memories sinking into these same predictable accounts that I have started to flip through like fading snapshots in an old family album. Although my memories are far from the elegance of Vienna's Ringstrasse, they have their own unique character and connection to world events. The kinds of deceptions used to lure Jews onto trains to go to "work camps" and keep their bank accounts stored loyally in Austria were also used to deceive Acadians. Acadians were asked to prove their loyalty to the British crown by giving up their arms and boats, which they did, just as Edmund de Waal's great-grandfather proved his loyalty to Austria by refusing to move his bank's resources to Switzerland. Both were misled and then trapped.

Today, the Acadian deportation is called a cultural genocide rather than a physical one. The deportations were designed to break communities and families by forcing individuals to blend into the wider society, stripping them of their language, culture, and sense of place.

The Canadian government would do the same thing in the twentieth century with residential schools for Aboriginal peoples. The goal was to extinguish the indigenous languages and culture, and force a "blending" with the dominant culture. It's a familiar story. Imperial cultures often try to protect their dominant position by suppressing competing cultures, but the most successful do not. This is one of the ways the Persian and Roman empires prospered so well for so long.

The Acadian deportation is worth remembering because it set the template for what would come later in other places. Churches and villages were burned, a law of no return invoked, and the men and women were physically separated, the sexes forced to board on different ships. It was this forced separation that became the inspiration for Longfellow's poem *Évangéline*. The details of the poem about a young woman, Évangéline, and her fiancé, Gabriel, separated on their wedding day are imagined, but the guts of the story must have occurred. Men and women, boys and girls were separated, and among them there must have been young lovers, pledged to each other but forced apart.

Through enormous personal effort, many Acadian families would reconnect, others never would. Paul-Marie Doucet was eight years old when his mother, father, brother, and sisters were loaded onto the ships at Beaubassin, the largest town in the Bay of Fundy. He would never see anyone from his birth family again.

There are only three Acadian villages in all of Atlantic Canada that survived the deportation. Everywhere else, people had to start again with nothing much more than their bare hands. Whether it was Belle Île en Mer off the northern French coast, Louisiana bayous, or remote Atlantic harbours like Chéticamp and Grand Étang, Acadians had no choice but to settle in places no one else desired. Patrolling British warships made sure the law of no return was enforced.

Twenty years after he had escaped the British warships, Paul-Marie would settle in Chéticamp with a wife and three young sons. Simon, one of his sons, would cut a small farm out of the forest along on the bluffs close to the harbour at Grand Étang and raise a large family there. Simon's grandson, Magloire, would open a store, not far from where I have found the field for sale.

CHAPTER 8

What Superpower Would You Choose?

One of the good things about the fish plant being closed is that the harbour water is now clear as crystal. You can swim in it. We just have to walk down to the boat launch at the end of the harbour and walk in. On the way, the children and I talk about important things like superheroes and dragons. Superheroes and the gaming world Dungeons and Dragons are new territory for me. My grandfather and I didn't talk about these things. Not once. So I don't bring much wisdom to these conversations, mostly I just listen.

    I am carrying the paddleboard and Clea is carrying the paddle. On our return, Felix will carry the paddle and I will continue with the board. (This division of labour has only been decided after much negotiation.) On the way to the boat launch, Felix asks, "Is school free, Grandpa?"

    I have no idea where this question comes from or why, but this is Felix's way. His curiosity skids around, landing hither and thither like a butterfly touching down before launching again. This question seems easy enough.

    "No, school isn't free. It's paid for by our taxes, which everyone must pay."

    "And swimming lessons? Are they free?" asks Felix.

    "No, that comes out of your mom and dad's own pocket."

"I don't understand," says Felix.

"Well, you've got two pockets in your trousers, right?"

Felix agrees that he has two pockets.

"Well, one is a collective pocket into which everyone puts some money and the other pocket is just for your own money."

"That's more like your allowance," says Clea knowledgeably.

"Correct," I reply, also feeling sure about this. "From the collective pocket, which is a lot bigger than your own pocket money, we pay for our schools, doctors, roads, street lights, buses, clean water, parks. A lot of things."

"But swimming lessons come from your own pocket," says Felix trying to fix the difference.

"And violin lessons," interrupts Clea, because she takes violin lessons.

"Yes, violin lessons your parents have to pay for from their own pocket."

Violin lessons do not interest Felix and he moves on to his favourite subject, superheroes. "If you could have any superpower, Grandpa, what would you choose?"

With the world at my command, I'm a little unsure what I would choose, and finally I say, "I'd like the power to make people happy."

Felix is immediately disdainful. "That's not a real power, Grandpa."

"I think it is. Imagine saying 'poof' and people's worries were gone and they were happy. Wouldn't that be a great power?"

Felix shakes his head. "That's a fake power. That's an evil power. You can't force someone to be happy. A real power is being able to save the planet from an asteroid or wrapping up a bad guy in a spider web like Spider-Man does."

"So what real power would you like?" I ask, curious.

"I'd like a car that flies."

I shake my head, disappointed. "That's not a real power. That's just an invention. Besides we've already got cars that fly. They're called planes."

"Not a plane. A car that that you can drive on the road like a real car, but it can take off into the sky whenever you want, without wings. Like in Harry Potter."

Clea says, "Grandpa's right. A flying car is just an invention. It's not a superpower."

Felix finds he must agree with his sister, which is always painful.

"A superpower would be, being able to swim under the water for a long time like a whale. So you never had to worry about catching your breath," says Clea.

We all agree this power would be useful, but neither I nor Clea is sure we want to swim underwater for long periods of time. Clea would prefer to fly.

"What about you, Felix? You haven't chosen your superpower yet."

Felix thinks for a bit, then decides he wants the power to immobilize bad guys with an immobility ball. He would start with his teacher, Monsieur Cyr.

Clea shakes her head. "Not possible, Grandpa."

"Why not?" I ask.

"Because Monsieur Cyr would always be stuck in his immobility ball and never be able to teach anyone."

Felix allows that could be a problem.

"How about we keep your immobility superpower but just for asteroids flying toward Earth," I suggest.

Felix thinks this has possibility, but he still likes the idea of immobilizing Monsieur Cyr.

"What about The Flash?" I say. "Then you would never be late for school."

Felix thinks about this and decides he does have a problem with being on time for anything. Super speed would help. He decides to take Flash speed.

When we arrive at the boat launch, we push the paddleboard into the water and away we go. Felix and Clea immediately begin climbing and diving off the paddleboard as quickly and happily as otters. The salt water feels pleasant against the skin, a gentle scrub with each dive. I play with Felix and Clea, pushing each other back and forth across the board and falling in the water as much as we stand on the board. Until, like an old seal, all I want to do is pull myself up on a harbour rock and bathe in the sun.

I didn't want to mention it to Felix, but there was one superpower that I did chase after pretty hard in Ottawa and that was the office of the mayor. A mayor has important superpowers because he has a big role in deciding how the money in our collective pocket is used. As I sat at the harbour's edge watching the children play, their voices ringing out across the water with effervescent joy, it seemed to me that Felix was right. Taxes and the collective pocket aren't nearly as much fun as repelling errant asteroids. Perhaps that was the superpower for me.

The more I thought about it, the more it seemed to me that there is something even more powerful than repelling errant asteroids, but I've never seen any superhero with it. Repelling asteroids is about preserving life, but life has to come from somewhere to be saved and no superhero has the power to create life, the greatest power of all.

A fish in the sea or a human being at the table doesn't just happen by executive fiat. It is related to some invisible, inscrutable spirit that impels life forward everywhere. It is this spirit that creates the soul, and the soul finds a home in the land and then the land creates life. This is a superpower so powerful I cannot even imagine the words to describe it. It can defeat even colliding asteroids.

CHAPTER 9

Lost Landscapes and Safe Harbours

From the lone shieling of the misty island
Mountains divide us, and the waste of seas;
Yet still the blood is strong, the heart is Highland,
And we, in dreams, behold the Hebrides.
—Poem fragment outside the Lone Shieling, Cape Breton Highlands National Park

Where is the thatch roofed village, the home of
Acadian farmers,
Men whose lives glided on like rivers that water
the woodlands,
Darkened by the shadows of earth but reflecting
an image of heaven?
Where are those pleasant farms and the farmers
forever departed!
Scattered like dust and leaves...
—Excerpt from *Évangéline*, Henry Wadsworth Longfellow

My favourite pub in Chéticamp is the Doryman. It serves a great fish and chips and has a big dance floor, a small stage for musicians, and lots of windows on the ocean side. It sits at the northern edge of the town, and if so inclined you can watch the boats coming and going through the mouth of the harbour. One evening as I was going to the tavern for a pint, I came across a man sitting alone on some steps at a side door that no one ever used. He was crying. His face was buried in his hands and his shoulders were shaking. I decided to put off my pint and sat down beside him.

He wiped his tear-streaked face. He was younger than me, perhaps fifty, and looked to be well kept with fine summer clothes. He did not seem drunk or in some chemical distress, but he was certainly upset. He did not look at me. For a long time he stared out at the harbour and the island that forms the western side of it. He did not say anything. I did not say anything. He began to take long, even breaths. The tears stopped.

"It's my first time home in…twenty-five years," he said with a deep, rattling sigh. For a moment, I thought he was going to start crying again, but he did not. Instead, he said, "I don't know what happened. One minute I was fine, the next I was crying. I'm a film producer in Toronto," he said, as if this would explain things.

Not knowing what to say, I said nothing.

Then he asked as people often do, "Are you from here?"

"Grand Étang," I said pointing down the road.

"What's your name?" he asked.

I told him and he said, "Oh yes, I've heard of you."

I nodded, appreciating that he had. We shook hands. He smiled a crooked smile, stood up, and said, "Thanks for stopping. I'm okay. It was the shock of seeing the place not in my memory. Memory is more reliable. I should keep it that way," he said, and his smile took on an ironic twist as if he both believed and did not believe what he was saying.

"I understand."

He looked at me curiously. I thought he was about to say something more, but he just nodded and walked away toward the town. I didn't get his name and never saw him again.

The truth is I'm not sure I do understand. Behind those tears is a mystery of connection and disconnection with a place, with a landscape, which I've certainly been able to feel but never really understand. I think it has something to do with the brevity of life and the feeling of our own vulnerability in the face of the looming crevasse of eternity—that, and the fact that we learn to feel sheltered by some landscapes, to feel like this is home. This doesn't mean the landscape of home is benign or easy. I don't think the Hebrides is, for example. It's the feeling the landscape gives to people who grow up there.

Whatever it may be, it's the same mystery that inspired the poem on the cairn in front of the Lone Shieling in the park. The Lone Shieling is a thatch-roofed, stone reproduction of a Scottish Highland crofter's cabin. It stands alone beside the road in the centre of Cape Breton Highlands National Park. Its thatch roof is rarely in good repair. Often it has holes in it. One end of the cabin is walled off as a stable for animals. On the other side of the wall is a cooking and sleeping area. The Lone Shieling is not much more than a cave with man-made walls. It stands by itself at the edge of the road, sheltered by the canopy of an old-growth Acadian forest. No other human habitation is nearby.

I've seen it many times but it never fails to fascinate me. The idea of people living in this little stone "croft" scratches at the inside of my soul. Life here seems much harder than a Mi'kmaw encampment. The sugar maples that shelter the Lone Shieling go back 350 years. Their trunks and branches stretch up and out of sight toward the sky. Walking on the surrounding forest paths, I can find the same sense of wonder that I do in a grand cathedral where the stone pillars stretch toward the light of the clerestory windows, which is curious because the Lone Shieling is so simple, so poor. Surely no one would live here unless circumstances had forced them to. Life would be too hard.

The hundred acres of the intervale where the Lone Shieling stands were gifted to the government by a successful son of Pleasant Bay. It was an important gift because it became the impetus for the creation of the park itself.

When I read that poet's words on the plaque beside the Lone Shieling or hear the plaintive chorus of "The Skye Boat Song" I feel the haunting fragility of time and place. "Speed, bonnie boat, like a bird on the wind, Onward! The sailors cry. Carry the lad that's born to be king over the sea to Skye." "The Sky Boat Song" is supposed to be about bonnie Prince Charlie escaping the British. I don't think so. For me the song celebrates the Scottish landscape and its loss—taken away by war, land clearances, and *la force des choses*. Loss of a home can happen to anyone, like that man I found crying beside the Doryman. The reality is we all lose the landscape of our childhoods, even if we never leave home. Inevitably, we become strangers banished to a distant shore. If we're very lucky, we get the chance to revisit that distant shore through our grandchildren.

Acadians and Scots are both refugee peoples from imperial land clearances. Lord Cornwallis, in charge of the Highland clearances, instructed his soldiers to nail the doors shut and burn the shieling to the ground if the inhabitants of a Highland croft were suspected of being Stuart supporters. Admiral Cornwallis put a price on Mi'kmaw scalps and oversaw the deportation of the Acadians and the burning of their communities. Not surprisingly, in Cape Breton, there has always been a complicity between Scots, Acadians, and Mi'kmaq.

Like the Hebrides, the Acadian marshland fields of the Bay of Fundy exist only in my imagination. They weren't cut from the forest as happened in Cape Breton but were borrowed from the sea by bending nature with earth dykes and an ingenious one-way gate called a *clapet*. These gates were hinged so that they responded to pressure from the rising tide that pushed them shut automatically, thus preventing the corrosive salt water from entering and damaging the fields beyond the dyke. But when the tide sank and the external pressure disappeared, the two-way hinge allowed the gate to move in the opposite direction, and the fresh water that had been damned behind the dyke was released to flow into the sea. In this way, the marshland fields did not turn into an insalubrious bog, which happens when fresh water remains bottled behind dykes.

These tidal fields didn't require the hard work of fertilizing each fall. In the spring, the land was renewed simply by leaving the clapets open for a couple of days, permitting the fields to be flooded by the high spring tides, which deposited tons of rich alluvial soil, enriching them with only the slightest effort from the farmer; then the clapets were returned to their normal two-way operation. It was a sustainable, renewable agriculture that simply slightly rejigged the ordinary forces of nature.

The original dyke technology came from France with early settlers like Charles d'Aulnay, but it must have been re-engineered to fit the New World environment where the tides were so much higher and more powerful than anything in France. At the village of Grand-Pré (Great Meadow) these coastal, ocean fields still stretch as far as the eye can see, and the memory of the Acadian villages they supported has endured.

At the beginning of the twentieth century, when Canadian Pacific was advertising their new transcontinental train service they used images of "Évangéline" with pastoral scenes of the countryside around Grand-Pré to tempt tourists to take the train east. It is a measure of the powerful nature of Longfellow's poem and the pastoral beauty of old Acadie that three centuries after the deportation, images of Acadian marsh fields still evoked a vivid response in people's hearts and minds.

Canadian Pacific wasn't alone in exploiting the memory of Évangéline's Acadie. The Cajun villages of the Mississippi Delta have also become tourist attractions and are advertised to good effect. Visitors love to wander around the central squares of towns like St. Martinville and Abbeville. The simple elegance of these small urban places—the church on one side of the town square, stores and cafes on another, the broad verandas and solid town hall on another—endures. And in the Louisiana countryside, the humble Acadian cabin with its steeply sloping roof and simple porch has entered the architectural vernacular of the American south.

There are more Doucets, Leblancs, and Boudreaus in Louisiana than there are in all of Atlantic Canada, and they speak French with the same accents and cadences as we do. It is a curious thing, this sense of a connection across so much distance and time. I have a powerful memory of a baking-hot August night in St. Martinville. The night air of the Mississippi Delta was saturated with rich tropical perfumes. It seemed as if the sun hadn't so much set as parked briefly behind a tree where it rested like a sleeping lion waiting for the dawn. From the far end of the square came the familiar sound of the fiddle and a street dance. It felt exotic and familiar at the same time.

I had been invited to the Congrès mondial acadien, a gathering of Acadians from all over the world, to read some poems from my collection *Looking for Henry*. I had never been to Louisiana before, and everything about it interested me, even the August heat that sat upon the land like a hot ladle. Like the Mississippi Delta itself, Louisiana is a rich and marvellous place. At the Congress, I met Choctaw Indians, Creoles, long-lost cousins, artists, musicians, politicians, lawyers, businessmen, folklorists, storytellers, and poets; but at night the formality of the Congrès mondial acadien dissolved, leaving only this heavy languidness in the soft Louisiana darkness, which hushed the soul's murmur.

Somewhere in the dark, I heard a woman singing a lullaby to her baby. Tears suddenly sprang from my eyes and began to course down my cheeks. It was as if the night itself was sobbing a wondrous hope that had no beginning and no end.

My guess is that the tears of the man sitting on the stairs at the side of the Doryman came from the same place mine did in St. Martinville. Untouchable and unknowable like the light of a sunset. As much as you cherish it, you cannot hold it.

We don't have beautiful village squares like St. Martinville in Cape Breton nor great marsh fields like at Grand-Pré, but we do have small harbours and they have their own charm. I have a cousin, Roger Doucet, who grew up in the little half-hip house beside the Co-op overlooking the harbour of Grand Étang. Grandfather's farm was only about a mile from the harbour, but Roger's childhood was completely different from mine. His family had no land, no barn, no animals to take care of. His father, Calixte, was the manager of the village Co-op, just a hop, skip, and a jump from their house.

Roger's idea of work began early. When the fishermen came in with the morning's catch, he would hustle down from his house to the wharf to meet the boats. There was always some fisherman who had run out of smokes. Roger would quickly find himself a commission and sprint back up the hill to the Co-op, order in hand, to buy the requested the cigarettes. Today, a boy cannot buy cigarettes, but in those days everyone knew smoking was a harmless habit.

Roger would be given a nickel for his efforts, and at eight years old he was already a successful entrepreneur with his own money jingling in his pocket for ice cream and soda. Whereas I was totally dependent on the goodwill of my grandfather and our weekly trips to the Co-op. At the Co-op, which was filled with imposing, busy people who wanted to talk to Grandpa, I was shy and never asked for anything, thinking an orange soda cost a lot of money. Grandfather, not wanting a soda or ice cream himself, rarely thought his grandson might like a Sussex Orange Crush or Cream Soda, or perhaps some striped vanilla, strawberry, chocolate Neapolitan ice cream from Scotsburn Dairy.

One morning, Roger and a chum were scavenging around the pillars of a wharf looking for crabs and discovered a dead man floating there. The RCMP were called in from Chéticamp to examine the corpse. They studied the matter for some time before deciding the man had slipped and fallen, hitting his head on the rocks as he fell. The blow had knocked him unconscious and he had drowned under the wharf. Today it would not be possible for a body to float unnoticed under some decking until discovered by two vagabond boys. But such was the intensity of the old harbour's life, the close construction of many buildings and docks, that there were all kinds of narrow, hidden places out of sight of people passing by.

Today, Roger is a computer guy and lives in Idaho. The last time we talked in the village he was on his way to England and Ireland. He wanted to visit fishing coves in Cornwall and Wales that still sheltered small inshore fishing fleets. This was more important to him than all the art galleries of London. Last time we walked around the harbour at Grand Étang, which is as pretty as ever but empty of activity, Roger explained if he were a high-tech billionaire, he would rebuild all the smoky, smelly, fishy busyness that he remembered from his childhood.

It would be no small task. The harbour was ringed with dense layers of rough, unpainted buildings, shingled barns, storage sheds, a fish processing plant, and fancier painted houses higher up the hill. I've counted twenty-seven different buildings in old photographs. The wharves themselves are crowded with handcarts and stacks of wooden barrels, with at least a dozen men variously engaged and others loafing in the summer sun. Closest to the water, there are rows of simple shacks where fishermen rested up before the next shift on the ocean. I didn't know it then but have learned since that the oldest profession in the world found trade there.

Yet, in spite of all that activity, the harbour was no more than a teaspoon of salt water nestled under the mountains. A thirty-five-foot, two-masted schooner like *Richmond Queen* was the largest boat that could berth at the dock without scraping bottom.

Roger knows his ambition to rebuild the harbour is a pipe dream, for not even a billionaire could recreate anything more than a Disney version. Without the seasonal round of the inshore fishery with each species giving way to the next in a long slow symphony of marine life, there can be little activity in the harbour. Even the blue and white seagulls, which used to crowd the sky above the wharves in peeling clouds, have flown elsewhere, leaving only a few vagabond cousins to patrol the harbour shore.

I often wonder if politicians have the slightest idea what they are talking about when they speechify about the importance of sustainability, climate change, and such. Like goldfish swimming in a bowl, they aren't capable of imagining a different bowl than the one they are in. When a new fish stock like the Arctic cod is discovered through climate change or an old fish stock starts to recover, deep-sea trawlers arrive from distant harbours to begin vacuuming up the new "resource." The ships return to their ports of origin, their holds filled with fish, but the local harbours, the local fish processing plants, the little farms, the villages and culture that fish used to support do not rekindle.

When I was a boy, the fishermen in the village had a visceral understanding that one fishing season did not make a life, that each year the fish had to come back and not just one species—all of them. The village needed all the fish tribes to return each year as faithfully as they had the season before. The idea of relying on one or two species as fishermen do today would have seemed ridiculous. I have a memory of a man who was well-known for fishing out of season and generally disregarding catch limitations being shown what the ocean looked like from the end of the wharf—upside down. After this experience, he decided that maybe the fishing regulations were for him also.

Who holds the corporations upside down when they strip-mine the sea and bend the laws of sustainability to suit their own pocketbooks? This is the connecting thought in my mind when I think of the beautiful, little bayou towns of Louisiana, the dyked fields of *Évangéline*, and our own small harbours along the Atlantic coast. They were all safe, sustainable places that people had invented with the sweat of their brow to shelter their families from the dyspepsia of war, greed, and religious conflict.

Where will our safe harbours, our renewable fields, our stable towns and villages be in the future? Where will we go when the malls and parking lots of our city environments can no longer be filled with cheap Third World goods or gasoline prices that rise faster than income? The landscapes that my generation has created are not safe landscapes. They are vast *chantiers* of exploitation, from the tar sands to the malls and parking lots of franchise America. This is what my generation has created and is leaving our grandchildren.

Sometimes when I wake, I wonder if something vital has broken inside me. Even on a beautiful summer morning, surrounded by the comforting scenes of my youth, these despairing thoughts well up. I've become repetitive and boring in my thoughts, and unlike Cassandra I'm not young or beautiful. I am just an old guy with old stories that trap me as much as illuminate. My son is right, I do need to escape these cycles of thought. I'm like a war veteran whose mind keeps returning to the same incidents in the same war; I can't seem to shake them.

My memories of failing to save Lansdowne Park in Ottawa and the north/south light rail line flow from my days on city council to the country without missing a beat, because the truth is that the landscape matters. It matters a lot. Like the walls of a house, the kinds of landscapes that we create in the city and in the country form the physical framework of our lives. City problems do not exist in isolation from the country, nor vice versa. Farmers need cities that are successful and cities need farmers to feed them. All of our human landscapes are connected because at the end of the day, we all share the same safe harbour, our planet. It's how our lives fit within that larger harbour that will determine whether or not our grandchildren will have an easy or a hard future.

CHAPTER 10

Fundraiser for Fort Mac—Tonight

> *Sometimes I think I should have a "press one for fundraising" on my phone; "press two for house painting"; "press three for paying gigs."*
> —Bruno Bourgeois, musician, The Phantoms and Le Group Lelièvre bands, house painter, Chéticamp, NS

The autumn is coming. You can't put your finger on it yet, but it's coming. The days are lighter and more airy. The shades of green are changing. In the Ottawa Valley, some trees have already budded and the valley is beginning to show the first speckles of the colours to come. In Grand Étang, the maritime summer has not let go yet. The sea is still warm. The children and I can still swim easily. The sea is tranquil, as if it knows also we are approaching summer's end, and it's decided to take a breath before playing with the storms of winter. There is an eagle sitting lazily in the grass of the bluff, not far from our front door. He is regarding the world. Everyone is waiting.

In Chéticamp, there is a big fundraiser for a young woman who has lost her house in the great wildfire at Fort McMurray, Alberta. Her house was not insured and Bruno Bourgeois has organized a party at the tavern to raise money to help her to start over. Bruno is a musician at night and a busy house painter during the day. Much loved in the community, he has played in many bands. The best known one is The Phantoms. The Phantoms play old rock tunes with an infectious joy that brings people to the dance floor faster than you can say, "Do you want to dance?" This summer they're having a fifty-year reunion, which will reunite the many singers and musicians who have played with The Phantoms over half a century of rock and roll. The entire village is looking forward to the band's reunion.

The Doryman sits at the mouth of the harbour like a square lighthouse. It seems as impermeable to change as the church, but there are no statues of saints here or pictures framed on the walls. It's just one big room with a long, narrow stage in one corner, which makes for an interesting arrangement of musicians because it forces them to play in a line. The drummer isn't hidden behind; he's at the centre of the band bracketed by guitarists, with the singer just slightly to the front between the drummer and the lead guitarist. It's an intimate, powerful setting.

The dance floor is directly in front of the stage. The rest is tables, chairs, and a battered bar. Unlike most bars, the Doryman is not dark. Sunlight pours through the large windows and fills the room with light from the sea and the sky. In the evening, you can order a decent fish and chips, a beer, and watch the sun go down, but the "Fundraiser for Fort Mac" isn't a casual evening.

Bruno has called in some favours and put together a great lineup for the night. The room is jammed and no one is looking at the sun going down. Draft beer flies, the music rocks, and I'm thinking if the town's volunteer fire department wasn't at the party the pub would be in trouble for overcrowding. There are a few brief, heartfelt speeches, but mostly the room just rocks. It's one of those moments in life when it feels good simply to be alive. By evening's end, $6,000 has been raised.

The community rallying to help a local girl living far from home is a fine thing. Nonetheless, I must confess to having mixed feelings about Fort McMurray. I'm happy to contribute but not so happy with the tar sands. This vast extraction project takes lakes of crystalline water and turns it into sick cesspools to separate the tar from the water. At the same time, the project has vacuumed up the younger generation from Atlantic Canada. Everyone has a relative in Fort McMurray. Why couldn't we find ways to employ the young at home in projects that return something more enduring than pollution and a new truck? I find myself grimacing at the thought of the tar sands, but what can you do when there is lots of money out there and none here? The young have no choice. They get on a plane and go west.

The tar sands are Canada's largest entry in the cash-and-carry earth stakes. Saudi may have gulf oil, but Canada has the tar sands; that's the line a proud Canadian is supposed to toe. Nonetheless, I can't help but feel our future isn't written in Saudi Elephant oil fields or Canadian tar sands. It's somewhere else.

Today, young people commute to and from Fort Mac for six weeks or six months. It's expected because that's where you get your truck money. This wasn't my expectation. In the 1950s, there were over two hundred children in the St. Joseph du Moine school. It never occurred to me to think that we lived in an isolated place. I had cousins and friends ready to play and go swimming on Sunday afternoon. The main road was busy with people coming and going, but if I had been an adult in the 1950s perhaps the village would have seemed more like a still pond without a breeze to ruffle the surface, as if the people were waiting for something to happen, as if Fort Mac was already calling.

The old expression is "times change," and I guess it's that simple; but when I think on it, it doesn't seem so simple. We are always living both in a time and moving simultaneously. Science now seems to be confirming that light waves move but the atoms inside the wave do not move, which seems inexplicable; something cannot move and not move. But it makes a kind of rough logic to me. We live in a time and are part of that time every morning when we get up. At the same moment, we are part of this river of moments that never stops moving, that leaves each morning moment behind even as it is being lived. This is roughly what people mean when they say "time changes." They don't mean the quality of light or time. They mean the river on which they both float and sink.

When my grandfather was born there were less than two billion people on the planet, and most of them lived as he did in the country, and much of the planet was pristine wilderness. Now we are close to ten billion, more than half live in cities, and the wild places are becoming parks rather than unbounded wild. The differences between the city and country have shrunk away. When the eighteen-wheel trucks do not arrive on time at the stores in Chéticamp and Grand Étang, the shelves become empty, just like in the city.

When my grandfather was raising his family, 80 percent of Canadians lived and worked in the country. Today 80 percent live and work in cities. This massive internal migration went into hyperdrive when the boys came home from the Second World War, and it continues to this day. The young people with good educations go first. Then it is the skilled tradesmen's turn, then the farmers, and finally the fishermen. Today everyone is "from away." Home has become where you are, not where you're from. In my father's family, out of ten children, only one brother and one sister stayed in the villages of North Inverness. At the same time, the scale of human activity has changed so utterly that the old economic life of a country village is now regarded as a quaint memory rather than real.

The planet's physical elements have become resources to serve urban populations. Entire mountain ranges are decapped for coal. The diversity of tropical forests is being replaced with plantations. The earth's greatest river systems are being turned into canals and holding ponds for hydro and irrigation projects. Ancient underground aquifers are pumped dry to irrigate crops. In biological terms, humans have become a plague species.

Everyone wants a piece of this global action. Money itself has become a commodity to be traded like pork bellies. The curious thing is money itself has no intrinsic value. It is just a facilitator. Money represents wealth but it is not wealth. Money is just another mediated reality. You can't eat, drink, or wear it or even use it to write on. Real wealth remains the processes that create the products and substances upon which human lives depend. Small villages like Grand Étang were once loaded with real wealth. They produced milk, butter, cream, eggs, construction lumber, vegetables, fruit, fish, wool, meat, people, and educational and cultural accomplishment.

One small harbour and one little village may seem trivial in the grand world of tar sands and Elephant oil fields, but multiplied by thousands across North America, rural villages gave the continent resilience, character, and a complex, assured food supply. What will happen today if a climate and/or economic disaster strikes as it did during the Great Depression? Today, if the plantations of California's central valley, the Prairies, or Florida crumble and people begin to go hungry, they won't be able to return to the villages and farms of my grandfather's day; the culture and small-scale production that made them work are gone.

The idea that Canadians could starve without food imported from distant places would have seemed bizarre to me as a boy—most of the food on our daily plate was local. But this is the reality today. Even a great food-producing area like the Ottawa Valley does not produce enough food to feed its own urban populations. There's no more than three days' supply of food in Ottawa, a city of a million people. When the big rigs stop rolling, the shelves empty fast. The world is connected not just by the internet; it's connected by how we use the earth—land and oceans.

It is these things that I can't help thinking about when I think of Fort Mac's wildfire. The thought harasses me that no amount of tar sands oil or fabulous new trucks will solve the problem of living in an unsustainable way. The only way we can do this is to live differently than the way we do today. The daily plate should be mostly local. Cities should be built for sustainability not the quickest, largest possible profit. Buildings should be no higher than the highest tree. Cars should be a choice, not a dire necessity. City blocks should be peppered with small parks so that urban environments are places people want to live in, not escape from, and the countryside needs to have work, not unemployment cheques.

The difference between Cape Breton and a city like Ottawa is mostly about remnants. There are more remnants of the old, small-scale economy in Cape Breton because there is less of the new to disguise its passing. Desiccated apple orchards still line the road. Some beautiful, old summer pastures can still be seen snaking along beside a salmon river. The skeleton of the old economy still rattles in Cape Breton. Like an old soldier with trembling hands who can't let the explosions of his old war go, these well-trodden paths burn the same routes in my mind, no matter that I am at the Doryman, surrounded by fine music and good cheer, the pleasant evening washing happily around me, raising money for Fort Mac.

Someone at the table asks me, "What's wrong?"

I reply, Nothing, because I'm troubled more than sad, although these conditions are sometimes difficult to separate. So I deflect the question and say, "I've bought some land in Grand Étang on the Old Cabot Trail. I'm going to build a house."

No one looks surprised. I guess people have figured it out faster than I have. Nonetheless, it's the first time I've admitted such an ambition beyond the confines of the family. I find it a happy thought. The land was more expensive than I wanted, but I am content with it. It has fine views of the sea and the mountains. Grandfather's old farm is not far away.

CHAPTER 11

Never an Issue to Our Happiness

No better place or better time to open this diary than the Beaver Club in the company of Sgt. Waddell, Cpl. LeClerc, and Don Wellhandes while spending a nine-day leave in the Metropolis City of London.
—Fern Doucet, November 1943

I have inherited a few oddments from my parents' house. Not much more than a shoebox, as much as de Waal received from his father before embarking on writing *The Hare with Amber Eyes*. There is a diary with a red leather cover that Dad kept during the war, and from Dad's office I took a model boat of a herring seiner, a gift from Nova Scotia fishermen when he retired, and a Haida talking stick that used to sit in a corner beside his favourite chair. I had never given either object much thought, but now that he's gone, I do.

Carved at the top of the talking stick is an eagle with its wings flared. The eagle is landing on a whale's head, which curls below the eagle unperturbed by the outstretched talons. The whale's tail joins to the hat of a Haida man who stands straight and resolute. He is holding a walking stick with a snake curled around it. I keep the stick by my own chair now. I take comfort in its silent presence. The Haida may be on the other side of the continent, but we also have whales and eagles on this side. Most days, I can see them from the window.

The talking stick tells me not to forget that we are all connected—even to trees. It is telling me to find strength in this. I took it once to a protest walk where developers were cutting down a century-old wood for more monster homes, and I used it to frame my speech. But I no longer have to make speeches, and the talking stick stays quietly by my chair.

My father's war diary was a great surprise because he was not a man who cared to keep track of his days. He was a man of deep practicality, rarely given to personal reflection. This small book from the war is the only diary of his that I know of. The entries in it reflect his character. From the death of a friend to a dance at the YMCA, the day's events are recorded in a few jerky phrases.

September 1, 1944. Boarded a cattle train for Naples. Stayed in yard all night. Our rations consist of bully beef, hardtack, beans, bacon, and turnips, tea, jam, and marge.

September 3, 1944. Arrived at Naples. Reported to No. 3 B.P.O. Sleeping in pup tents on dusty football pitch, near Vesuvius. Significant poverty everywhere here.

October 17, 1944. Day off. Went up to the front. Had dinner with Canadian Artillery men. Bags of shells falling all around. Gave me a good idea what sort of life soldiers have up at the front.

Fern Doucet was an air armourer, one of the men who kept the planes armed with bombs and bullets. His squadron flew Spitfires, Hurricanes, and later, Mosquitos. In Italy the airmen lived mostly in tents as the fighter squadrons flew from airfields close to the front line. In the diary, the locations of his airfields, often just a field, are never identified, and it's impossible to know exactly where he was both in England and Italy. The diary entries are not literary events. They read like paper tweets from 1943. When Fern actually takes the time to compose a full sentence with a subject, verb, and object, the completeness of the thought comes almost as a shock.

March 30, 1943. Today is my mother's birthday anniversary. May God bless her with a long healthy life.

The cryptic entries at first annoyed me because of their brevity. (For example, he never explains what phrases like "usual routine" mean.) Nonetheless they start to capture me. They give an unconsciously intimate view of a time when Canada was a much smaller country and of a young man without any family encumbrances or obligations except to himself. The diversity of his interests and the simple joy he takes in almost everything surprises me. People do get killed around him, but that is the nature of war. Death doesn't surprise him. It is life that interests him, not death.

In England, he goes to a Knights of Columbus bingo in a church basement and the same evening attends a music appreciation lecture, which he "enjoyed tremendously." With his time off, he sometimes teaches French to those in his squadron who have asked for lessons. He becomes a language student himself. In Italy, when the Allied troops are jammed on the coast outside of Naples, he finds an out-of-work Italian teacher in the town above the beach and hires him to give him lessons. The Italian is impressed and offers to give the lessons for free as he has nothing else to do, the schools being closed, but Fern insists on paying. I can't help but smile every time I think of these two men teaching and learning Italian while a war roars on around them. Fern learns enough to speak to girls and write notes.

More than anything, he looks forward to letters from home. One day, he records happily that he received twelve letters! He misses his family. A river of cigarettes crosses the Atlantic from his parents, brothers, and sisters. No wonder Canadian troops could give away so many. On one occasion, his brother Philias, an inveterate smoker himself, sends him six hundred, his mother three hundred, and his sisters send parcels with more cigarettes. Cigarettes were obviously good for you.

The young man I discovered in the war diaries is both the same and different from the father I knew. He's much more carefree. Life rests easily on his shoulders. He loves the company of women and has a busy social life (this never changed), and he is disciplined (this doesn't change either). The violence and drudgery of the war are kept at bay by focusing on the daily tasks of keeping the planes flying.

One night in the grand metropolis of London, he meets a young nurse with raven hair and a movie-star figure, Katherine Oliver. London is awash in young men and women. Kay has many beaus. Her principal cavalier is a handsome Spitfire pilot named David Thomlinson, but he's not at this dance. All's fair in love and war, and Fern asks if he can walk her home. Kay agrees but it's midnight and pouring rain. They walk, arriving at 48 Bute Gardens, soaking wet from hat to shoe line. Elsie Oliver, Kay's mother, takes one look at the bedraggled looking boy in the soggy airman's uniform and says, "You'd better stay the night." He sleeps in the spare bedroom.

Kay and Fern see each other when Kay is not otherwise occupied and Fern is not dancing elsewhere, but there's no indication in the diary that either Kay or Fern have met their happily-ever-after partner. Fern is shipped out to Italy. Kay works at the hospital and continues to dance with her beaus. As Fern climbs the gangway of his troop ship, he has no idea where they might be going. Some think it's France, others Spain; Italy seems too far away. They are finally headed to the front, wherever that might be. The balloon has gone up. There is going to be a second European front and they will be part of it.

It turns out they have guessed wrong about the destination. The troops are going to Naples and the start of the long, ugly Italian campaign, which finishes for the Canadians at the Battle of Ortona. More than a thousand Canadian boys are killed at the town of Ortona. In the press, it's called "little Stalingrad."

The Canadian boys fight with courage and a determination that is the equal of their foes, but curiously there are no protests of patriotism in the diary or even vitriol against "the enemy." The character of being Canadian is proclaimed by how the men conduct themselves, not by what they say about the soldiers on the other side. On his day off, Fern travels north to visit a childhood friend who is fighting on the ground.

November 3, 1944. Went up to Reccione to see Stanley. Had dinner with him. Spoke to a fellow who was with Leo Cormier when he was killed while trying to capture a house with his Tommy gun.

He admits to no emotion but the next day his normally clear handwriting becomes shaky.

There are no diary entries for a few days thereafter. It seems that he has been in the hospital but he doesn't explain why. A few days later, he returns to his squadron. The entries and steady handwriting resume.

The Canadians keep in touch with each other. They hang out together. Fern writes that they put up a Canadian soldier in their tent who was travelling south. There are no questions, no hesitation. They enjoy and respect each other's company in a natural and spontaneous way that feels genuine and powerful, but there is none of today's familiar patriotic symbols to buttress their emotions. Canada has no national flag. No national anthem. The red and white maple leaf hasn't been invented yet. "God Save the King" is never mentioned either. There's lots of genuine Canadian diffidence as they fight their way up the spine of Italy.

The American air force has a good deal of equipment, not so much the Canadians. Fern's ground crew is sometimes reduced to scavenging in American dumps for spare parts. It doesn't occur to either the pilots or the ground crews that they should quit because they don't have enough parts for their planes. There's a simple and deep confidence here. If they need to scavenge for replacement parts, they do. They intend to prevail.

Fern complains twice, once about the lack of food and once about mail from home after he arrives in Italy: *Received no mail. It's rather tough to be away from home without mail. Hope I get some soon.*

At six-one and 140 pounds, he's so thin that today we would think he was on the edge of starvation, but they are all rake thin. It's difficult to put on fat when you're constantly on the move, sleep in tents, and the food is canned, dried, and repetitive. Many entries finish with "dead tired" and some days are worse than others. *December 10, 1944. Bad luck all day. H pranged. F and C collided in mid-air. F/O Al Shannon and P/O Rideout got killed. I worked on Al's kite for three months. Nice kid – Too bad.*

There was no television, no Skype, no email, no online conversations. All they had to communicate with were conversations, paper, pen, radio, and memory. There was no virtual reality. The reality was the day beginning.

In his diaries, Fern treats the war not much differently than ugly weather that you have to endure, like a bad southeast storm back home. His diary entries are full of the books he's reading, films, concerts, and plays he's attending, and of course the girls he's meeting. Death, injury, and loss he notes quickly and passes on. This feels not so much callous as blunt, a practical acceptance of reality. They are at war and people get killed in a war. Expecting it to be otherwise would have struck him as ludicrous. Today, I sometimes get the impression that politicians think it's only "the enemy" who is supposed to die in conflicts.

September 30, Sabato, 1944. Rained nearly all day. Had to stay down at field (crash tender). Took a book with me. Read a lot. S. A. F. crashed in a Spit. We pulled him from beneath burning kite. Cut up pretty badly. Studied Italian all evening. Quite cold in tent.

October 27, 1944. Had to move out of tent. About a foot of water in tent. Moved into town, Fano. Four of us in a room. Taught French for two hours to an airman. Studied Italian.

It took me some time to realize that none of the stories my father told of the war were in his diary. Not a single one. In the stories he told for public consumption no one ever dies. He never gets hungry. His hands never shook so hard that his writing disintegrated into an unreadable mess and then stopped entirely, and his twenty-first birthday was not celebrated with one line in a wet tent. The diary made me realize that the stories he would tell of the war were all carefully edited pocket adventures that he trotted around the party track then packed back into his memory box until the next time an engaging war story was required.

I liked his public stories. There was one he told of driving a truck loaded with bombs and ammunition as they moved up closer to the front. The truck was an ambulatory ammunition dump and carried huge signs above the cab and over the tailgate announcing "Explosives. Stay back."

His truck was supposed to be widely separated from the rest of the convoy so that if anything went wrong only his truck would be blown up. But the road was muddy and the trucks in the convoy had crept close together. Instead of being separated from the others, his truck loaded with explosives was sitting bumper to bumper with the rest.

As the convoy tipped over a hill and began a long descent toward a valley floor, an enemy Messerschmitt appeared on the other side of the valley and began flying directly toward the long, thin line of trucks. At that moment, the Canadian trucks were perfectly exposed and perfectly defenceless. They had no air cover and no armaments set up with which to defend themselves. They were the proverbial sitting ducks. All Fern could do was keep driving and hope that the pilot would not spot the frigging great signs mounted on his truck.

He peered through the windshield, craning his neck, watching for any sign that that the enemy pilot had spotted his mobile ammunition dump. But the Messerschmitt pilot just kept flying lazily across the valley's blue sky while the convoy chugged serenely along below him. By the time Fern arrived at the bottom of the valley, the following truck had retreated twenty metres back and was retiring further—but the Messerschmitt was gone. It was a lucky day.

Another story he liked to tell was about a track and field meet in the middle of the Italian campaign. The back office had decided that the men needed something to divert them from the possibility of sudden death and had decided an impromptu track and field event would serve the purpose. All units were invited to select a couple of athletes to compete. It was an all-Canadian event.

Fern was tall and could run so it was decided he and two other airmen who had the same qualifications should represent their squadron. Taking the competition seriously, the three young men cut back on their smokes and did some early morning sprints back on their grass runway. After two weeks of this intense training, they considered themselves ready.

To everyone's surprise, the "forget-death track meet" was a great success. The sun was shining and there was a dance and local vino after the races. What more could you want? The mile was the last race to be run, and Fern lined up against guys from other air and army units. He knew nothing about track racing but was naturally fast and ready to run. The gun went off and Fern's long, graceful stride quickly took him to the front of the pack where he stayed for three laps. He could hear another runner directly behind him, following him stride for stride, but he couldn't tell who it was or what condition he was in.

Coming into the final turn with only a sprint to the finish remaining, he thought he had the race won as his legs were beating out a good rhythm and he felt strong. Then, the runner behind him, who had been calmly drafting him, breezily accelerated past him as if Fern was standing still. As the more experienced runner bolted by, he hailed my father with the friendly salutation, "Sucker!"

It is this race that he lost to Sergeant Lightfoot from Winnipeg that Dad remembered more vividly than anything he ever won. "How could you beat someone with a name like Lightfoot?" he would recall with a smile.

But the story I always liked the best, and I think he did too, was about chickens. Some squadron mates had "liberated" some hens from a farmer for supper. Fresh anything was very rare and word quickly got around the squadron that there was something exciting happening for supper.

The boys who had "liberated" the chickens asked Fern if he could cook up the hens. The liberators were from Toronto and therefore regarded a chicken's natural habitat as the dinner plate and had no idea how to actually clean and cook one. Fern looked at the freshly killed chickens and at his friends who had gathered around to examine the prizes. But instead of agreeing to cook them, he asked each one of his mates this simple question: "What does your father do?"

It turned out about half of the Canadians were farm boys. Then he asked another question of the boys who had "liberated" the chickens.

"Did you pay for them?"

"No."

There was a silence. The boys who had stolen the chickens were all from the city. Fern turned to them and said, "We'll cook them up this time, but only this time. A farmer is a farmer, and we don't steal from farmers."

That was the end of it. The country boys cleaned and cooked the chickens up and the squadron never stole another hen.

Four of Dad's seven brothers joined the RCAF. When they began to leave home in 1939, there were seventeen people on the family farm. These were the days when there were no seniors' homes and a family often had to support three generations. Both of Fern's grandmothers lived in the family house. Cecile Deveau, my great-grandmother, still used her loom to create cloth, and one of Dad's first memories is of watching his grandmother's shuttlecock spin back and forth as the loom magically created cloth from a few thin threads.

Seventeen people in one household was too large for Dad's mother to manage alone, and she hired a young woman named Annie to help her. Annie was so charming that Alex, Fern's eldest brother, proposed, and Grandmother lost both her helper and her eldest son.

It is said that all families that are happy are happy in the same way, and I think the Doucet family was happy in all the ordinary ways. Fern maintained a great affection for his parents, brothers, and sisters all his life and visited them whenever he could, which wasn't easy for they were spread out across the eastern half of the continent.

My father's world became divided into before the war and after. When Dad returned to the village, both his grandmothers had passed on. The loom and spinning wheel had left the house and were stored in a shed, soon to be sold to an antique dealer. Dad's oldest brothers, Gerard and Alex, had both married and built their own homes. The youngest, Armand, had departed to attend a commercial college. Uncle Denis had taken his powerful physique to Montreal and found a job in a factory. La belle Bernadette had found a handsome husband, an Acadian from Maine.

After the war, there would be no more fouleries.[1] The carding mill and grandfather's sawmill would become the

---

1 A foulerie was a kitchen work party held to shrink cloth in the homes where cloth was weaved. The shrinking was done by stringing the cloth up into a long roll, wetting it, and then beating it back and forth on planks with a team of people on each side to lift and bang the cloth between them on the table. Someone would sing traditional songs to keep the rhythm going, and in this way the cloth would be shrunk for washing and wearing.

names of roads, not destinations. Slowly, the many community and economic activities that had animated the independent existence of the village began to wink out. It was as if an invisible bomb had gone off in the village, hollowing it out.

December 20, 1944. Aerodrome traffic control. Pretty cold standing at the end of runway all day. Saw a show at Windsor Club, Captain Blood. Wrote a letter to Bernadette. Listened to radio until 11 p.m.

An ordinary day in an extraordinary war.

I also live ordinary days. I work. I read. I listen to the radio. I meet some friends for coffee. In winter, I skate on the canal. In summer I ride my bicycle in the hills. I find much joy in each day, but there is one essential difference between my life and that of my parents.

Unlike Fern, I don't believe that I'm part of a generation that is leading the world anywhere good. Somehow between his generation and mine, the world has entered a space where the simplest conclusions are impossible to discern. My thoughts always come back to the same place. Our priority shouldn't be arms or war; the national project should be focused on developing economies and lifestyles where people can live well but without denuding the oceans and the land like a picked-over pasture.

It seems so blindingly obvious that you can't create safe harbours based on more consumerism and exhausting the planet's resources, but this is what business leaders are still trying to do. And they complain when they cannot. Nor can politicians create a peaceful future based on walls and fear of other people. The Romans couldn't, nor will the Americans.

My father's generation believed that the war would be won and people would be freed of tyrannies to live better lives. Their confidence was not misplaced.

August 27, 1945. Went to RCAF HQ to draw some pay. Getting married tomorrow. Kay and I saw Father McCarthy in p.m. He granted me dispensation to marry Kay, who's non-Catholic. I'm sure religion will never be of issue to our happiness.

CHAPTER 12

Flora MacDonald and "The Gaelic Ship"

Eternity is made of wishes.
Society is composed of stories.

The field that I have bought hasn't been farmed since the Depression when every acre in the village was under the plow or feeding cows. By rights, the field should have gone back to bush years many years ago as so many others have, but the grass has been reasonable enough that a neighbouring farmer has cut it each year for hay. In this way the field has been preserved from the coyotes and the invading bush. Except for the fencing, which is now gone, it would have looked much the same in my father's childhood when one of the defining events of his life began.

On Black Tuesday, October 29, 1929, the New York stock market crashed and did not rebound. Millions of people lost their life savings, and in the west, a dust bowl of Biblical proportions began to scour the land. Families sundered and the most unfortunate starved in profound "grapes of wrath" misery as the Great Depression sunk its talons into North America. Young people who had left their little Nova Scotia villages for opportunities elsewhere came home, for there was no work in the cities and little food. Dad was six years old when the Great Depression began.

The Depression was followed by the 1940–45 war. Dad's generation would be marked forever by those two world events. From those experiences came an amazing sense of personal independence, but that independence was always tempered by a powerful sense of community and country. It wasn't the Hollywood backlot, Ronald Reagan consumer question: "Are you better off now than you were four years ago?" Dad's animating idea was the same as another veteran of that war: "Ask not what your country can do for you, ask what you can do for your country." And they did.

It was the children of the Great Depression and the veterans of the Second World War who pioneered almost all the programs and institutions that today we think of as distinctly Canadian: national health care, access to a university education, national public broadcasting, UN peacekeeping. Their attitudes and vision would bring Canada much renown as a peaceful, compassionate nation.

Those qualities of self-help and community were forged in very hard times. During the Depression, even parish priests had to run small farms in order to reduce the costs of maintaining the church and parish presbytery. There was no money in the parish and thus no money for them. The most important person at the presbytery was the housekeeper who managed the kitchen and kept the house going. To help the housekeeper with household chores like filling the woodbox, weeding the garden, and milking the cow, a boy was given free room and board.

My uncle Phileas and later my father were sent to Broad Cove to work for Father Archie McClellan, a tall, strong Scot. In 1935, Broad Cove was a long, bone-crunching, mud and gravel drive from Grand Étang, where the primitive condition of the road forced cars to heave and bounce along not much faster than a horse could walk. In winter it was impassable for weeks at a time; the villages simply closed in on themselves. Today, you can drive from Grand Étang to Broad Cove in about forty-five minutes on a two-lane asphalt road. In the Depression years, even going home for Christmas from Broad Cove was seen as too difficult.

Nonetheless, to be the "priest's boy" or the *domestique du prêtre* was a much sought-after position by parents. The priest was one of the few well-educated people in the village, and the boys benefited from that association. Both Uncle Phileas and Fern would go to university. The boys who were chosen to work at the presbytery usually did.

The curious thing is that in spite of the many deprivations of the Depression, it was a time of great local economic and social effervescence. Everyone had large families and the villages were packed with activity. When Dad recalled his childhood birthdays (which were on May 28), he remembered them as the time when the family planted potatoes. At the end of May, everyone in the village was planting potatoes and a child's birthday didn't stop the work.

When he was a teenager, on Friday afternoon my father would say to his best friend, Wellington Levert, "Should we try the beans at your house or mine tonight?" Catholics were supposed to eat fish rather than meat on Fridays, but in a fishing village fish was the normal fare, so on Friday everyone ate beans. As circumscribed as life was, people were not without hope and looked to the future, seeking ways to prepare for it.

Nor were the villages animated just by the sweat of people's brows—they were also alive with ideas. The co-operative movement spearheaded by activist priests like Moses Coady, Joseph DeCoste, and Jimmy Tomkins advocated for community-based capitalism that would free people from the controls of banks and large corporations. In Grand Étang, the parish council voted to replace the bank, which had fled the village during the Depression, with a credit union. Legend has it the first deposit was ten cents.

It was a very different world. During the 1930s, consumerism was an "ism" that had no meaning. Because there was no money and few goods, life was organized around producing what was needed, not buying things. People knew down to the last barrel of potatoes, flour, oats, salt pork, beef, cod, herring, milk, sugar, and summer preserves what it would take to get a family through the winter. This self-sufficient tradition continued long after the Depression ended.

After the Second World War, it took a long time for consumerism and the outside world to reconnect with the little fishing villages of Cape Breton. Children were still educated with very little help from the outside. In the 1960s, my cousin Roland had the school janitor, Joe Delaney, for a teacher, and he remembers Joe with affection. My father counted himself very lucky that he had Edmund Chiasson and Alex Dan Doucet, two young schoolteachers from the village who he remembered as central to helping him build the knowledge and confidence he would need to go to university. Edmund and Alex Dan were barely out of their teens themselves.

When I reread these words, it sounds like I know what I'm talking about, but I'm not sure that I do, because neither my father nor anyone of his generation ever talked openly about their lives. They kept a great deal to themselves. I remember Pierre Trudeau, when he was prime minister, responding to a question about the breakup of his marriage to Margaret Sinclair. The journalist was complaining that he had not said anything publicly about it. Didn't he think the public had a right to know? Trudeau's response was, "Why? Those who have gone through a divorce don't need to be told what it is like, and those who haven't don't need to, so what's the point?" He said nothing more.

My father and mother would have understood this attitude completely. The more painful something was, the more it was kept quiet. It wasn't a share world. The adult thing was to keep your troubles to yourself. There was a firm line between the private and the public domains. They weren't of the Facebook generation. I only knew that Dad had kept a war diary after he died, when, to my surprise, I inherited this little red book with a steady stream of entries from those years. As for the tough times during the Depression, it was all "Good night, John-Boy," very similar to the Walton television family vignettes. The tough stuff was quietly interred.

There's a good deal to be said for simply suppressing bad memories. In the short term, it can permit you to carry on without being harassed by thoughts that can't lead you anywhere positive. But like everything else, suppression has its costs. After Fern had successfully completed a four-year Bachelor of Arts program in three years and a summer with marks good enough to get him into graduate school at the University of Toronto, he began to cry inconsolably. He didn't leave his apartment for two days, all the while sobbing.

I am sure he was intensely embarrassed by this breakdown. After all, he was a grown man, already twenty-four years old, a veteran of the war with a wife, a son, and another baby on the way. What was he doing crying like a baby? He should have been stronger. The event and memory of it simply disappeared.

I heard about it many years later from Bernadette, my father's youngest sister. We were talking about something else entirely different, yet somehow it surfaced. She was the only one to repeat such a tale. For my parents, it no longer existed. The same thing goes for "The Gaelic Ship." If it truly happened, it's best forgotten. I understand, but ignoring the true nature of the past has its costs, and sometimes they can be steep. Where is the balance between the "share" generation and the "keep calm and carry on" generation?

A physicist searches for answers in the movement of atoms, but for me the world is composed of stories, not atoms. This is the way we remember our families, the history of nations, and imagine a future. My image of Canada was formed by stories that I heard growing up, stories that I scarcely noticed at the time but turned out to have powerful, life-long resonances.

Stories are never entirely "true." The line between truth and invention is often blurred. Even stories that seem resolutely imagined, like fiddling for the devil, are never entirely fiction. Sometimes the line drifts more toward the fiction side, sometimes less so; the distinction is never clear. Of all the stories I have ever written, the line between fiction and fact is most blurred in "The Gaelic Ship."

THE GAELIC SHIP

The first school days at Broad Cove would have been difficult for the French boy, for English was the only language of instruction. It was made bearable by Neil McNeil, who was equally miserable. The two boys must have been little islands of silence in the schoolyard, unable to talk to each other or anyone else. Neil's family were Gaelic speakers. He had red-tinged hair. His shoulders were already broad and strong beyond his years, and it was clear he was going to be tall like his older brothers. But unlike his brothers, he didn't take to English at all. His mother had died when he was born and he had been raised by his grandparents. The grandparents had never bothered speaking English to him, and his father was often away; when he returned home he slipped back into the old language.

Neil had a naturally slow, careful way about him and like other mountain children was regarded as a hick by the more worldly boys and girls of Broad Cove. The French boy, seeing the writing on the wall, heeded his parents' advice to learn English and set about doing it. Not so Neil. The crude jokes about his accent and manner of speaking did not inspire him to do anything except to become taciturn. He rarely talked unless he was forced to by the teacher.

Neil's older sister had learned English quickly and she pestered him to learn faster, but the more he was harassed, the more stubborn he became. The French boy became a translator for Neil.

On stormy nights, Neil would stay at the rectory where he was a great favourite. Mrs. McIsaac was very fond of him and called the teacher a savage, which pleased Neil although it wasn't quite accurate, as the teacher was a McLeod whose own English was also burred with the old language.

Wednesday night was a card night, and Mrs. McIsaac had friends visit. They all ganged round the kitchen table to play, and the language of the game was the old language. There, Neil McNeil became a different boy. Instead of solemn and watchful, his face was animated and flushed, his bright blue eyes sparkling. Here, he talked a great deal. None of which the French boy understood, but it frequently sent the ladies into gales of laughter. Mrs. McIsaac said Neil could tell a story like his grandfather who was known to be a great storyteller as well as a fine figure of a man.

While the ladies played cards and Neil entertained them, the French boy did his homework and then did Neil's. At the end of the night he gave the completed homework to Neil, explaining what he had done and why. Immediately, Neil's face grew grave.

One Friday night, the French boy was invited to climb the long track with Neil and his older sister to their homestead. The sister had thick waves of auburn hair and bright blue eyes like Neil. From the doorway of their house, which was high on the mountain, they could see the entire sweep of Broad Cove all the way to Inverness and then back up north toward Grand Étang beneath the mountains.

Neil's sister asked the French boy sympathetically how he was liking school. The French boy blushed under her frank gaze and scarcely replied, because he did not want to embarrass Neil who was not doing so well. "Do the girls tease you?" she asked. "I've heard that they do." He shook his head because they teased Neil more.

"Neil doesn't like school much," said his sister and sighed a little. "He can't seem to get the hang of English. There's nothing much to it. Neil needs to practice in front of a mirror, that's what I did. You must make a different face when you speak English. When your face looks like the backside of a hen, then you're speaking English," she said, grinning.

Neil's grandparents appeared and the girl went upstairs to her own room. Neil and the French boy went out to catch the cows for milking. Neil's father was away in the woods working for Bowater, pulling logs. The big horses were gone and there were only three milking cows in the barn and a one-year-old colt. The boys finished their chores quickly and went back to the house with the milk. They had supper, the evening ending in laughter and Neil's grandfather telling stories. Neil's sister did the translations for the French boy, which set the old people laughing even more. Their merriment infected the younger ones.

At Thanksgiving, Neil failed his tests, and as the Christmas exams approached, Father Archie began to sit with Neil, coaching him in a mixture of Gaelic and English. It was only then that Neil started to learn how to read, because it transpired that he could not. He had been pretending. He had memorized the alphabet in a straight line from A to Z but could not recognize the letters when they were out of their alphabetical order. Father Archie figured this out and taught him how to recognize them when they were placed in a different order to form a word.

Neil said afterwards that it wasn't Father Archie who taught him. It was Mrs. McIsaac. She taught him how to use the alphabet to read in Gaelic, and once he understood how to read Gaelic, he figured out how it went for English.

One day, at the back of the schoolyard, some bigger boys circled the French boy demanding that he say "three." When he could not make the "th" sound correctly, they began to punch him. Neil came round the corner of the schoolhouse, howled a Gaelic war cry, and in a fury charged the boys, proceeding in a few seconds to bloody the nose of one, blacken the eye of another, and rip the shirt off a third.

When all five boys appeared in school with banged up faces and torn clothes, the teacher was told it was Neil McNeil's fault—and the French kid.

That night, John McLeod, the teacher, came to the rectory, and he did not waste a minute before crossing swords with Father Archie. The whole house could hear him. "Do you think I like it? But I canna teach in the auld language, Father. The Gaelic is dead! Dead as a doornail. Do you think they speak Gaelic in Ottawa? Do you think they speak Gaelic in Toronto? There's no future for the auld language. And you know it as well as I do!"

Father Archie said something, but no one but the teacher heard it.

"Do you think Neil is going to live on a mountainside for the rest of his life?"

Father Archie, who in spite of his size was a mild-mannered man, responded in a way that no one could hear.

"You're not helping me, Father. His brothers learned English. His sister is one of my best students. You must be giving the boy the illusion that there's some future in the auld language, because that's all it is, an illusion."

"McLeod, you'll not be yelling at me in me own house," said Father Archie, now loud enough for others to hear.

"I'm sorry, Father, but there's a reason Gaelic is not allowed in the school. How do you expect Neil McNeil to learn English if he is always speaking Gaelic?" And he looked hard at Father Archie. "Are you speaking Gaelic with him?"

Father Archie looked uncomfortable and did not reply. The teacher continued. "And what about your boy fighting? The priest's boy is supposed to set an example for the others. What kind of example is fighting?"

"His marks are fine."

"That's not the point."

"Boys will be boys," shrugged Father Archie. "I seem to remember you getting into a few scrapes, and I don't remember yelling at you for it."

This time it was the teacher's turn to look embarrassed and they left it at that.

At school, Neil McNeil and the French boy were separated with Neil on one side of the class and the French boy on the other. Neil was prohibited from playing cards with Mrs. McIsaac on Wednesdays. He did homework with Father Archie and they tried not to speak Gaelic. Things seemed to return to normal.

In the New Year, Neil was allowed to go back to the storytelling group, which began as soon as a second pot of tea was made and the card game finished. Then, it was Neil McNeil and Black Donald McIsaac who were the stars, both having the knack of telling stories. The *Brenagh* sailed in on one of those evenings.

"Not long ago, there was a ship called the *Brenagh*, captained by Angus Joe MacDonald. He crewed the *Brenagh* entirely with Gaelic speakers. Captain Angus didn't much care if a man had ever been on a ship before, because he figured sailing could be taught but not Gaelic. You spoke it or you didn't. Once you had crossed over the gangway of the *Brenagh*, the only songs were Gaelic, the only stories were

Gaelic, the only language was Gaelic. It was as if you were in a Gaelic country. On the *Brenagh*, no other language but Gaelic was heard.

The *Brenagh* was known as a lucky ship, and there were many who would have liked to sail with the captain if they'd had the old language. The captain sailed the *Brenagh* from one end of the globe to the other, from China to Africa, Africa to South America, and back again. There was no port he didn't know or where he wasn't welcome. They say the *Brenagh* never hailed a bad harbour. The captain always had a lineup of men wanting to sail with him. They came from all over: Brittany, Wales, Ireland, Scotland, Nova Scotia. Everywhere there were Gaelic speakers.

Now one day his wife, who sailed with him (for captain's wives sailed with their husbands in those days), put her foot down and said they had to stop sailing. The *Brenagh* went up for sale and went quickly for a good price, being known as a lucky ship. Now here's the queer part. Captain Angus tried to sell her to a Gaelic-speaking captain but couldn't find one that suited his fancy. So instead the *Brenagh* went to an English captain who had coveted the ship for a long time. But the new captain and his English crew foundered off Madagascar, losing all hands on their first voyage—and that was the end of *Brenagh*.

"Why did the captain quit?" asked Neil

"It was the wife. When they had a fourth child, she didn't want them to be sailing anymore. But here is the interesting thing: they say the captain's oldest boy is putting together a ship's crew in North Sydney this winter with nothing but Gaelic speakers, just like his father used to do. Won't that be something? Make a little money and do it in the old language."

The *Brenagh* story was Neil McNeil's favourite, and he was always pestering for more stories of the *Brenagh*. Black Donald obliged him, the *Brenagh* having sailed in many strange places and having had many great adventures. She had even run into Captain Joshua Slocum, the first man to sail around the world alone.

Now normally the spring seal hunt is far out in the gulf when the pack ice sweeps down from the Arctic and stays somewhere between Newfoundland and the Magdalen Islands. Millions of pups are born directly onto the ice, far away from any predators until they're ready to swim back home with the herd. It happens only rarely that the really big herds come as far as Cape Breton, but in March of 1935, the ice was exceptionally strong and it packed up against the shoreline in a vast field along the entire coast. The men began to leave the villages to walk across the ice to join the men from the ships in the hunt, which was taking place at the edge of the ice in clear view of the shore.

Neil McNeil decided he would go too, just to watch, and he asked the French boy to go along. Now the French boy was from a fishing village, and he knew hunting seals was not as easy as it looked. The winds can shift, breaking the ice up, and suddenly you're trapped, caught between ice floes and open water with nowhere to go. It's nervous work. You always have to have one eye on the wind and one eye on the ice, watching it in case the ice begins to shift out to sea or break up under your feet. But this Saturday was especially inviting, for the sun was warm and the ice perfectly flat, stretching toward the horizon.

Neil and the French boy stood on the shore looking out. The ice looked as solid and secure as the day is long. "I bet we could walk straight to your village and be back in time for supper," said Neil. And suddenly, the French boy had a great longing to go home.

"Maybe we can find this Gaelic ship," said Neil, looking not toward the headland that marked the French boy's village but further north toward the smoke smudge on the horizon that marked the hunt. It was warm, sunny, and clear, with the ice so smooth that the boys began to gambol across it like young colts let out from the winter barn into a spring pasture. In no time at all, they were running past the mouth of Margaree Harbour, moving quickly in a dead straight line for the French boy's village. In the distance, beyond the ice, they saw a sealing ship steaming north toward Bay St. Lawrence, toward the vast herd that had drifted down from the Arctic.

They were able to move so quickly that they were soon so far out it was easier to just keep going toward the French boy's village than to return to Broad Cove. At first, when the boys walked in the kitchen door, Marie-Claire did not know whether to be angry or happy to see her son home. After some chiding about walking on the ice, she decided on being happy and served them a grand meal after which the two boys promptly fell sound asleep, although it wasn't yet midday. They slept sitting straight up in rocking chairs and when they awoke found themselves in the middle of a kitchen party with music, food, and lots of neighbours who had dropped in to celebrate their surprising arrival.

When Neil McNeil recognized a tune, he would sing in Gaelic with a fine, clear voice and the others would just listen.

That night, the French boy's brother, Denis, hitched the farm's fastest horse to the Sunday cutter and drove them directly back over the ice to Broad Cove. Denis was not a great talker and the boys did little but watch the vault of the winter sky and listen to the sled's runners flying over the smooth ice. Later, when he was older and living far away, the French boy would sometimes recall the night flying over the ice as if they had drifted off the planet and were floating in the sky itself.

In the village of Broad Cove, everyone had heard about the boys walking across the ice all the way to the Acadian shore, and it conferred on them a certain notoriety that they both enjoyed. The next day, they received their Easter marks. Neil did not go directly home. He sat on the small dock below the presbytery, gazing out at sea. "I want to go to sealing on the *Brenagh*," he said, "and never hear English again."

The French boy did not know what to say, so said nothing.

"In your village, can you speak French in school?" asked Neil.

"There are lots of books in English."

"But speaking French wouldn't be forbidden?"

"No. We speak French."

"You can speak it in the schoolyard?"

"Yes."

"So why can't we speak Gaelic in Broad Cove? The teacher speaks Gaelic to Mrs. McIsaac, but he speaks English to me. What is wrong with our language?" Neil McNeil said this slowly as if it was costing him a lot to form the words.

Again, the French boy did not know what to say, so he said nothing.

On Thursday, the French boy did not see his friend before school started because it was a morning when he had assisted Father Archie at the early Mass and was late himself. It wasn't until noon that he realized Neil was not in school. He went and asked the teacher where he might find Neil. The teacher did not know; Neil had been marked absent.

The French boy walked straight down to the shore. He thought that he could see a small dot, far out on the ice, moving steadily toward the north. From there, he went directly to Father Archie and said he thought Neil McNeil had gone looking for the Gaelic ship. Father Archie sent for Neil's grandfather, and he came down from the mountain with horses and sleighs along with some neighbours. They waited at the presbytery until Neil's father, who had been called in from the bush, arrived.

It was like a McNeil clan gathering. Every McNeil who owned a horse was at the edge of the ice in a great circle of men and beasts. What little was said was in the old language. Neil's father was a tall, thin man with a hawk face whom few dared to approach, so dark and grim did he look. Suddenly with a shared Gaelic cry that seemed to rise from the bottom of the Earth, the men in one surging mass left, the horses galloping furiously toward the horizon across the vast, white plain of the frozen sea.

Later, it began to snow with great white flakes. The snow was fat and warm, and slowed their progress, for it began to be hard to see. But the men did not stop, even when they could not see. The first night, they camped at Fishing Cove, and the next day Neil McNeil's father drove his horses all the way north to Bay St. Lawrence where the ice ended and the open sea began. At Bay St. Lawrence he lost his best horse to the water where the ice suddenly became thin and separated under him. The noble animal floundered down into the frigid waters. He was the strongest, fastest horse that Neil's father had ever owned; his great violet eyes shrank into the white edges with fear as he thrashed and struggled to get back on the ice. In spite of the horse's great strength and determination, he kept slipping back into the frigid water. The men became soaked and frozen trying to cut the terrified animal free from the harness that attached him to the sleigh, but they could not free him for fear of going in themselves.

It was three days before the men came home, silent, ragged, and worn out.

They had found no Gaelic ship, no Gaelic-speaking boy, just inshore sealers and a couple of English-speaking crews out of Sydney and St. John's.

And so the story ends. How much is invented or not, I can't say. A Gaelic-speaking ship did exist and it did sail out of North Sydney. I first heard of it in Flora MacDonald's apartment overlooking the Rideau Canal in Ottawa. The renowned politician and I would meet from time to time to chat about nothing much in particular. She was in her elder years and still greatly engaged with life. In winter, we both liked to skate on the Rideau Canal. Sometimes we would talk politics but not much. In spite of being Canada's first female Minister of External Affairs and a life-long Progressive Conservative, she found herself upset by the reigning Conservative government and preferred not to talk about it. She would always make the point, "I am a *Progressive* Conservative."

Mostly, we would talk about Cape Breton. Flora was born and grew up in North Sydney. She told me about her childhood and about her grandfather who had been a sea captain and had insisted on hiring only Gaelic speakers for his ship. Her grandmother had voyaged with him as was the custom of the day on commercial ships and they had three children at sea, but when the fourth came along, she had insisted they settle down in their home port. Her husband's ship was sold and they raised their children in North Sydney. The cost to him of abandoning the *Brenagh*—and those who wished to sail on the *Brenagh*—is not known.

Euripedes wrote, "There is no greater sorrow on earth than the loss of one's native land." Socrates preferred to take hemlock rather than go into exile. Cicero did much the same. A ship was waiting for the old lawyer after the Republican defeat and he escaped the city to join it, but on the road toward the port he changed his mind; instead of continuing to flee, he simply waited at the side of the road for his pursuers to catch up.

Cicero was a man of words, not swords, and was never known for being physically intrepid. Charging enthusiastically toward the enemy, gripping a sword and buckler, screaming with blood lust, was not his idea of a useful way to pass his time. He liked to figure things out from behind a desk or from the speaker's podium. It is a testimony to his state of mind that facing exile from all he knew and loved was less appealing to him than keeping his head on his shoulders. When his assassins finally caught up with him, he quietly held out his head to make it easier for them to sever it.

Sigmund Freud was forced to flee Vienna to escape the Nazis, but when he was interviewed by BBC, he did not celebrate his escape. Instead he lamented the loss of his native language, German. A native language is called "native" because it is like a country. It's the place where one understands and expresses most easily what it is to be human. Without it life is never the same.

The native language of Flora's father and grandparents was Gaelic, but Flora could not speak a word. Her father refused to speak Gaelic with his children, regarding the old language as a disadvantage his own parents had saddled him with; he did not want his children to have it. This wasn't an unusual attitude. All over Cape Breton, Gaelic speakers "protected" their children from the old language. As in "The Gaelic Ship," the schoolteachers were often native Gaelic speakers themselves but refused to let the children speak their home language. They were convinced that to be successful in the world meant speaking English.

Flora remembered classmates who spoke English with a strong Gaelic inflection who were teased, and on at least one occasion she joined in the mocking laughter at a country boy who had trouble responding in the correct way. She never forgot this moment and frowned when she remembered it. When Flora returned to private life after politics on the national stage, she had many choices for a second career. She could have seen her name mounted on many a corporate masthead and been paid a great deal for attending a few meetings a year. This is often the route for well-known politicians when they retire. Instead she settled on spending the rest of her life leading a not-for-profit group that builds schools and water systems in remote mountain villages.

Young men and women need heroes. In "The Gaelic Ship," the tragedy for Neil McNeil was that the context in which he could have found a hero was being taken away from him. He felt alone and without direction. I was very lucky to grow up with many heroes. Flora MacDonald was one. She was better than Spider-Man. Her power was the ability to knit together distances between people and circumstances and help children get an education with nothing much more than the force of her personality. She would have made a great prime minister, and if the men who had previously made commitments to her at her party's leadership convention hadn't switched their allegiances when it looked like she might win, she would have been.

Flora had a grand funeral. A ton of famous political figures showed up to say goodbye at Christ Church Cathedral in Ottawa. From time to time, nations need funerals large enough to put a comma on time's endless flow. Flora's was that kind of funeral, where in spite of the size of the church, many people were obliged to stand outside in the street. If tears can be happy they were in this instance, for everyone remembered Flora with affection. Nonetheless, I would have preferred if she had taken a break from saving the world and put off the funeral for a little longer, for I had something to show her in Cape Breton that she would have delighted in.

The following summer my house began to grow magically in the field like a mushroom pushing up from the ground after a rain. The two sides of the house arrived from Bouctouche, New Brunswick, on the backs of two enormous trucks, along with a crane that came from Sydney. It was something to see, these two massive boxes being lifted like giant loaves of bread, swivelling in the air from the back of the truck, and being dropped onto the foundation as if they weighed no more than a feather. The thing that worried me wasn't the moving, it was whether they would fit on the foundation. If the foundation and the two boxes didn't fit together exactly, we were in trouble. There would be no easy way to fix such a mistake. We all held our breath as the first box came down. Would it rest securely on the foundation or be slightly off?

The fit was perfect and the two boxes were winched tight together. There were still months of work to be done, but the basic frame, basement, walls, roof, windows, were all magically in place. The floors remained to be laid. The siding had to be put up, the doors hung. All the ceramic work for the basement and bathroom floors remained to be completed, but the basic skeleton of the house was set. It could storm away outside and the men could work inside dry and protected from the elements. It felt solid, strong. The windows were large and impressive. From every room there was a fine view.

I would have liked it if Flora could have seen my new house by the sea. We could have gone for walks along the Old Cabot Trail and on Saturday night hived off to the Doryman to hear Lola and Clarence LeLièvre sing. In the tavern, I would have watched her hold court and talk with people in her bright, decisive, no-nonsense kind of way. To be in her company was a fine thing.

CHAPTER 13

Myles from Nowhere

Sweet Auburn! Loveliest village of the plain,
Where health and plenty cheer'd the
labouring swain,
Where smiling spring its earliest visit paid,
And parting summer's lingering blooms
Delay'd
Dear lovely bowers of innocence and east,
Seats of my youth, when every sport could
Please—
How often I loiter'd o'er thy green,
Where humble happiness endear'd each
scene
—Excerpt from "The Deserted Village"
by Oliver Goldsmith

Myles from Nowhere is a weather-beaten house and an equally battered barn at Margaree Forks in the Margaree Valley. The old buildings have been converted to something between a junk and an antique store. It wasn't so long ago that Cape Breton homes and barns used to be treasure troves of old, interesting things that were no longer needed, but the island has been raked over for so long by antique dealers that there's little left. I can remember my grandfather giving away horse-drawn equipment, a loom, spinning wheel, and other oddments for tokens. Grandfather's thinking was he didn't need these things anymore but the antique dealer did, so maybe they would get some good use elsewhere. This is the conserving nature of all good farmers.

Myles from Nowhere is exceptional just because it's still in business. Myles knows everyone on the island (or as close to make no difference), and in spite of years and years of exodus, his store still harbours some surprises. Not long ago, I found a worn brass theodolite in used but excellent condition. It was once owned by a prominent Nova Scotia road engineer. His name was still inscribed on the box and there was an old, yellowed newspaper cutting describing the man's distinguished career and the many projects he had worked on. The heavy brass instrument gleamed in the worn box, and you could imagine him setting it set up on a tripod at the road edge for some grade measurements. I was tempted to buy it, but what would I do with a nineteenth-century theodolite in excellent condition? I hadn't the slightest idea. Nonetheless, it was a beautiful piece of technology and I couldn't help but admire it.

On my last visit, I found a small collection of very thin books from the early part of the twentieth century. They were not much more than linen covered pamphlets. Each book consisted of one long poem, and a hundred years after their first publication only cost two dollars a book. The most famous poets of the age—Keats, Byron, Sir Walter Scott—and their poems were commemorated in this little series published out of London, England, by a long ago company called Johnson and Hickborn. The little books were confidently called a "deluxe edition" and did have some fine qualities. The paper was thick, of good quality, the print heavy and bold. A full-page, handsome portrait of the poet was featured inside of every cover. A portrait of Oliver Goldsmith appeared on the front page of his famous poem, "The Deserted Village."

Today perhaps some students of English literature would be acquainted with Goldsmith's "Deserted Village," but it no longer belongs to the common lexicon as it did when it was published. At the beginning of the twentieth century, trench soldiers like my Grandfather Oliver carried the *Oxford Companion of Verse* in their vest pockets. They memorized poetry, read or declaimed verses to each other, and often tried to compose poetry themselves. George Oliver could recite verses from "The Deserted Village" with the same ease a man today quotes sports statistics. First published in 1770, "The Deserted Village" has never been out of print. One edition has just followed another. In today's world, there's often no more than a year between a book rising to the *New York Times* bestseller list in the spring and descending to the publisher's remainder list the following spring. The lifespan of a bestseller has become seasonal.

In 1915, "The Deserted Village" needed no explanation. People understood viscerally that the poet had used the life of one imaginary village to capture the collapse of a way of life across the length and breadth of the British Isles. The enclosures of common lands marked the first stirrings of the global economy, which began with ocean trade, distant plantation production, and the shrinking of small-scale, rural society everywhere.

Goldsmith never revealed the name of the village he was thinking of when he wrote "The Deserted Village," giving it a fictional name, Auburn, but the village didn't need any particular identity. Readers understood "Sweet Auburn" was just a metaphor. In the century between 1770 (the year of the poem's publication) and 1870, seven million acres or about one-sixth of England was privatized (i.e., changed from common land to fenced land controlled by one owner). This privatization took four thousand separate acts of Parliament.

These four thousand acts were passed by parliamentarians who benefited directly from the Acts of Enclosure; that is, the same men who voted to fence village lands then received private ownership of the land they had voted to enclose. Conflict of interest wasn't a problem for these parliamentarians. They had the power and they used it. It's not quite so transparent today but it still happens. Vital public services like water, health care, and land are still coveted, and there is an unrelenting pressure on all elected officials to convert the common realm to the private for personal profit. I saw it happen in Ottawa throughout my tenure on city council. In order to make cement at bulk rates, construction companies received half a million tons of clean water annually at a cost so low that it's the same as giving it away. At its essence this is exactly what happened in Ottawa with the conversion of Lansdowne Park to a private mall or with the appropriation of Algonquin islands in the Ottawa River for more condos.

Chéticamp is one of the very few places I know of where a "commons" has been created instead of appropriated. The Chéticamp commons is a community cattle pasture on Chéticamp Island just opposite the village. During the effervescence of the 1960s, the large island pasture was cut out of the woods and is still used by local farmers to graze their cattle. On hot summer days, the whole herd meanders down to stand in the cooling breeze on a rocky peninsula that sticks out from the island into the harbour. Many a tourist photograph has been taken of this little herd of cows as it stands in the summer heat shimmering on the rocks, calm and safe from flies, their large, colourful bodies reflected in the still water.

Land held in common for the general use of villagers and farmers may be little known today, but its history is as ancient as agriculture itself. This shared land or "the Commons" as it was known in Britain, was always available to any villager to graze cattle, sheep, ducks, hens, to stroll, socialize, pick wild mushrooms, and so on. This was the way village life worked once the species switched from hunting and gathering.

One of the most thrilling moments I have ever experienced in my travels was walking up the steep hill to view Hattusa, the ancient capital of the Hittites in central Anatolia. The city/fortress of Hattusa was the capital of the Hittite Empire. The city was built on a massive isolated mountain promontory and has the same lonely grandeur of the much better-known Machu Picchu in Peru. Yet, while the Peruvian city suffers from too many tourists, Hattusa suffers from too few. During several days spent there, we met one Turkish family driving in a little car. The only other visitors were a couple of tour buses that rocketed around the walls of the site, unloaded their visitors at the Lion Gate for photographs, and then departed in the blink of an eye.

There is something uncanny about walking around a place where thousands of people once lived and ruled a mighty empire now that there is little but denuded rocky outlines of their long ago existence. The famous Lion Gate, an opening in the wall framed by two stone lions, is still there as are the battered basement walls of the royal library, the contents of which are now stored in museums. But on the site you need to have considerable patience and imagination to decipher even the skeletal vestiges of the old city.

The moment I remember best from my visit to Hattusa had nothing to do with the remains of this desolate imperial relic but with something that is much older than the Hittite capital. It was a commons at the edge of the modern village of Bogazkale, which borders the ancient site. I had always assumed that all village commons had been eaten up, that there was nothing left but this memorial poem of Oliver Goldsmith to an older way of life, and that the forces of mass production and individual wealth had wiped them all out. But as we walked up the hill toward the wreck of the ancient city, a large, closely cropped, unfenced field suddenly appeared before us, running between the rebuilt walls of Hattusa and the village.

A band of children was playing on the field, their voices rising gaily to the sky. Several groups of women were sitting in circles on the grass, chatting and doing some hand work. Together, they casually supervised the playing children. I could easily imagine playing with my own grandchildren here. Around and about the field itself, an odd collection of animals was scattered, a couple of lazy horses, donkeys, a few cows, some waddling geese. At the edges of the field, several women were collecting greens with what looked like a paring knife but was hooked and sturdier. They carried a forage bag slung over their shoulders. I stopped to ask one of these women what she was collecting, but my Turkish being limited it was hard to understand her quick explanation. She offered me a taste and I tried them. The leaves were coarse but pleasant tasting.

In the distance, an older man emerged from the woods with a wheelbarrow stacked with wood, trundling toward the village. A dog loped along beside him. It was then that it struck me with a thrilling rush of recognition! We had stumbled upon a village common working much as it would have in 1770 England.

Today, I find Goldsmith's poem overly sentimental, but when I first read it I was still under the spell of my own Sweet Auburn. In Grand Étang, in the 1950s and '60s, from my bedroom window at Grandfather's house, you could see a village vista as beautiful as anything in Goldsmith's poetic recollections.

All along the coast were farms. A steady, unvarying row of half-hip roofed houses lined the Cabot Trail. The front door pointed toward the sea, the back door toward a barn and the high fields for grazing cattle. Dotted here and there among the hayfields, where the earth was especially fertile, the land was plowed for small crops of potatoes, turnips, and oats.

I never got tired of this view. Among our closest neighbours, I could see who had let their barn go unpainted, whose was freshly painted, whose crops were doing well, who had the fattest looking cattle. And my aunt could check the whiteness of neighbours' laundry, which flapped in the wind beside the houses.

City planners now refer to land use like this as "pattern language." Pattern language refers to the pattern or form land and buildings take when their design is related directly to their function. For example, in Grand Étang the farms were narrow because every farmer wanted direct access to the main road and a mix of low land for cultivation and upland for grazing. Houses were hipped at the peak because that created a dense, rounded cap, which was much stronger than a simple straight roofline and thus more robust during winter storms. Each barn had small pastures fenced immediately around it in order to give the milk cows a place to stroll comfortably at night but leaving them within easy reach for the morning milking.

As a youngster, I didn't need any planning term like "pattern language" to understand what I was seeing—the view spoke for itself. The houses, barns, fields were all there because they worked to make the land and the farm productive. It all served a purpose.

Today, this Acadian coastal landscape has vanished like "the Commons" has in Europe. Most of the fields are now covered with dense, small, green conifers that pack down over the land like grass. Most of the old barns have been dismantled. They are too big and too difficult to maintain. The few that remain look odd and out of place, like terrestrial icebergs sitting alone in a green sea of scrub. The fields that remain now sprout summer bungalows.

Nor do I have much patience for Goldsmith's nostalgic, elegiac poem. His elegy masks the harsh reality that rural life has always been subservient to: money, greed, and power. It was in Goldsmith's day and it is today when global corporations routinely take governments to court and win for limiting their ability to amass land and use chemicals for industrial farming.

The alienation of the commons is an enduring story. In 1549, more than two hundred years before Goldsmith wrote his "Deserted Village," a peasant revolt against enclosures took place in Norfolk led by a Robert Kett. Thousands of people began to return privatized fields to the commons by physically taking down the enclosing fences. The Kett revolt was far too large for even the great Norfolk landowners to contain, and they called on Edward VI to send in the royal troops. He obliged and sent thirteen thousand soldiers north. The peasants were duly defeated and Robert Kett and the principal rebels were hung, drawn, and quartered for treason.

Protests over land use and land ownership, whether they are Aboriginal or non-Aboriginal, are treated as crimes against the state. Louis Riel, the great Metis orator, was executed as Robert Kett was—for treason. His treasonous act was insisting the new Canadian government's land surveys respect the farms and land divisions of the Metis people in the Canadian west. Natural justice would suggest the longevity of their claims, and the Metis's European/Aboriginal provenance gave them a legitimate claim to retain their lands, just as English villagers had natural rights to retain their common lands. The reality is there is no such thing as natural justice when it is confronted by raw power and the desire for personal wealth.

The story behind the disappearance of the humble streetcar from North America was another story about land use and profit. Streetcar lines create an urban landscape that is much more conserving of land than an expressway/parking lot landscape. Asphalt and cement make mall and tract housing easy to build and immensely profitable because it is the public or "the commons" that assumes all the principal costs (i.e., sewer, water, roads, parking).

The judge who ruled against the tire and car companies for colluding to close down city streetcar systems imposed a fine of one dollar. It was intended to be nothing more than a symbolic judgment. In his closing remarks, the lawyer who received the dollar judgment in favour of his clients (the streetcar companies) called it a tragedy of the commons.

This is a tragedy that I have felt very personally. My whole life has been about trying to convince others that we, the people, don't need to live in such land hungry cities. Assuming that the people are sovereign, ordinary people can decide tomorrow to bring back the village commons and have central parks in our towns and cities. We could easily build fast, efficient streetcars for our city streets instead of more expressways to suburbia. Nor do we need to cram people into towers like battery hens. There is nothing written in the stars that says we have to live in our cities or the country the way we do. There are other choices.

Rural Canada could be populated with small, ecologically healthy farms that rely more on people who care for the land. This rarely happens now because the small-scale spreads profits more evenly across the population and thus reduces profits for the largest corporations. Small-scale versus large-scale is not just about costs. It's about the balance of benefits. Being more like Sweden and less like the United States is a philosophical and environmental choice, not simply an economic one.

It is no accident that the fiercest opponents of responding to climate change are the ones that profit most from accelerating it. Just as it was those who fought hardest for enclosing the Commons were also the ones who benefited most from it.

Myles from Nowhere is a state of mind as much as a place. I don't at all feel miles from nowhere when I go there. I don't feel the need to be any place other than where I am. In winter, I continue to live in the old part of the city of Ottawa where I grew up. My daughter and her family live in the same old neighbourhood. As a child, I walked to the neighbourhood public school as my grandchildren do now. In Cape Breton, I live in a village that in spite of everything still manages to survive. Today, from the kitchen window, I can count sixteen boats out fishing lobster. They spin and pop around the ocean surface hauling and dropping their lobster cages, busy as tinkers.

I do not live in these places because they are quaint. I live in them because they are where I can best imagine my own past and a more secure human future.

Myles from Nowhere is just a country antique store, but it also represents the memory of a more sustainable way of being in the world. From the seeds of that memory we can build a society that can better combine the best of the old and the best of the new. "I think therefore I am," said Descartes. "I choose therefore I am," said Sartre. From these two ideas arose the idea of existentialism and the corroding thought that only the individual really matters.

"I connect therefore I am" has a very different quality. It's not a stand-alone existential thought. "I connect" cannot exist alone. A connection requires two or more people. It implies that life is not about going through it alone but how we go through together. If I have learned anything from my Acadian ancestors, it is that we define ourselves not just through thinking and choosing but by how we connect to others; and this is a complex, shifting universe that has no iron rules.

My father's thoughts about fishing, fishermen, and the global economy were very different at the end of his life. His career gave him the chance to see first-hand what happened when the "traditional" fishery got replaced by global supply chains. Everywhere the corporate trawlers arrived to vacuum up the sea floor, the fish stocks were exhausted.

As my father approached his last days, we discovered that our views of life and its meaning had come to be similar. We no longer contended in any way. He had changed his thoughts about small boats versus large boats. He no longer trusted the mantra of his youth, that bigger was better. I am trying to leave my grandchildren the same things that my father left me—

a commitment to our species by respecting the quality of life of all living things. No doubt, this "Myles from Nowhere" chapter has too much history in it, but I can't see how to avoid these stories. The future will require us to find different ways to connect with each other, and how we connect depends on what history teaches us is essential. The story of the loss of the commons should not be forgotten.

CHAPTER 14

The Undertow

The day is cloudy, and the remains of yesterday's big storm still roll in at the beach below the cliffs. It's cloudy and the end of summer heat is sultry rather than pleasant, but Felix wants to go to the beach. Soon he will be going back to school and the city. Clea is not so sure it's a good day for the beach.

If I had known anything at all about undertows, I would have known you don't go in the water for twenty-four to forty-eight hours after a big storm, because the storm's waves can carve long trenches in the geography of the ocean floor, and powerful undertows emerge, barrelling down these underwater trenches. But I didn't know this. The beach at Chéticamp Island is on a long sandbar and deepens very slowly into the sea. It is shallow and safe.

In the afternoon we drive to the beach. The day is still grey. The sea is choppy and angry with the leftover power of the storm. There are not many out. A few teenagers and that's about it. The day doesn't look inviting, but like Felix I'm thinking the summer will soon be over and the children gone back to the city; better to take advantage of what we can. The teenagers are playing in the waves, laughing and shouting as they try without much success to body surf. The waves are too choppy.

Clea isn't certain if she wants to go in. Felix is already walking into the water. At this moment, the only thing I know about undertows is literary. In John Irving's novel *The World According to Garp*, Irving uses the undertow as a metaphor for any unexpected, chaotic accident that can change a life forever.

We approach the water cautiously, or at least Clea and I do. Clea is afraid. She is intimidated by the surf, which is more rough than high. Felix is already in the water up to his waist and heading out farther. I call to him to come back. He hears me and turns but still keeps walking out. He is going out too deep, too fast, and I call to him again to come back.

I've been swimming at this beach since I was Felix's age. There's nothing to worry about, I tell myself, but I am worried. Something about this day doesn't feel right. Felix keeps drifting out. I'm not mistaken. He's going out too far, too fast. I pick up Clea in my arms and chase after Felix. Felix is young but he's already a good swimmer and totally unafraid. Clea doesn't want to go out, but I have to bring Felix back.

Suddenly, the sand disappears from beneath my feet and I'm treading water. It all happens so fast. The waves are hitting me like some enormous washing machine. The smash of the wave pushes me toward the shore, which I expect, but it is followed by another force that drags me back to the sea. Each wave has this reverse power. I swim after Felix, holding on to Clea.

Then I notice there is another current coming at me. This one is forcing me not out to sea but parallel to the shore, and it's really strong. The waves are simultaneously pulling me out to sea and parallel to the beach; that's why Felix went out so fast. It wasn't just him. He was being pulled and pushed toward the sea. I paddle with one arm as fast as I can toward Felix, screaming at him to turn back and swim to shore. Now! Go! Go! Don't wait for us! Swim now!

He hears the urgency in my voice and turns back toward the beach. I'm still carrying Clea and do what I can to follow him in. Felix swims hard and makes a few metres toward shore but then comes quickly drifting back toward me. He can't get himself to shore. I hold Clea with my left arm and catch Felix with my right arm as he is going by me. With Felix in my one arm and Clea in the other, I have little power to move anywhere. All I can do is tread water. The danger of the moment is overwhelming. It feels like we might drown.

Felix is still oblivious to the danger, but Clea isn't. She asks, "Grandpa, can you touch the ground?"

I can't. Holding the two children and only able to use my legs, we're not going to make it to shore. I call out to the teenagers, but I can't even see them. No one can hear me and the waves are high enough to hide us. I remember that a brave woman recently died a little farther down the coast after saving her own child and two others from an undertow. The exertion was so intense, she made it to shore with all three children but died.

In my mind is the thought that I can't be that far from the sandbar where I was standing just a few short moments ago. I had been standing there and holding Clea with water up to my hips and then suddenly I was over my head. I realize that in spite of not being able to touch bottom right now, the sandbar must be close.

There is a still moment slotted between the push of the wave toward the shore and the undertow pulling us back toward the sea. In that interval, I pump my legs like a crazed cyclist, trying to reach the sandbar. There is nothing. I can't touch the bottom. I have no choice. I have to find that sandbar. The story of the woman who died saving three children resonates in my head.

My right toe suddenly touches something. It's there! The sandbar! I lean forward using the children as dead weight to cantilever me forward, redoubling my effort. There is something there! I am able to paw at the sand with my right foot and pump in the deeper water with the other. Right, left, right, left, my legs flail as if I'm back on the football field. I don't seem to be moving anywhere. All I can think of is getting both feet onto something solid.

My breath is coming in great heaves. My heart is pounding like crazy. I can't tell if I'm touching the ground or not. Is the water deeper or shallower? Was it my imagination? Did my toe touch something? Then I feel my right foot hit something solid enough to find a foothold and pull myself forward. Suddenly, both feet are on the sandbar and I can get enough purchase to fight the backwards drag of the undertow. Suddenly, I'm bursting toward the beach, and the water is showering from my legs. The water falls away from me and I'm free. On the beach I collapse onto the sand and the children roll away from my arms. A cold terror rises inside me making me shiver.

Clea is silent, white-faced, and breathless. She asks if I'm okay. I'm so shaken I can't answer. Felix is calm and already thinking ahead asks, "Should we tell Mum and Dad?"

CHAPTER 15

Wars and the Family Forest

> *The part of duty I am now upon is what though necessary is very disagreeable to my natural make and temper as I know it must be grievous to you who are the same species.*
> —Lieutenant-Colonel Winslow reading the Deportation Order, Grand-Pré, 1755

One morning I was beachcombing not far from the house, looking for salt-preserved logs, which are useful for all kinds of things, and had found an excellent one, which I began to wrestle up the trail toward the old road. A man appeared at the top of the bluff, watching me struggle with the timber. He called down, "You need your grandfather's horse."

I shouted back, "But I don't have it, so why don't you come down and help me?"

He did. It transpired in the course of carrying the log that he was a Chiasson, now living in Boston, but we were related because his grandmother and mine were cousins. This is common enough among Acadians. The Doucet tribe goes back to 1632 and Captain Germain Doucet. The Doucet family tree may have started with one man and one family but is now more like a forest where the roots of each tree touch other roots and in this way are connected to all the other trees in the forest. Someone's grandmother's sister married someone else's grandfather's brother who is somebody else's cousin and so on, down through five hundred years. In the end, whether it's in Louisiana or Atlantic Canada, if you're Acadian you probably share a grandmother somewhere.

I was always sure that some of my grandmothers were Mi'kmaw, because the Acadians and the Mi'kmaq often intermarried and were neighbours and friends. One of the reasons Acadians refused to carry arms for the British was that it would have meant being pitted against the Mi'kmaq, who were ferociously opposed to the English. They didn't want to carry arms against their neighbours. It's hard to find an Acadian family who doesn't have a Mi'kmaw connection somewhere.

William Roach, the famous wood carver who lives in Petit Étang, a village on the north side of Chéticamp, flies the Acadian flag and the Metis flag from his studio beside the Cabot Trail. He does it so that people will not forget he has Mi'kmaw grandmothers.

I always took it as gospel that I also had Mi'kmaw grandmothers. How could I not? Captain Doucet's fourth child was an adopted Mi'kmaw boy who later married into the Acadian community. His children carried the Doucet name. My father always said that the wife of Pierre, the captain's oldest son, was a Mi'kmaw from whom our family line is descended.

So I had always just assumed that I had Mi'kmaw grandmothers, but now I'm not sure. Cousin Edgar had his DNA tested and apparently no North American Native markers showed up, which is very strange because we are first cousins.

The surprise was total. Here I am being convinced for three score and ten years that our line of the Doucet family all had Mi'kmaw great-grandmothers, but apparently some of us don't. After a few moments of shock, I realized this didn't change anything. I had no desire to have my DNA checked and felt the same connection to the Mi'kmaq that I always had. My feelings had not changed a whit.

Captain Doucet didn't remain in Nova Scotia. He returned to France after being defeated in 1652 at the siege of the fortress of Port Royal where, outnumbered five to one, he lost the final battle against the Americans. He was given the choice to surrender his arms and remain in Acadie or keep them and return to France. He decided the more honourable choice was to return to France with his arms and he did, leading his small band of soldiers onto a ship and sailing away. He never returned but left all of his children and grandchildren in the New World. He would have been surprised to learn that his descendants did not take up the cudgel and seek revenge. Instead they took a radically different course. They refused to join anyone's army, to the point of losing their lands. It was this refusal to fight that caused the deportations during the Seven Years War and led to centuries of isolation and the Acadians' indifference to the wider world.

It was another war that ended that isolation and began the Canadian story.

My grandfather, William Doucet, was born with a suspicion of all governments, which was characteristic of Acadians of his generation. They had no reason to trust any government and didn't, but he died thoroughly Canadian. He became Canadian through small gestures and experiences that changed his view of what we now call Canada. Being able to own land and vote, rights that had been denied Acadians, was central to that transition, as was seeing his uncle win a seat in the provincial legislature.

Another was being able to hear a Cape Breton fiddler on national radio. This changed his sense of what Canada was, as did following the careers of great hockey players like Maurice Richard and Jean Beliveau with Acadian names and French voices.

Prime Minister Mackenzie King journeyed all the way to Chéticamp by train and motor car to make an election speech using incomprehensible French, but making that effort impressed people. It made people feel connected to the federal government in a way that they never had been. All these things impressed Grandfather. It changed him from someone who regarded the hanging of Louis Riel as an assassination by the state (about which he never changed his mind), to someone who thought Canada was a good idea. So when his sons signed up for the war, he did not protest; instead he wished them well and prayed for their safe return.

Wars, like the family forest, are all related. The twentieth century began with the Kaiser's War, which generated the Second World War, the Holocaust, and Israel as a refuge country, which in turn spawned the Palestine/Israel standoff, which has morphed and spread across the globe like a virus. As much as leaders like to portray each war as a singular event, they are not a collective version of two men duelling. They have a shared pedigree. Each war becomes kindling for the next.

The Seven Years War of 1756–63 was part of French/English confrontations that had been going on for seven hundred years. These wars were all about controlling land and wealth by militarized aristocrats, often with one branch of the family aligned against another. It began with the Norman invasion in 1066 and never really stopped until the 1914 war. The principal difference between the earlier French/English conflicts and the Seven Years War was new marine navigation and ship size, which gave this war a scale never possible before. With the new technologies, the war crossed oceans and grew to become the first global conflict, being fought in Europe, India, Asia, and the Americas.

The war had been much anticipated. Both the French and English were anxious to fight each other and had been preparing for it for years by building ships and fortresses, and training and assembling troops. Like the Sioux versus the Cree peoples, it was a familiar grudge match that both sides were comfortable with, and it spread along the sea lanes like a new strain of flu, like a plague across the planet. On the island of Cape Breton, the French crown had constructed a massive fortress and named it after their king. It was designed to be their first line of defence in protecting France's "possessions" in the New World.

In spite of its cost, size, and intimidating character, the Fortress of Louisbourg didn't calm Acadian nerves or inspire loyalty to the French crown. Anticipating the carnage to come, Acadians began to move northwards looking to put distance between themselves and the European combatants. The Acadians had been down the warpath before, and their experience was clear. It didn't lead anywhere good.

By the 1740s, Louisbourg's soaring walls were creating as much consternation in London as Russian missiles in Cuba did in Washington in the twentieth century. It was a formidable place. The entire harbour was bracketed with canon, walls, and embrasures. The construction costs were so heavy that Louis XIV is said to have expected the walls of Louisbourg to rise above the Atlantic horizon and be visible from Versailles.

In the short term, the war came close to bankrupting both England and France, and in a sense France was. The taxes needed to fund it contributed to the overthrow of the French monarchy and came close to doing likewise with the English. But the winning side gained a global empire from which vast wealth began to flow toward the centre.

Samuel Johnson (1709–84) was one of the few prominent personalities of his era to understand that the 1756–63 war was a new phenomenon. It had nothing to do with protecting national boundaries or safeguarding human rights of the oppressed. It was a war about which European nation would control the flow of slaves and wealth from "the colonies" to Europe. It didn't come cheap. Aircraft carriers cost more than most nations can afford today, and Britain built the equivalent of several fleets of aircraft carriers. The costs were such that the King of England couldn't fund it. He was totally dependent on Parliament's willingness to vote to fund it.

Johnson opposed the war in England in a brilliant series of essays where he disparages the government's willingness to suppress native populations in the service of greed. His opinion of slavery is excoriating, and he's not afraid to say so either with his pen or in his private life. He is the first celebrity to adopt a dark-skinned man as a mark of affection and as a political statement.

Although the Seven Years War is now recognized as a trade and resource war, it began with the familiar lacquer of honest John Bull versus the Frogs, the "Frenchies," the Papists, etc., and this is how the Acadian deportation was sold to the Boston militia. They responded enthusiastically to the call. Young Boston men saw "the Indians" and "the French" as enemies, and to this day the Seven Years War is referred to in American history books as the French/Indian war.

Like the famous Noam Chomsky today, Sam Johnson had the force of character, position in society, and intellectual confidence to stand up to both his government and popular sentiment. Johnson's reputation as a brilliant scholar and thinker was similar to Chomsky's today. Nonetheless, neither Johnson nor Chomsky, in spite of their courage, clarity, and reputation, had any discernable effect on the government of their day. The Bush *père et fils* prosecuted their Middle East wars with the same ebullient spirit as William Pitt *et fils* did their colonial wars.

What strikes me is how little the essentials of wars over resources have changed. In 1756, the East India Company was pushing for a war for the same reasons Haliburton Oil Field Services does today—for profit. The allure of Iraqi oil fields had the same coin in Washington prior to the Bush wars as the wealth the East India Company's executives had acquired in Westminster.

The Marquis de Montcalm and General James Wolfe, who confronted each other on the Plains of Abraham, remain postcard representatives of the two European sides. Montcalm is remembered as a brave and elegant marquis whose personal wealth was anchored in rural estates. Although frequently outnumbered, he managed to secure victories confronting more numerous forces with his Indian allies at battles like Fort Ticonderoga.

Wolfe is remembered as a brave but dour man without the élan of aristocratic title. He was a career soldier from a career military family. He lived and died army.

The great Fortress of Louisbourg with its impressive armaments and battlements guarding the entrance of the St. Lawrence was at the top of the British list for places that must be extirpated, and the war started out very well for young James Wolfe and the British. In spite of the millions invested in the Louisbourg fortress, the limestone mortar that had been used to secure the stones of the fortress's thick walls turned out to be defective. It hadn't set properly and the great walls crumbled like sand under the detonating force of the fortress's own enormous canon.

Nor did the Goddess of Fortune smile on the French. Two magnificent French flotillas, handsomely provisioned with munitions, soldiers, and supplies, were sent to resupply the fortress and lift the British/American siege; both were violently dispersed by hurricane winds as the ships approached Cape Breton. The French garrison at Louisbourg went hungry and suffered the many maladies the confinement of a siege brings, yet it still held out.

An attack from the sea wasn't considered a realistic possibility by the builders of Louisbourg, and along the Atlantic shore, the fortress's defenses were weak. Wolfe led his men from small boats to charge the weak ocean defenses and won a foothold inside the fortress, allowing the British to enter. The battle for Louisbourg was over. Overnight, the young Wolfe became a hero, but he never developed Horatio Nelson's capacity for personal drama or seducing the media eye. He would have made a good Canadian. He got the job done and didn't pay much attention to praise. His success at Louisbourg made him the logical choice for the invasion of Canada.

As his fleet sailed up the broad back of the powerful St. Lawrence toward Quebec City, his letters home reveal a sensitive man. The grand estuary of the St. Lawrence was a very different scene from Louisbourg, which was impressive but isolated. The further Wolfe's fleet sailed up the river, the less confident of victory he became, and his letters are filled with cautionary admonitions. He had good reason. The fields, mountains, and majestic power of the St. Lawrence dwarf even magnificent southern rivers like the Hudson. His ships were harried and fired upon constantly.

As the summer ended and the autumn advanced, Wolfe knew he was in serious trouble. His navy captains were threatening to take their ships home regardless of what he wanted. They predicted disaster if their wooden ships were trapped in the ice, which would make them sitting ducks for attacks from the shore and bombardment by canon from the citadel.

Internal disagreements among the British senior officers escalated, the sea captains on one side, the army on the other. Wolfe's letters reveal that he had begun to despair of any success. Then at the last moment a possibility emerges. Through an informant, he learned of a narrow path that climbed the cliff face directly from the river to the heights behind the Quebec fortress. The small cove where the path began could be reached only by men in rowboats, but Wolfe had done this before in more difficult circumstances, running through rough ocean surf and over a sharp, rocky shoreline.

He quickly assembled some Scottish troops and sent them scrambling up the cliff. They had no trouble securing the summit, and his regular troops quickly followed.

If the Marquis de Montcalm had simply poured himself another cup of coffee and sat on his élan and waited for his greatest ally—winter—to arrive, there would have been no battle and Wolfe would have been forced to retreat. Both the Marquis and the General would have survived, and Canada would have better food today. But when Montcalm awoke to find his enemy neatly arrayed in the fields before his walls, waiting for his response, it was a challenge he could not resist.

Scottish troops played a pivotal role in capturing both Louisbourg and Quebec's citadel. This has always seemed slightly absurd to me. Just sixteen years earlier, in 1746, the British army had defeated the clans on Culloden Moor with canon and racked musketry in an easy battle, as the Scottish clans carried nothing much more than enthusiasm, swords, and pitchforks. It wasn't a whole lot different than North American Indians taking on the American cavalry with bows and arrows.

As a young officer, James Wolfe had also been at Culloden and later participated in "pacification" of the Highlands. In spite of Wolfe's roles both at Culloden and during the subsequent clear-cutting of Highland crofters, he enjoyed considerable popularity among the Scots for refusing to shoot a wounded man at Culloden after a direct order from the Duke of Cumberland. It's still debated today whether this actually happened or not, but that was the perception of his actions at the time and it fits a man whose personality was tempered by a strong sense of personal honour.

Nelson would get a statue on top of a tall column to commemorate his victory at Trafalgar. Wolfe would get half a continent.

The fall of the fortresses at Louisbourg and Quebec were jubilant moments for the winning side and deserved the headlines they received. Nonetheless, life in New France (now Canada) would not change much. The peace treaty between the English and the French negotiated in Montreal guaranteed the French-speaking population all the basic individual and collective freedoms, including religion, as well as guarantee of a 50 percent share of the fur trade pie to be divided between the Hudson's Bay Company, which was English, and the Northwest Company, which was French Canadian. The role of the church remained secure, as did land rights.

The contrast between the way French Canada and the Acadians were treated was stark. In Acadie there was no treaty that recognized any of the Acadian losses or any future for them—at all. Like in the Highlands after Culloden, the persecution did not end with the war. If anything, it intensified. The Acadians become a non-people without any rights or recognition except in the negative. It would be years before they were permitted to own land anywhere in Atlantic Canada and then only in marginal areas, not desired by anyone else.

Not unlike the Ephrussi family, the Doucets had experienced many years of good fortune. Prior to the deportation, their families had been large and healthy, their society prosperous and happy. Paul-Marie Doucet's birthplace, the town of Beaubassin, was large and busy with shipbuilding, trading schooners, farming, and fishing. After the war it disappeared to be replaced by a British fort named after Colonel Lawrence. It is only very recently that archaeologists have begun to reconstruct even the memory of its existence.

More than a decade after the deportation, one of Paul-Marie's brothers in Louisiana reported to a priest who was taking a parish census that he had heard his youngest brother Paul-Marie was living in the Madawaska region of what is now New Brunswick. How he knew this, in the days when communication between villages just a few miles apart was difficult, is a mystery, but this is not an alternate reality story. This all happened, and it changed the lives of thousands of families for centuries. From one young boy's life would come my Acadian ancestors and our Cape Breton home.

The older I get, the more wars of all kinds seem like nothing more than the human equivalent of wildfires. They clear-cut society. The family forest is engulfed in flames, and once the fire is rooted no one can do much except try to survive until the flames burn themselves out. Then slowly from under the ashes, green shoots emerge and new life begins. Families are formed, children raised, and the family forest tended again.

CHAPTER 16

The Nerf Wars

The famous educator A. S. Neill described the years ten to thirteen as the gangster years for boys. They pack down into wildness. When girls are learning skills that will endure all their lives, boys don't have much more on their minds than running, tumbling, wrestling, and shooting.

I speak from experience. On my tenth birthday, I received a wonderful gift—two cap pistols with (plastic) ivory handles carried in two black holsters, which made me instantly the revered leader of my gang as everyone else had only one holster. There was something wonderfully satisfying about pulling out both pistols simultaneously, fully loaded, and blasting away at some furtive enemy.

"You're dead! I shot you first!"

"No, you didn't. I shot you first!" The voices rang out happily as we patrolled the back alleys of St. John's, looking to win the cowboy wars.

Felix is always up for some shootouts, but the armaments are considerably more sophisticated than cap guns, which required nothing but a small round roll of caps to be fitted into the pistol chamber. Today, no self-respecting ten-year-old has a cap gun. Today they have Nerf guns. These are plastic facsimiles of submachine guns and are loaded with foam bullets that actually come firing out of the barrel hard enough to hit and bounce off a target.

Felix has given me some training on his Nerf guns of which he has both a pistol and a submachine gun. It's not as simple as pulling the trigger on a cap pistol. The gun actually has a Nerf bullet magazine that looks much like the real thing, safety catches, and barrel extension accessories "to precise the shot." There are no outraged cries of "I shot you first!" because Nerf guns shoot real foam bullets that can hit their target.

Watching Felix and his buddies hollering around the house, setting up in sniper position with extra magazines and whatnot, I'm reminded of lion cubs tumbling around their mother, practising what will become the deadly charge, pounce, and throttle of their adult hunting lives. These boys all understand what "locked and loaded" is right now. The basic moves needed around adult guns won't change.

On the other hand, foam bullets do no worse than sting, and after a battle everyone has to help collect the bullets because they are too expensive to be left hidden under a lilac bush. No doubt someone, sometime, somewhere will call for a ban on Nerf guns, but I'm not sure that's the right approach. What about requiring terrorists and the Western allies to fight with Nerf guns, and who ever loses the battle has to collect the bullets?

We could extend this idea of cleanup after a battle to nations and an exchange of nuclear detonations. We could require the winning side to be responsible for decontaminating the site, providing housing for the homeless, health care for the radiated, and so on. Maybe the appetite for collecting nuclear arsenals would diminish then.

Felix and his buddies certainly can't quite grasp the difference between real bullets and Nerf bullets. My father-in-law was hit by a real bullet in a real war and spent a year undergoing various surgeries in hospital and never really recovered. His kidneys were damaged and as the accumulated scar tissue slowly began to shut his kidneys down, he slipped into the agonies of post-traumatic stress. Real weapons have real consequences.

The great thing about Nerf wars is that the exhilaration of the hunt for the enemy remains, but afterwards the boys get to clean up and compare notes on their own success. Nerf wars are a good deal of fun, but why not require adults to play like children instead of worrying that children will turn into adults?

CHAPTER 17

"Harry the Whale" and the GAMS Cooperative

I cannot overestimate the importance of observing every little thing and of reasoning upon it. The history of invention is full of incidents in which apparently trivial observations have proved of immense value to the world.
—Alexander Graham Bell

Alexander Graham Bell would have liked the little Gulf Aquarium and Marine Station (GAMS) Cooperative in Grand Étang. It occupies what used to be a restaurant in the harbour that fell on hard times and had to close. On the ground floor, there is an Ocean Discovery Centre for children, with a touch tank, eels, crabs, and the kinds of things that go bump in the water. Upstairs holds the office and research and meeting area.

GAMS sits at the edge of the harbour a few steps from the sea, kitty-corner from the Mi-Carême Centre. They co-exist uneasily. The Mi-Carême belongs to the days of magical thinking: light a Candlemas candle to save a sailor's life; hide your face behind a mask and disappear; expose your face and identity magically returns.

GAMS is the stuff of measurement, not the imponderable world of music and magic. Each summer, the temperature of the sea and the saline content of the water are recorded, as part of the attempt to understand what is happening to the ocean with climate change. All this brings a passionate light to the eyes of Gretchen Noyes-Hull, the director and founder of GAMS. Her research station is the world of measure it, weigh it, test it. Do your best to relate cause, effect, and context, and always be skeptical of your conclusions. If there is magic to it, it's a different kind of magic from the Mi-Carême.

It's not that GAMS is in competition with the Mi-Carême Centre. Summer tourists visit both. It's just that they are very different. The Mi-Carême is about the culture of a people, and culture is rarely measurable. GAMS is about the biology of the sea and the Descartes model of "I think therefore I am." Nonetheless, together, GAMS and the Mi-Carême are helping to redefine how the little harbour can continue to be useful in the future.

Gretchen is the mother of three children and, like me, a grandparent. Her day job is teaching oceanography at the University of Maine. She is now seventy and has devoted many years to trying to understand what is happening in the Gulf of St. Lawrence off northern Cape Breton. She's done it all on a shoestring, cobbling together summer research grants each year for students and volunteering her own time and expertise every summer season.

A few years ago, her little marine co-operative won an Atlantic Canada Co-op Award for her proposal to build a research and teaching aquarium in Grand Étang's harbour. The design is now complete and she's trying to raise money to build it. If she does, she will have accomplished something deeply astonishing. In the little village of Grand Étang in the remote vastness of northern Inverness, there will be a small but important research and education aquarium fed naturally by the sea it sits beside.

If Gretchen is successful in building a permanent aquarium and research station, this will change life in the village forever, for suddenly little Grand Étang will have oceanographers from all over the world wanting to live here to do research. With them will come new houses, new thoughts, and new ways of doing things. In the process, little Grand Étang will join the circle of science that is unravelling what climate change is doing to the ocean and how life there is adapting to climate change and how fishermen can adapt themselves.

Gretchen and I first met when we rented her house on Chéticamp Island, and we quickly became friends. From the beginning, it felt as if I had known her for a long time. My father had the same kind of irrepressible energy Gretchen does. I have learned through her and through shore clambering expeditions with grandson Felix how to appreciate the intertidal life of the harbour. The nose edge of the harbour is filled with many fascinating lives: crabs, starfish, mussels, oysters, snails, eels, wandering mackerel. There is as much life as you're prepared to look for.

Felix takes delight in capturing little crabs and holding them in his hands. He gives them names and deciphers their personality. This one is Herman the pacifist; this one a boxer who dances and tries to bite. Felix and I can spend a whole afternoon just prying free shore rocks, looking for things that jump. Felix thinks he might like to be a marine biologist, which I take to be a great compliment to Gretchen because until recently his only ambition was to be Spider-Man.

The old wooden house Gretchen owns on Chéticamp Island is a relic from the vanished village of Cap Rouge. Parks Canada expropriated the entire village of Cap Rouge in the 1930s. A few houses escaped the expropriation by being floated down the coast. Gretchen's little house is one of them. Her house was towed down the coast to Chéticamp Harbour. The expropriation order was done to create an unencumbered entrance to the park. It remains a sore point among Cape Breton Acadians because no English-speaking community was ever expropriated by the federal government for the park.

The Cap Rouge villagers received $1,800 for their houses and land, and were free to take away their houses if they could; but it wasn't their first choice. The village of Cap Rouge, which occupied some of the most famous and picturesque land in all of Cape Breton that appears in endlessly reproduced photographs, has vanished into memory. A small part of that memory is Gretchen's blue house. It's the only building that's left from Cap Rouge. She hasn't changed it that much and now rents it out. Anyone who does live there quickly learns a great deal about the history of North Inverness, for the house is full of it. Gretchen has done more for the Gulf shore than she will admit and more for me than she knows.

At GAMS the explanations about the ocean are always more complex than you expect, which I don't mind at all because Felix is ten and most curious about how the world works. He likes detail and asks questions from sunrise to sunset. Why do you use baking powder to make waffles, Grandpa? How does a starfish eat? Why does the wind blow? Sometimes I can answer. Sometimes I can't. Felix is on a mission to understand the world. He is tall for ten and has the energy of titans. Fortunately, he is very good-natured, even when he's breaking things, which is frequently because he hasn't learned yet to blend his energy with his curiosity. He reminds me every day about how little I know and how much fun it is to think.

I have learned that how a starfish eats is gross and violent, especially if you happen to be an innocent mussel. The starfish lands on the mussel's shell, wraps its arms around it, and steadily pries it open with its tentacles. Once the shell has been pried open, the starfish ingests the mussel's innards directly into its own stomach. I had no idea the quiet starfish had such a violent character and was as surprised as Felix was when it was explained.

Nonetheless, Felix still thinks I'm wise, which isn't true at all. It is just that there is a difference in experience between ten and seventy. At ten, Felix thinks the world is comprehensible through knowledge. I do not. Knowledge is seductive but limited in its uses. What knowledge is there when I sing "Harry the Whale" with Évangéline? This little song is one we have composed and is immensely satisfying to sing, which Évangéline and I do lustily whenever I pull out my guitar. "Harry the Whale" makes us smile, but it also helps us understand why GAMS and the ocean are important without ever doing much but making us smile.

The grass in my hayfield grows up to the edge of the cliff and flows down the face of the cliff itself. Grass is a powerful plant. It leans right over the cliff and challenges the sea to come and get it. It's a battle that never stops. On a summer day, the grass appears to be winning the battle to reclaim the land from the water. Then, slowly, in autumn the tables are turned and autumn storms begin to destroy the grass that in summer tumbles over the edge of the cliff so boisterously it looks as if you could walk on it when there is nothing beneath it but air.

In winter, the plants are defeated and retreat, but the victory isn't final. In spring the war between roots and water begins all over again. No one can explain this endless conflict between green and blue. Why does it happen, or which will win? Nor is there anything that can explain why a woman lights a candle in a window or why her man looks anxiously for its light as he sails toward home, except that the light is comforting.

Ocean life must not extinguish; the life of the planet depends on it, so we must understand our relationship with the ocean better. Nor is it all about disappearance and extinguishment. There's hundreds of thousands of mussels in the pond behind the harbour. It should be possible to have a sustainable mussel fishery there without jeopardizing anything. I'm betting my father would think this would be possible.

Climate change and ocean warming means that some of the old species won't return. It's not clear if the cod will, but the warming seas will bring new species from the south. They are starting to arrive already. For a harbour to be useful, it needs to be able to do more than shelter boats from a storm. It should be the centre of a harmonious relationship with the ocean that connects us all, and GAMS can help us do that. It may be small but the spirit is large and the goal important.

CHAPTER 18

In the Shadow of Évangéline

> *D'Aulnay accused Nicolas Denys's sawmill foreman of treason and threw him into a deep dungeon in which he could see no light with fifty pounds weight on his feet and he was made to die of misery.*
> —Fortune & La Tour, M. A. MacDonald

There is more history that has been forgotten than will ever be remembered. This mostly doesn't matter. Who cares whether the weather was fine or ill on Friday or that Grandpa's crepes were especially delicious this morning? Yet these small things are the heart of all our memories, we remember them better than who won a battle or what political party was elected. And so we should, for these simple memories are more reliable. The crepes were really good on Friday. They were just right and Clea and Felix did smile with pleasure. It is not clear with politics and wars waged. The memory of battles and politics are manipulated by who wins. If Germany had won the Second World War, it is Dresden and Hamburg and the Allied bombing that would be remembered as a crime against humanity. Not a pleasant thought for anyone, but I doubt that death camps would be front and centre.

More than anything else, Acadians are remembered because they refused to fight for either the French or English during the Seven Years War of 1756–63. Everyone else did or was conscripted, but the Acadians refused. Their refusal and its consequences became the stuff of legend, and every Acadian grows up in the shadow of that refusal and the story of Évangéline. I grew up thinking that Acadians had been gifted with some special elixir that allowed us to be peaceful when others were not, that in this way we were different from all others.

It wasn't until I was a university student that I would learn that the Acadian story began not in a peaceful refusal to fight but in the unchained violence of a religious and civil war so devastating that it wiped out entire communities and suffocated the old connections to Europe. Critics of the Acadian refusal to fight for either the French or the English sometimes regard the Acadian position as defeatist or subservient to a greater power. On the contrary, it was the reverse. The Acadians were confident enough to refuse to be bullied into doing something they didn't want even by the greatest power of the age, and they didn't want to fight anyone. When the Acadian deputies met with Lord Cornwallis and expressed what they considered their rights versus the King's rights, the admiral's response was amazement. "It seems you want to deal with the King as equals?"

This thought seemed as bizarre to Admiral Cornwallis as Louis Riel's request was to Ottawa, that the Metis be treated as equals with sovereign rights to their land. The Metis leader was able to put it more eloquently than anyone else: "We are a people different in power but no less equal in rights."

The Acadian position was more nuanced. They gave up their arms and boats when requested without protest. They never disputed the idea that the British were sovereign, but they wished to retain authority over local land division, freedom of worship, and freedom from military conscription. This is all entirely exceptional. It's a nascent form of federalism, not that dissimilar to the federal/provincial division of powers today. Nothing remotely like it was occurring anywhere else. Politically, the Acadians were generations ahead of their time, and it was new to Acadian society also. They didn't have it all figured out but were in the exciting process of devising a different kind of society.

The early French colony in Atlantic Canada wasn't like this at all. When Captain Germain Doucet arrived in 1632 with Charles d'Aulnay and Charles de La Tour, the Acadian leaders were not local. The leaders were aristocrats and reflected the aristocratic order and culture of France from whence they had come. The violent religious intolerances of France (Huguenot versus the Catholic) also accompanied the first expeditions and soon found an ugly echo in the new colony in a bitter conflict between two French leaders, Charles de La Tour on the Huguenot side and Charles d'Aulnay on the Catholic.

La Tour and d'Aulnay were both creative, energetic, ambitious men. D'Aulnay was the richer and made many trips back and forth across the ocean to recruit skilled tradesmen, stone masons, carpenters, smiths, and farmers for the new community around Port Royal. La Tour depended on Protestant (Huguenot) funding from Nantes.

D'Aulnay could have easily lived a quiet, luxurious château life in France, but court life didn't interest him and the new colony started well. D'Aulnay and his superior, Isaac de Razilly, were enchanted with this new world and they had a strong team—men like Nicolas Denys, who was an extraordinary entrepreneur but in spite of his success would be forced to return to France because of the d'Aulnay/La Tour war. Isaac de Razilly was the senior, the richest, and the most stable. His early leadership kept the various factions under his command from imploding. Unfortunately, he died within a few years of arriving, and without his calming presence the younger leaders quickly barricaded themselves behind the old religious fracture lines.

D'Aulnay especially showed no interest in modifying his religious convictions. It was his way or no way. He was Catholic with a capital C. He and his wife, Jeanne Motin, were a powerful force; they raised seven children and are credited with introducing dyke farming in the new colony.

Charles de La Tour and his wife, Françoise-Marie Jacquelin, had the same ambition to see the New World populated with a vigorous new society but with himself as its leader, not d'Aulnay. Without de Razilly to control their ambitions, a war between the two men was inevitable.

The violence of the d'Aulnay/La Tour war had all the marks of a European war—guerrilla raids, pitched battles, sieges, torture, and violent death—but it was so small and so personal, it feels more like a family feud gone crazy. Although divided by religion, both men had many reasons to have been friends. In France, their families had lived in the same Parisian quartier and they probably had attended the same school separated only by time, but this didn't stop the violence. D'Aulnay killed Françoise-Marie Jacquelin, La Tour's brave wife, the same way he eliminated Nicolas Denys's sawmill foreman—by imprisoning her in the ugliest of circumstances. Chaining a former colleague's wife to a wall and waiting until starvation and the cold killed her is up close and personal in a way that a drone attack can never be.

The war between d'Aulnay and La Tour was a reflection of its times. In Paris, the St. Bartholomew's Day massacre in 1572 left Huguenot corpses stacked like cord wood beside the Seine. On that day, France's entire Huguenot leadership was exterminated, including the king himself. In rural France, Protestant congregations were massacred, children included, or imprisoned as d'Aulnay did, leaving the prisoners to starve in extraordinary misery. It was similar to the recent Rwandan massacres between Tutsi and Hutu. It was a genocidal war before the word had been invented.

The 1598 Edict of Nantes from the Huguenot King Henry IV slowed the violence down, but it continued to bubble along beneath the surface, and in 1685 when the edict was revoked, new waves of genocidal violence immediately swept the country. This was the European context in which the d'Aulnay/La Tour war played out in Nova Scotia, New Brunswick, and Maine.

Both men had powerful connections. Charles d'Aulnay was related to Cardinal Richelieu, and Charles de La Tour had the backing of Huguenot merchants in Nantes who were some of France's most successful. Recognizing that this was a problem for his colony, Louis XIV divided the land and governorship of Acadie between the Huguenot-backed La Tour and the Catholic-backed d'Aulnay. It was one of those "it seemed like a good idea at the time" decisions, but it worked to increase violence not reduce it. It gave both factions a sense of legitimacy to justify their side of the war but not enough resources to govern and grow the new colony successfully without co-operating, which they wouldn't do.

The scheming and fighting finally ended in the siege of Fort La Tour. It was a winter siege and must have been miserable for everyone. D'Aulnay blockaded La Tour's little fort with privately hired warships, which cruised back and forth in front of the fort.

La Tour's wife, Françoise-Marie Jacquelin, was in charge at the fort, her husband being in Boston trying to raise money and troops to lift the siege. She fooled d'Aulnay into thinking the fortress was well defended by having her men wear different hats and walk in changing patterns along the parapet, making the defenders appear more numerous to the crews of the blockading ships. With very little but her wits and courage she held d'Aulnay's ships off for months while his crews shivered on frozen decks, patrolling the frigid sea. The blockade exhausted d'Aulnay's fortune. When he finally broke into Fort

La Tour with the help of a traitor, he was enraged to discover there were only eight defenders. He hung all eight and forced Françoise-Marie Jacquelin to watch their twitching demise. A few weeks after her men were hung, Françoise-Marie Jacquelin herself died in the silent penumbra of an unheated cell.

The devastation was quite complete. By the end of the war in 1645 there were fewer settlers in Acadie than there were at the start. Dynamic, successful leaders like Nicolas Denys had been obliged to stand by and watch their sawmills and communities torched. It is reported that d'Aulnay's side of the war cost him the extraordinary sum of 800 pounds a month. Nor was he regarded as a hero. The great hero was the amazing Françoise-Marie Jacquelin. She became a media star in Paris through sensational reports of her brave and creative defence of Fort La Tour while her husband was in Boston.

Despite his victory, Charles d'Aulnay didn't die exultant. In Port Royal, he attended Mass daily and went to confession obsessively, overwhelmed by the feeling his life had not unfolded as it should have. He was only forty when he won the war and forty-five when he died in 1650 from hypothermia after a canoeing accident. He didn't die a happy man. His last will and testament requested that he be buried under the church steps at Port Royal and, according to M. A. MacDonald in her book *Fortune & La Tour*, asked that those who walked over his grave "have pity for a person who merits only the chastisements and thunderbolts of a justly angry God."

D'Aulnay's fears about the futility of his own life are realized. His four sons all return to Europe where one after another they die on the battlefield. His daughters enter a convent for the daughters of impoverished aristocrats, and the d'Aulnay family name is extinguished. The new colony remains Catholic, but the connections to France and Versailles wither after the civil war. No one comes to replace d'Aulnay, de Razilly, or Doucet.

On hearing of Charles d'Aulnay's canoeing accident, La Tour hastened back to Port Royal from Quebec City where he had fled after losing his wife and his fort. Boldly, he asked d'Aulnay's widow, Jeanne Motin, to marry him. La Tour was already sixty but unlike his younger rival didn't appear to worry about his life being over at all. He had the vitality of a buccaneer. The proposal seems absurd, for La Tour had been her husband's mortal enemy, but La Tour argued that this would be their opportunity to put an end to the conflict and bring peace to the colony by ending the enmity between their two families once and for all.

It would be interesting to know what was going through Jeanne Motin's mind when her husband's great enemy proposed marriage. I'm guessing she would have consulted with Captain Germain Doucet, because Doucet had been appointed by d'Aulnay as her children's guardian. He and d'Aulnay had a long friendship. They were together on the first Isaac de Razilly expedition of 1632. Their friendship probably preceded even that, because Doucet came from Loudon (Vienne), the same area where the d'Aulnay estates were held. Both men were Catholic and on the same side throughout the Acadian civil war, although Captain Doucet did not participate in the winter siege of Fort La Tour. During this siege, he was the commander of another small fort at Pentagouet in what is now Maine.

Just what the thoughts or conversations were on the d'Aulnay side of the marriage proposal remains unknown, but the outcome was simple enough. D'Aulnay's widow agreed to La Tour's proposal. They married and buried religious toxins in the marriage bed. Although the Jeanne Motin/La Tour *volte-face* is astonishing considering the violence and enmity between d'Aulnay and La Tour, these kinds of things did happen.

For example, in Chéticamp the ancestor of Clarence Lelièvre of The Phantoms fame was a Huguenot and suffered five years in a French prison for his faith before finding refuge on the Channel Islands of Guernsey and Jersey. At the time, Jersey was the fishing camp of Robin, Jones, and Whitman, a company that operated a fish plant in Chéticamp. Clarence Lelièvre's ancestor came to work at Chéticamp and ultimately married a Catholic girl there. He converted and his children were raised Catholic. His story isn't as dramatic as the La Tour/Motin one, but the story has not been forgotten. It has resonated down through the generations of the Lelièvre family.

Charles de La Tour and Jeanne Motin had five children together. Their children would go on to have large families of their own, and the La Tour name lives on in Nova Scotia to this day. Charles de La Tour finished his days in pleasant retirement and died a patriarch in a quiet, coastal village. Unlike d'Aulnay, he doesn't appear to have had any strong religious convictions. His Huguenot connections in Nantes seem to have been more about business than religion. Like many early Acadians, it seems he was comfortable with Mi'kmaw spirituality, the Huguenots' faith, and Catholicism. Jeanne Motin remained a Catholic and their children were raised in that faith.

The d'Aulnay/La Tour war may have been ridiculously small, but it was brutal. It took the little colony decades to recover. In contrast, by 1650 when Charles d'Aulnay died in the boating accident, New England had become so populous and powerful that it was like a Puritan cat sitting on the doorstep of the Acadian mouse. One can't help but speculate: What if La Tour had been able to win the war and the new colony had drifted into the Protestant sphere instead of the Catholic? Would the New Englanders have then become friendly co-religionists and co-settlers instead of enemies? Would there have been no deportation? Would Halifax have become the capital of a Protestant but French-speaking Nova Scotia?

We will never know. With d'Aulnay's victory at Fort La Tour, the Acadian community staggered but remained Catholic, and the violence between the two Puritan communities and the Acadian settlements continued. For almost 150 years, Protestant raiders from the south regularly swept over the little Acadian coastal communities, burning and looting. In many ways, the deportations of 1755–63 are just a larger version of something that had been going on since 1613 when the Governor of Virginia dispatched a privateer, Samuel Argall, in three armed ships to dislodge and destroy the first Acadian settlements. By all accounts he did an excellent job, looting the little houses and burning fields at harvest time so effectively that people starved to death in the winter of 1613. No wonder Samuel de Champlain decided Quebec was a better bet.

Not surprisingly, after the d'Aulnay/La Tour war, the remaining Acadians became adept at avoiding conflict and came to be called "the neutral French" (*les Français neutres*) to differentiate them from French Canada. Historians like to refer to the Treaty of Utrecht in 1713, which transfers Acadie to the British, as the moment when the Acadian communities irrevocably withdrew from the international conflicts that swirled around them.

I disagree. I've always thought it was fifty years earlier in 1654 when Germain Doucet was besieged and defeated by General Robert Sedgwick. When this happened, the last connections to France were severed and the process of becoming a unique New World society began. When the captain and his soldiers returned to France, no one took their place. The leaders of the Acadian community became entirely local, and they developed very different ideas about governance and life in general.

It's not known where in France Captain Doucet's days ended; the location of his grave is not recorded. How would he have shared his memories of a grand world with vast virgin forests stretching toward every horizon and seas filled with uncountable wealth? How would he explain he had a Mi'kmaw son?

I can't help but feel it must have been a very lonely exit. He would have been irrevocably separated from his children and grandchildren and all he had known on the western side of the Atlantic Ocean. His eldest son, Pierre, after his father's defeat at Port Royal, travels to Quebec, where he seems to have become a *courier de bois*, travelling the northern river systems of New France. But these are refugee years for the Doucet family, and it is not possible to know what exactly was happening or where people lived. Records are not kept. During this time, Pierre's first wife dies. It is not clear when or why, except that she was young. He does not remarry for a long time.

Twenty years after Germain Doucet returned to France, Pierre returns from Quebec to Port Royal. He's a widower now with a strapping young son of his own. Not long after coming back, he meets and marries a local girl, Henriette Pelletier. This marriage is a very different kettle of fish from his first. They do not wander. She is clearly not Mi'kmaw but now has a brother-in-law who is. She is not alone in having Mi'kmaw relatives within the young Acadian community. The newlyweds settle down in Port Royal where they produce ten children. Pierre Doucet lives into his nineties and dies a patriarch at Port Royal. In 1713, when his own days draw to a close, there are now four generations of Doucets in Port Royal, with the younger members of the family already moving to newer communities like Beaubassin farther up the bay.

I doubt if anyone at Pierre's wake in 1713 paid any attention to a European Treaty being signed at Utrecht. Even if Pierre's descendants had been aware of it, why would anyone care? European title to Nova Scotia had changed nine times between Germain Doucet's defeat at Port Royal and the Treaty of Utrecht in 1713. What could another European treaty possibly mean for ordinary people's lives?

Life went on. In the years between Germain Doucet's defeat and return to France in 1654 and the Treaty of Utrecht in 1713,

Acadians resolutely avoided any European conflict and they enjoyed peaceful, prosperous times. There were fields to be taken from the sea, crops to be sowed, boats and houses to be built, marriages to be celebrated, children and grandchildren to be welcomed. Life was good. This was a magical, peaceful, prosperous time that will be celebrated by Longfellow in his poem *Évangéline*.

The lens of history tends to freeze the past into sets of frozen images and give it labels, often around monarchs. This is Victorian, that is Georgian, and so on, but the reality is like everything else, society is always shifting and changing. My father was born into the most devout Catholic society imaginable. His world and education were defined by the Catholic Church and its calendar. Protestants were considered interesting but not really plausible. Yet he learned to be just as happy sitting in an Anglican pew as a Catholic. He remained nominally Catholic but had lost all conviction of his own religion's perfection.

There are always beginnings and endings, for that is the nature of life itself. Seasons have beginnings and endings. Wars have beginnings and endings. Powerful societies have beginnings and endings. Life's dance is complex. Finding your own place in that dance can surprise everyone. It must have surprised Charles de La Tour and Jeanne Motin.

When I think of the years that separate the tiny d'Aulnay/La Tour civil war, which ground to a halt after the siege of Fort La Tour in 1640, and the global conflict that started in 1755, the Acadian civil war seems so miniscule and so old that it can't matter. It all happened long before Canada was even envisaged as a nation. In 1640, the indigenous peoples still occupied and ruled most of North America, including Nova Scotia or Acadie, and were still fighting for it in 1755. It wasn't until 1867 that the new Canadian provinces got together to hammer out an accord that set out the parameters for a new country.

But in 1755, stories from the d'Aulnay/La Tour civil war weren't ancient, forgotten history; that war was still within living memory of the community. Many families would have had ancestors who had suffered in that conflict. Those family memories would have become part of the subtext of the collective memory when the Acadians convened in their villages to talk about how they should respond to the British demand to swear allegiance and carry arms. One of the lingering effects of the d'Aulnay/La Tour war must have been to make people suspicious of conflicts emanating from European ambitions, no matter what their guise.

Lord Cornwallis, the British admiral, would have seen just a collection of ragged farmers and fishermen when Acadian deputies came to meet with him. The Acadians saw an independent people with their own history and their own way of being in the world. It was two strong but different realities colliding.

I apologize for troubling the reader with so much history when recalling the life of one small family, but a family story, be it ever so insignificant, doesn't happen in a vacuum. It didn't for the Ephrussi family of Vienna and it didn't for the Doucets of Grand Étang.

CHAPTER 19

Goodbye Grandchildren

Emma and Sebastien came to pick up the children today. They made a pretty picture when they arrived in their car. They drove so slowly up the lane that the children were running to them as fast as the car was moving. Emma was able to get out of the car and walk along beside it with the children. It was a joyful little parade. Clea and Évangéline's hair and dresses were blowing in the wind; Felix was so excited he didn't know whether to climb into the car with his dad or just circle the slow-moving vehicle at Flash speed so that he could simultaneously be both inside the car with his dad and outside the car with his mother.

It was one of those moments that I know will settle in my mind forever. My throat was dry and eyes damp with happiness at seeing my daughter and son-in-law coming toward the house surrounded by their children.

Ach! It's been a fine summer, but it's time for them to go back to the city. I remember when I left to go back to school in the fall, Grandfather would stand very straight, his eyes moist with silver tears. I know now what was on his mind. There was that worry. When would we see each other again?

The great stars of your life are parents. They are the sun in your firmament. Whatever they say and do carries great weight; their influence endures all your life like no other. Grandparents are not in the same league. They are slighter, smaller. There was only one occasion in my life when they weren't, and that was when Grandfather and I were alone out of sight of the rest of the adult world, tramping about field and forest.

Then we had the chance to be a little different from anyone else. It was as if for a brief moment we could define the world on our terms in our way. I remember Grandfather making me stilts on a rainy day and both of us clumping around the barn floor. He bet me that he could run across the field faster on stilts than I could, and he did! Grandfather had learned when he was a boy and had retained his agility. He was as quick as a cat on stilts. Maybe Felix will have some memories like this someday. They won't be quite the same but they won't be that different either. Although I still do things that adults are supposed to do—drive a car, write "concerned" letters to the editor, cook meals, and so on—the adult world interests me less and less.

There is a quality to grandparenting that is not particularly adult. It has something to do with the passage of the years and the approaching of life's curtain. I have trouble taking the adult world as seriously as I once did. I don't miss it.

CHAPTER 20

Russell Daigle, His Farm, and "The Bishop's Candlesticks"

Russell Daigle lives in Terre Noire. It's a small village down the road from Grand Étang. To me as a boy it was unknown territory because it was too far away. Today, through the magic of the automobile, blink and you've jumped the distance from Grand Étang to Terre Noire, but by the old measures Terre Noire was a long way away. It was entirely outside of the ambit of our parish.

My grandfather's village, Grand Étang, is part of the parish of St. Joseph du Moine, which is comprised of three villages: Grand Étang, St. Joseph du Moine, and Cap Le Moine. If you're driving in a car, you can zip by hardly conscious that they exist, but they do. Each has its own character and history.

Grand Étang is centred on the harbour and the saltwater pond behind the harbour from which it takes its name. St. Joseph is the middle village and centred on the little farm valley of Le Moine. This village is home to the church and parish hall, the volunteer fire station, a couple of garages, an extension unit of Université Saint-Anne. It used to have a large primary school as well as a butcher shop and a dairy. (The dairy has been converted to a popular art gallery.) I always thought that St. Joseph du Moine was by far the largest village in the parish and that's why the parish was named after it, but that's not so. I was surprised recently to notice that there were about the same number of post boxes for St. Joseph du Moine as there is for Grand Étang.

Cap Le Moine, the third village of our parish, sits in a swale of land that curves around the cape on the other side of St. Joseph. Here the coast road dips and rises, curves and bends with the houses of the village blending harmoniously with the land, the coastline, and the road. People often stop at the look-off in Cap Le Moine to take pictures of how the road, farms, and land meet the sea.

After you pass by Cap Le Moine, you arrive at Terre Noire. It's a very small village, so small it's missed on most maps. At the same time that I was passing summers with my grandfather in Grand Étang, Russell Daigle was passing his with his grandfather in Terre Noire. Like me, he used to use a bench to jump on the back of his grandfather's farm horse and ride down to the sea looking for adventure. We never met, then being separated by so much territory, but we do now. I frequently go to his garden to buy vegetables and talk about this and that. He lives in his grandfather's house, which he has bought and restored. The house is tall and quite beautiful in the old-fashioned clapboard way.

This is the story of how Russell came to leave Cape Breton.

"In 1963, I was in the army where I was learning how to be a bandsman. I had left school for the army even before I completed grade 11. It looked to be my future, but my uncle, Vincent Deveau, called. He had an offer for me. He was working with Edmund Chiasson over at St. Ann's driving a bulldozer to cut trails for pulp. St. Ann was too far away to get home and he had a big farm. There was no one to take care of his milking cows, and he had nine. Would I come home and help out with the chores? Then I could go back to school and finish off my schooling. So I got out of the army and came home. I was nineteen at the time and too old to be in school, but I decided to try it.

"In the morning, I would throw hay down from the mow for the cows, then separate the milk for the dairy, because we sold the cream for butter; the skim milk would go back to the calves."

"We did the same thing," I said, remembering.

"Everybody did. The cheque from the dairy was a big deal. Then I'd wash up and go to school. I was always a little asthmatic, and being around so much hay that fall began to bring on attacks. After Christmas, I had a really serious attack. Couldn't breathe. I was driven in to Chéticamp to see Dr. Samson. He got out his stethoscope, listened to my chest, then said, "Your lungs have collapsed. You're not going home. You're going to the hospital right now.' And he walked me across the street to the hospital.

"In the hospital, he took out this enormous syringe that looked like it could kill a horse. It took five minutes to inject something called aminophylline. Then they rigged me up to an intravenous steroids drip. This wasn't a plastic bag like you see now. It was a glass bottle and it was attached to something that looked like it should have been in a garage. I don't remember feeling any better, but after that Dr. Samson said, 'That's it. That's all I can do.'

"The nuns set up some candles on a table near my bed and I asked them what for. They said they were praying for me. I suppose I wasn't conscious all the time because I began to dream that I was all curled up in a little ball inside a box. I didn't want to be there, so I sat up to break out of the box and broke everything, the glass bottle for the intravenous, tore the needle out of my arm. It was a mess. Blood and glass everywhere, but I could breathe!

"I went back to the farm and the first night there had another bad attack. Back I went to the hospital. A storm set in, and it was nine days before anyone could get to Chéticamp to visit me. It wasn't that storms were worse then than today.

What's changed is the equipment. A single-axle truck with a plow on the front could get locked in a snowbank just like a car. If the driver tried to take a run at it, snap, the plow broke. The storms today are still cruel, but the double-axle trucks are so much heavier and more powerful. They can blast through.

"I didn't go back to school until after Easter. Grade 11 was the time we faced provincial exams, so there was no way I could fake it and get my year. I was going to lose my year, but Archie Neil Chisholm, who was my teacher, found a way to drive from Margaree to coach me. Edmund Burns came from Grand Étang. My classmates brought me the assignments, and when I went back after Easter I found that I was just fine. I wasn't behind at all. I was ahead!

"After high school, I went to work in Sydney as a carpenter and got my union card. The job I was working on had a lot of sawdust blowing around, and bang! Back the asthma came. It was really bad. At the end of that episode, I decided enough was enough, and I went to see Norris Matheson at CJCB, a country and western station in Sydney. I had always liked music, could play some, and figured radio would have less sawdust blowing.

"Norris listened to my pitch and said, 'I'll hold a job for you, but first go to Ryerson and take a course they have in Radio and Television Arts. When you've done that, come back and you've got a job here.'

"So I went to Ryerson to take this three-year course in Radio and Television." Russell smiles wryly. "It took me forty years to get back."

On the hillside behind the house, Russ has created a wonderful garden filled with all kinds of magical things, like moon flowers from Tibet. He calls them moon flowers because they only bloom at night. During the day, they are limp and dead looking. If you want to see them bloom you have to come out at night.

He also has many ordinary flowers—hosts of red geraniums that circle less dramatic plants, and white hydrangea blooming by the house. The hydrangea, unlike geraniums, don't have to be coddled. They grow well in Cape Breton, having little fear of either wind or sea salt.

Root vegetables grow well, but the surface ones must be tended carefully. They are a cranky constituency. I'm always telling Russ that he should price his vegetables higher than he does, for his garden takes a lot of knowledge and a lot of work. He says he will, then doesn't. I'm not sure why. Perhaps because when he has an abundant crop of beans or beets, carrots or lettuce, it all looks easy. He rarely sells flowers, preferring to keep them in the ground to admire.

The soil of Cape Breton is acidic. It's excellent for potatoes and turnips, but the acid will stunt all those plants requiring an alkaline base. To grow many vegetables, the soil must first be limed to bring the acid content down, then fertilized with organic material to bring the pH content up. Then there's the salt wind, which can damage and break plants even in the softest summer.

Cape Breton farming is so different from the fertile earth of the Annapolis Valley where Acadian farmers first experimented with dykes that it can scarcely be imagined. When I first visited that great valley and saw a corn stalk pushing its green shoots straight up through asphalt at the edge of a gas station, tears sprang unbidden to my eyes. It seemed like a miracle, for growing corn is not possible in Cape Breton. You have to be smart like a fox to be a farmer in Cape Breton. Russ Daigle is smart like a fox. He has started and succeeded in creating many successful businesses. His son still operates the family recording studio in Toronto, but gardening in Cape Breton is a very different story. At the end of the growing season, Russ does well if he can pay himself a small wage for his own labour, his fertilizer and seeds. Nor is his garden some fancy movie star creation.

It's a plain field of plants arranged in beds according to the needs of the plants and access for the gardener. There are no ornaments but the plants.

Russell is doing something very few others will. Commercial gardening is dominated by migrant labour on industrial-sized farms. Russ doesn't buy his plants from a nursery. He grows them from seed. He's the only one I know who does this. In Cape Breton, to grow vegetables and flowers from seed is not easy but necessary because a Cape Breton gardener can't wait for spring to determine whether Mother Nature is going to be early or late this year. Russ must be ready for the field with his plants already germinated in his greenhouse windows.

When the time to transplant to the garden arrives, then you need an intimate knowledge of how and where the tiny plants will thrive. Some will need to grow behind the shelter of stronger plants or be carefully hilled with organic material. There are dozens of little tricks Russ has developed through trial and error. Nor is it easy knowledge to acquire, because each plant is its own universe and not many have this knowledge anymore. Gardening has become a decorative hobby, not a lifeline. Even potato patches, which used to be beside every house, are rare.

Nor does Russ see much help on the horizon when he lifts his head from the garden. The federal and provincial governments have steadily withdrawn from supporting small holders. Agriculture has become agribusiness. The small holder is regarded more as an eccentric problem than a necessary advantage. They are not regarded as "efficient."

Without ever intending it, Russ has become a link between the knowledge of the old farming communities and people today. When I start a garden at my house, it is to Russ that I will turn for help to make it happen.

The story about the bishop's candlesticks is from the time when Russ's grandfather and mine were young men and had large farms themselves, larger than anything that exists today.

THE BISHOP'S CANDLESTICKS
(first published in *Cape Breton's Christmas*,
Breton Books, 2015)

Christmas in St. Joseph de la Mer began at Advent. By then the boats had all been pulled up on the shore. The nets hung in the sheds. The turnips and potatoes had been pulled from the earth. Indian summer had played itself out. There were no more gentle reminders of summer days. Houses were sodded between the walls and the ground. Those who could afford them put double windows on, and those who could not brought more wood in the house. Summer porches were closed in with planks. The last of the stove wood was stored in the shed, and the land settled into a grey stillness, waiting for the first snow. The days brief like a candle guttering out.

On the first of December, the women brought the Advent calendars out. They were hung by the stove, and people's minds began to turn toward Christmas and eating too much and drinking too much and getting cranky from too much company.

Late at night after the chores were done, the women baked fruitcakes and meat pies and cookies, and then hid them away in tin boxes in remote, cold corners of the house, where they would stay fresh and the little ones wouldn't find them. The men began to buy candies at the Co-op and secret them away in tool sheds, where they would ponder the Eaton's mail order catalogue, trying to juggle what was wanted against what was needed. The fishermen began to sew wreaths of pine with fishing twine for the front door and garlands of ribbon pine for the stairs.

At the presbytery, Father Aucoin and Mrs. Cross argued over where the Christmas tree should go. Father Aucoin thought the hall was about right. Mrs. Cross thought the library was about right. The choir began to practise "Adeste Fidelis," and there was jockeying for solo parts. Anselme Chiasson would sing "O Holy Night" because he had the best voice in the village and it was the hardest tune. But everything else was hard felt. Sophie Deveau was ecstatic when Father Aucoin picked her to sing the page in "Good King Wenceslas." Ulric LeBlanc was devastated, as he was sure he would have made a better page than Sophie Deveau, who was freckled, small, and a girl.

Philibert Aucoin began to tune up his reading voice for "And it came to pass in those days, that there went out a decree from Caesar Augustus that all the world should be taxed." Although he made it a point to tell anyone who wanted to listen that he didn't believe in God or Jesus Christ but felt obliged to read because his cousin, the priest, asked him. (His cousin always asked and Philibert always read.)

The church was strung with garlands of pine and spruce down the centre aisle, and red and green ribbons were tied there. Father Aucoin and the priest's boy, Daniel Boudreau, set out the crèche in front of the church. They brought the pieces in from the barn where they were stored all year. It was freezing cold, and the boy's fingers chilled through his mittens, and his breath blew in a frosty cloud. The priest hummed as he carried the carvings out. He did not seem to mind the cold or hear the boy stamping his feet and banging his hands to keep warm.

The crèche pieces had been commissioned by Father Aucoin from an old fisherman on Chéticamp Island. In the beginning, it had been another charity of the priest. Something to put a little money in the old man's pocket at Christmastime without him feeling it was charity. The old man was not expected to last much longer, but the old man had not died.

When he had finished the Three Wise Men and Joseph and Mary, people began to understand it wasn't just their imagination—the fisherman, who was old and fiercely independent, was carving the likeness of people in the village.

Marguerite Poirier, who was beautiful with piles of billowy hair, pale skin, and blue, blue eyes, was Mary. The fleshy, red face of Albert à Didier, the hotel-keeper of St. Joseph de la Mer, was added. The sardonic visage of Philibert, the matchmaker, came next, and at the back of the crèche crowd the thin curve of Jean à Basile, the village miser, was seen holding tight to his precious black mare.

The priest had not asked for these village reprobates to be in the crèche scene and argued against them. He did not want to pay for Marguerite Poirier to be Mary and suggested Marie à Adele LeBlanc, the young schoolteacher. There were many more worthy persons in the village the fisherman could use for models. The old man thought about this for a while and then looked up from his workbench to ask the priest, "Is it only worthy people who can come to the child's birthday?"

When he heard this, the priest felt a little ashamed, and from that day forward they did not argue, and Father Aucoin began to understand that the old fisherman was creating a history of the village in his crèche scene. For over the years a throng of silent figures began to gather around the crèche: fishermen and farmers, sisters and brothers, mothers and fathers crowding around the little manger in a circle that spilled beyond the corner of the church.

This year's addition was an altar boy singing from his hymnal dressed in his surplice. He looked like an angel, an angel in the image of that scallywag, Daniel Boudreau. It was the priest's gift to the boy, although the boy did not realize it was the priest who had chosen him for the crèche scene, not the old fisherman. Nothing was said, but the boy found himself wondering if the priest expected him to be like his older brother Robert, who had won a scholarship in Halifax. The boy was proud and at the same time uneasy when he looked at his wooden likeness singing among the other wooden people.

The Three Wise Men were dressed as fishermen with sou'westers and rain gear. Mary and Joseph were in sober browns and white, and the baby was tucked away in a trough of straw but was so bundled up one could scarcely see if it was white, black, or shellacked. (Father Aucoin took the biblical direction of swaddling seriously.) The entire scene was lit by two hurricane lamps, which hung from the corners of the makeshift shed and sent out comforting yellow beams.

Father Aucoin and the boy set the crèche scene up on the Saturday before Christmas, and from that moment on the baking and mending and building of wooden toys began to race at fever pitch toward the finish line of Christmas Eve.

Children woke early to mark the days off on the Advent calendar, and adults were too busy to notice that the sun had faded to a spark in the sky, and the southeast gales howled down the coastline, rattling window panes.

Throughout Advent there would be a terrible coming and going in the presbytery as choristers and actors in the pageant and visitors dropped by on their way to and from the church. Mrs. Cross would have a permanent kettle boiling on the stove and pans of gingerbread in the oven. For the boy, the smell of Christmas was always the sweet scent of gingerbread and the crackle of parcels being set down in the hall. There would be a holler from the porch, the front door would swing open, and a thud would reverberate throughout the house as something hit the floor. The door would then swing shut and a mysterious brown package would be found sitting in the hall.

Invariably, Father Aucoin would say, "Ah, Father Christmas has arrived early this year," and he would pick up the parcel and set it down on the dining room table without opening it, which was a great frustration for the boy.

Father Aucoin's temper, which was short at the best of times, at Christmas would begin to seriously fray. The choir sounded wretched. The bishop's candlesticks had not arrived as promised. The children could not seem to remember their lines for the pageant. The Christmas tree had gone up in the study as Mrs. Cross had wanted instead of the hall, where Father Aucoin had wished.

Then one day a large brown package arrived from Boston, and Father Aucoin shook it this way and that. When the priest handed it to the boy to open, Daniel felt a great bubble of excitement in his chest. Mrs. Cross gave him the scissors and there was much snipping of string and tearing of paper. The boy kept lifting the box, trying to figure out what would be inside, but he could feel nothing even after he had opened it. Inside the box, there was nothing but crumpled newspaper. Lots of newspaper crumpled up, and the boy kept taking the newspaper out until in the middle he found neatly packed, small boxes of red and white candy canes.

"There must be hundreds," said the boy, astonished at the size of his treasure chest.

Father Aucoin picked up the boxes and said cryptically, "Come with me." He put on his coat and boots and they crossed the yard to the church. "I thought we'd hang them on the boughs," he said to the boy. "Do you think God would mind?"

"Who will eat them?" asked Daniel, being practical.

"I thought the children would. They could take them home after Mass."

"I don't know," said the boy, uncertain because he had nourished the brief and greedy hope that they were all for him.

"Well, I think we had better try one first, don't you? To make sure that they taste as they should," said the priest, and he took one of the candy canes out of the box and stuck it in his mouth. The boy did the same and sat down in the pew opposite the priest. Neither said anything more for a few moments. The priest was tired and so was the boy. The candy canes were peppermint and sweet and tasted so fine that they decided to have a second.

"It looks nice," said the priest finally, breaking the silence with a small gesture of his candy cane toward the altar, which was covered in crisp white linen and was garlanded with green boughs around the base. There was another long, comfortable silence.

"I think I will put the bishop's candlesticks in the centre of the altar," said the priest. The bishop had never sent a gift or present of any kind to St. Joseph de la Mer, but this year there had been a little handwritten note in the November monthly circular: "Will be sending bishop's candlesticks for Christmas. – G."

Father Aucoin had been thrilled by this note, for there were some beautiful candlesticks in the basilica. In St. Joseph de la Mer, they had very modest ones, and Father Aucoin was confident the bishop's candlesticks would make a wonderful ornament to their liturgy of the Mass. He would light them only for High Mass.

Whenever he thought of the new candlesticks he felt like humming. They would need large holders, something noble so the candles could stand tall.

The boy looked up at the altar and did not feel as the priest did that the two of them were sitting alone in a very small boat balanced on the edge of vast seas. He felt only that it was late and he would like to get to bed to sleep away the dreaming night, but he dared not move, because he knew that the priest did not like to be disturbed in the church.

The priest finished his second candy cane and sighed. Christmas was almost here once more. The boy was growing up. He would have to see about getting him placed somewhere. Perhaps at St. Ann's or Boston. He must write to both of them and he must write to his brother and thank him for the candy.

He got down on his knees and began his evening prayers. He sometimes felt guilty praying. Prayers were so easy, so comforting. It was harder to write letters.

He found the boy outside arranging the hay in the crèche. They blew out the hurricane lamps and walked quietly back to the presbytery together, the stars spilling across the sky between the mountains and the sea.

On Christmas Eve, Daniel's father Marcel Boudreau arrived and brought his youngest son's present to the presbytery and tucked it under the tree. After Midnight Mass, with faces flushed from rum and eggnog, meat pie, and butter cookies, Daniel, his father, the priest, and the housekeeper all gathered in the study to open the presents. With a yell of delight, Daniel pounced upon the stilts that his father had made for him and immediately began stumping around the presbytery, teetering back and forth with his father laughing, delighted, and no one seemed to mind.

The priest opened his present from the bishop. It was a small package, a small book called *The Bishop's Candlesticks*. It was a play. On a small sheet inside the cover of the book was scrawled a brief note from the bishop saying he had enjoyed it and perhaps Father Aucoin might also. As usual, he signed it simply "G."

The priest held the book in his hands as if it was a small but very heavy weight. "Very thoughtful of the bishop," he said. He watched the boy swaying around on his new stilts and was grateful for the boy's high spirits.

Just before the sun came up, Marcel Boudreau went home, loaded down with Christmas food from Mrs. Cross, and they all went to bed except for the priest who went out to serve early morning Mass for those few who had missed the midnight service. He went to the church alone, leaving the boy to sleep.

On his way into the church, he stopped at the crèche where the priest stuck *The Bishop's Candlesticks* under the arm of one of the wooden wise men; then he changed his mind and stuck it under the arm of Philibert, his cousin, the matchmaker.

Philibert could become the keeper of the bishop's candlesticks. This thought made him smile. The sun was coming up, as if God was pleased. Like a storm at sea, another Christmas had been weathered.

CHAPTER 21

The Kitchens of Grand Étang and "Moving Ice"

C'est la Mi-Carêm', amusons-nous gaiment, Maman;
Il faut fêter ça, ça pass qu'un' fois par an, Maman.
Viv' la Mi-Carêm! Ma mèr',
Chantons, rions, dansons, Maman
—From the collection *Chansons d'Acadie*,
by Anselme Chiasson

When the fish disappeared and the fish plants in Chéticamp and Grand Étang closed, Gretchen Noyes-Hull's reaction was to start a research station to try and find out what was going on in the ocean. The reaction of the full-time residents of Grand Étang was equally immediate but different. They started something called the Mi-Carême Centre.

What can you do in a fishing village when there are no more fish? There were no easy answers. People spent many a night talking, talking, talking, looking for straws to grasp. It felt like the village was sinking. The old primary school had been converted into a makeshift community centre with a fire hall, a little library, and some general rooms used for storing masks and other artifacts of community life that now felt as fragile as a spring flower.

The church festivals that used to define the seasonal round were getting smaller and sometimes disappearing altogether. No one celebrated the Chandeleur any longer; it used to be as important as the Mi-Carême. If the festivals disappeared, what would be left? Would there even be a village? Perhaps it would disappear also.

The Mi-Carême was the largest mid-winter festival. It was held each year exactly halfway between the beginning and end of Lent. It's a festival filled with dance, music, and merry-making. The religious aspect has always been faint, for its principal purpose was to give relief and solace to people in the face of mid-winter's long dark nights and the penitence of the Lenten sacrifices. Some think this mid-winter festival is a Christian adoption of the Roman Saturnalia when slaves became owners and owners became servants; as in the Saturnalia, Mi-Carême revellers were masked.

To "run the Mi-Carême" was a favourite sport of the young. Small groups would run or sleigh from house to house, wearing masks to see if their neighbours could guess who was behind the disguise. Sometimes people would make a lightning trip, returning all the way from Boston or as far away as Toronto just for the fun of running the Mi-Carême.

Running the Mi-Carême is similar to running the *Chandeleur* (Candlemas), a festival that was held each year on February 2, just before the Lenten period started. The Chandeleur leader would be dressed in his Sunday best and carried a cane covered with ribbons, but his companions would be dressed in poor work clothes. When the Chandeleur runners arrived at the porch, the leader would say, "Are you going to give something for Chandeleur?" (meaning something for the Chandeleur party). If the response was yes, which it almost always was, the leader would turn back toward the other Chandeleur runners and call, "Come in!" Once inside the house, the Chandeleur runners sang and danced around the leader with his beribboned cane to an old tune called "Escaouette." (The origins of the Escaouette song are unknown. Some say it is Mi'kmaw, others not.)

The food collected was used for the Chandeleur party, but it also was distributed to those who were poor and needed assistance to get through the winter. In this way, both Chandeleur and the Mi-Carême festivals acted as a community food bank, redistributing food according to the capacity of the givers and the needs of others. For both festivals, people began arriving for the party while it was still light, at about four o'clock in the afternoon. Several fiddlers played for the dancers, one spelling off the other, and until around six o'clock when people ate, then the music and the dance continued. At midnight, people knelt down and prayed and the party ended, or so it was supposed.

La Chandeleur, like the Mi-Carême, was a complex festival with many strands. It was a religious event focused on the blessing of the candles by the priest during Mass, a community quest, a charity, a dance, and a massive party all rolled into one week. The candles were especially made for the festival, and on Sunday, the candles would be blessed by the priest. Chandeleur candles would be lit throughout the year to comfort the sick; when they were lighted in a window, it was thought they would help bring men home safe from the sea.

Although they were supposed to close at midnight, Chandeleur parties often lasted until the sun came up. Sometimes rumours circulated that afterwards there had been some illicit encounters between men and women. The Mi-Carême is still practised in the village but not the Chandeleur. It ended one Sunday when the priest refused to bless the candles because he felt that the party side of things had overwhelmed the sacred and charitable.

It was from the kitchens of the village the idea came of

creating a cultural centre dedicated to preserving the memory of the old festivals. Monique Aucoin sought funding from the government and she was successful in getting it. Then the work of creating exhibits and workshops began. The Mi-Carême Centre is now housed in a small building at the entrance to the harbour. The shape of the building with its cedar shingles and half-hipped roof fits perfectly in the harbour setting. It looks like it has always been there. Although, like its neighbour the little Gulf Aquarium and Marine Station (GAMS), the resources for the Mi-Carême Centre are slim and the future uncertain.

A future for the harbour has not been reinvented yet, but a start has been made.

My own hope is that the Mi-Carême Centre will evolve into more than a place of preservation but become a school of Acadian music, arts, and traditions like the Gaelic College at St. Ann's is for all things Gaelic.

One day, Monique Aucoin asked me if I would come to the Mi-Carême Centre and give a talk. I was honoured to be asked but had no idea what I might say or what people might want to hear. She said one of my stories would be a good idea. "Moving Ice" was the story I chose. It is a story from the Depression years when life didn't depend on much but yourself and the magic of hope, which you needed because money and concrete possibilities were in short supply.

This is not to say the old days were perfect. It was a world that was easy on the environment but hard on people. "Moving Ice" is about the hard-on-people side of things.

MOVING ICE

I will avoid the occasion for sin.
I will not look at girls.
I will avoid the occasion for sin.
I will not look at girls.

The boy scrawled in a brown paper scribbler at the kitchen table. It was the kind of scribbler where the paper is so rough that you can still find bits of wood chips flattened like moles on the pages. If he pressed too hard, the point of the pencil tore the paper and if he did not press hard enough, the words were so faint that they were difficult to read. Every time he finished a line, he looked up from the table to see if the lights in the church had been switched off. They remained bright rectangles of light.

Without closing his eyes, he could see Father Aucoin kneeling at one of the pews, his hands clasped in front of himself, praying. The boy imagined a river of prayers flowing out of Father Aucoin through the windows of the church toward heaven. Before he came down to breakfast, the priest prayed at a little prie-dieu in his bedroom. There was Mass at seven, the Angelus at noon. When he walked about the parish, the priest carried his breviary and read from it when he stopped to rest.

The boy pushed his pencil across the paper. *I will avoid the occasion for sin. I will not look at girls.* And he wrote a tiny 56 in the margin to indicate where he was. Writing the numbers down wouldn't help him to get to one hundred any faster, but he could not seem to help it. Fifty-six felt more solid than forty-six, safer. He was getting somewhere.

Everything for Father Aucoin was the occasion for sin. Swimming offered the occasion for sin. Square dancing offered the occasion for sin. Pocket watches offered the occasion for sin. The little injuries floated up in Daniel Boudreau's soul like the weeds that he pulled from the presbytery garden. Bitter and prickly, they peppered the space in front of his eyes until he could not write any longer.

What good did praying do anyway?

He had prayed for his mother every night, kneeling by the edge of his bed until his knees were sore and his back stiff. He had prayed to be allowed to stay home, instead his father sent him to the presbytery. "It will be good for you. The tea is fresh," said his father. Not a word about avoiding the occasion for sin. "The tea is fresh."

At home, they said grace before meals and a prayer before bed. On Sunday, like everyone else, they went to Mass. His mother had trimmed his hair when he had been chosen to be an altar boy. But he never got the impression that his mother thought a great deal about praying. It was just something you did, like brushing your teeth.

It was only when she began to cough that the boy began to think about praying. How many prayers equalled one cough? One night when his mother was coughing, coughing in the room behind the kitchen stove, he decided that he would make a deal with God. For every Hail Mary that he said, his mother would have one cough less. He stuck his hand up, open toward the ceiling, and shook hands with God. Each night the boy prayed fiercely until his throat was dry and raw from saying the words.

Not long after he had arrived at the presbytery, when they were sitting down to supper, he decided to ask the priest what he prayed for.

Father Aucoin squinted into the light of the kerosene lamp, thought for a moment, and said, "Different things."

"You pray to move the ice off the lobster grounds, don't you?"

"Did Peter à Peter tell you that?"

"Yes."

Father Aucoin stopped eating his breakfast and gazed off toward the window. "Each spring the fishermen ask me to pray for the ice to move off the lobster grounds," he said, shrugging his thin shoulders. "It's not something I choose."

"How does a prayer work to push ice? Is it like a big hand that just comes down and pushes the ice along?" the boy asked, trying to imagine "Our father who art in heaven" pushing along a great field of ice.

Father Aucoin pressed his lips into a thin line against his teeth. It was a sign the boy would learn to be wary of.

"No, I don't think so."

"Then how does it work?" persisted the boy, because he thought that surely the priest must know.

"I'm not sure," he said finally. He tapped the heel of his fork lightly against the table. "What about you, young man, what do you pray for?"

"I pray for a pocket watch. I would like a pocket watch like my father's. Then I would be able to know exactly what time it was when I work in the morning."

"How much does a pocket watch cost?"

"A dollar," the boy replied quickly, because he had examined it often enough at the Co-op.

"A dollar is a lot of money," said Father Aucoin, shaking his head sadly as if this was as difficult to attain as moving ice.

I will not look at girls. I will avoid the occasion for sin. The boy marked 71 neatly beside the last word. Then he put his pencil down and began to nibble his fingers, which were cramping. He stood up from the table, stretched, and went to the piano, where he began to fiddle with the keys.

He had lied, although he did not think of it as lying. He had said it automatically. He had wanted a pocked watch and the priest expected him to be praying for something, so he had said pocket watch. He was not conscious of lying, but the truth was he had given up praying for anything.

At the presbytery, he had quickly learned to avoid the occasion for prayer. At bedtime, he pretended to be asleep in his bed so that he would miss evening prayers, and during Mass, the boy prayed with such practised efficiency that he scarcely knew what he was saying. He drifted through Mass from the Confiteor to the Post-communion in perfect time without pausing, without hesitation, rarely missing a beat. The Mass was like an old tune that he could play in his sleep.

"I confess to Almighty God, to blessed Mary, ever virgin, to blessed Michael the Archangel, to blessed John the Baptist, the holy Apostles, Peter and Paul, and to you, Father, that I have sinned exceedingly in thought, word, and deed, through my fault, through my fault, through my most grievous fault."

He phrased the response just right. Letting his voice build in a natural, musical climax toward *grievous*, which rang like a bell when he said it and then resolved perfectly into *fault*. The other boys followed Daniel's voice.

Élodie Cormier sat in the fifth row from the altar rail. She was not from the improving side of the parish. Her father was not a pillar of the community. He had a small holding on which he kept a few cows, pigs, and chickens, but he was not much of a farmer. Theo Cormier mostly specialized in getting by. He avoided contact with anyone who showed signs of wanting to improve him. This included his wife, his daughter, and Father Aucoin. Theo Cormier wasn't exactly a sinner, but neither was he interested in applying for sainthood. Left to his own devices, he liked to sit on an overturned barrel, roll cigarettes, and talk. The idea of working at anything for a sustained period was not pleasing to him. Theo had seven daughters, one for each day of the week, he liked to say.

Theo Cormier would never have dreamed of asking the priest to teach Élodie how to play the piano. It seemed like a waste of time to him, for they had no piano in the house, nor were ever likely to get one. It had been the priest's idea, for Élodie sang in the choir and it began to seem useful to him that the girl should be able to read music so that she could help the others who followed her voice, which was sure and clear.

The boy did not pray for anything, but he did save money for a pocket watch. After Mass, the priest gave each one of his altar boys a five-cent piece. As soon as Daniel had saved a dollar, he went to the Co-op and bought himself a pocket watch. It was the first thing that he had ever bought in the Co-op. He kept it under his mattress at night and during the day in his front pocket tied with a string to his belt exactly the way his father did.

The priest did not notice the new watch, which was amazing because the boy consulted it at every opportunity, mostly to see if it was still working, for he had a terror it might stop.

When the priest did notice, he immediately flew into a great temper. How could the boy be so unthinking to waste a dollar on [a] pocket watch? How stupid could he be? A dollar could be spent in so many wiser ways. There was his schooling to think about. There was…and on and on, until the boy's great joy in his new watch was entirely spoiled.

I will not look at girls, the boy wrote carefully. What was he supposed to do then? Look heavenwards? He had fallen in love. He had not expected it. For the longest time, he was not even conscious of Élodie. She was just one of Theo Cormier's daughters. He saw her every Sunday in an absent-minded way. It was his father and older brothers that he liked to watch, for they always participated in the liturgy with clear, robust voices, and he would be filled with pride when he heard them.

Theo Cormier's daughters sat on the other side of the church from the Boudreaus, and the boy began to find staring at them to be a pleasant thing. For the longest time, he could not make up his mind which one he liked the best until, like a gate opening up inside of him, he discovered it was Élodie. She sang in the choir directly above her sisters, and it was above their heads toward Élodie that his eyes kept turning. Élodie had blonde hair, blue eyes, and a pale, clear complexion. When the sunlight came through the side windows and fell upon Élodie as she bent her head toward the music sheet, a halo seemed to dance about her. There were moments when the boy would not have been surprised if she had sprouted wings and begun to fly heavenwards.

The boy's fingers tore up the scales. He could play scales faster than Father Aucoin. It was the only thing that he could do better than the priest, and he enjoyed it. His fingers were more nimble. "Rhythm, Daniel, remember the rhythm. You're not racing a car. Music doesn't mean anything without rhythm," the priest would call from another part of the house as soon as he heard Daniel attacking the piano. Then he would come and stand at the piano until the boy had slowed down. It was the one sure way Daniel had of annoying Father Aucoin. He ripped up and down the scales for a long time, forgetting that the priest was still in the church and he was annoying no one.

He went back to the kitchen table and began writing once more.

I will not look at girls.
I will avoid the occasion for sin.

The boy pencilled in *80* at the end of *sin*. The desire to rip the pages into little pieces swept over him. Rip, rip, rip into little squares. He sat on his hands and waited for the feeling to pass.

Élodie's father was not a pillar of the community, that was the problem. He came to church, but mostly to talk with his friends. He paid little attention to the liturgy. He belonged to no improving societies. He was not a member of the Credit Union. He attended no study groups for parish improvement. Given the chance, he drank. Theo Cormier was an occasion for sin, therefore his daughters must be also. It had taken the boy a long time to figure this out, but once he had he was sure of it.

His own father worked whenever he could, but there wasn't much work. He remembered that the year his mother had died, his father had managed to earn thirty-three dollars.

"Thirty-three dollars!" He remembered his father's astonished voice telling the story to Philibert. It seemed like a lot of money to Daniel. His father laughed when he heard this and sat him down on his knee. The Boudreaus had not been lucky, but he was lucky to be taken in by Father Aucoin. Philibert and his father explained this to him.

They explained that Father Aucoin had a piano, that the priest would teach him how to play. He was musical like his mother. Father Aucoin was an educated man. All the boys who stayed at the presbytery did well. It was a great chance for him. The boy did not know how to tell his father he did not want to go. He was ten, almost eleven. His father packed up his bag and swung him onto his shoulders before they were even out of the house.

Philibert and his father were big, strong men and they came strolling across the fields toward the church, his father and Philibert singing, his father in tune, Philibert off-key. But they sounded fine, happy and full of life. It seemed like a grand arrival, as if he was a prince.

Mrs. Cross opened the door and Philibert lifted him off his father's shoulders and set him down on the porch. Father Aucoin appeared. He was dressed in his soutane, a long thin streak of black at the door. His blond hair and pale face accentuated by the dark soutane. Philibert and Daniel's father doffed their caps when the priest arrived and took off their boots at the door. They seemed to be dissolving in front of the boy's eyes. When they sat down for tea in the kitchen, he noticed that his father's trousers were patched and the sleeves of his shirt ragged. He'd never noticed this before but he did now, and he thought of what his father had said: the Boudreaus were not lucky.

Mrs. Cross showed him the chores. He must stoke the furnace before he went to bed, that was his chore. He must clean the stables when he got home from school and fill the stove's kindling box, these were his chores. He must put fresh hay in the cow's manger before he went to school, that was his chore. Mrs. Cross washed up in the morning, but he washed up in the evening, that was his chore. After breakfast, he served early morning Mass with Father Aucoin before he went to school, that was his chore.

He had a bedroom all to himself. Through the window, he could see the side of the church, which in the moonlight seemed like the side of great white ship, but the ship was stuck, it wasn't moving. He wanted to go home. He wanted his mother back, and he went to the window. There was nothing to see but the stars. It felt as if the stars were getting smaller and smaller and he was falling into a deep, dark hole.

I will not look at girls.
I will avoid the occasion for sin.

The boy marked *90* down beside *sin*. The lights went off in the church. The boy felt a rush of panic. He had not finished yet. He was still short of a hundred. He bent his head down and tried to write more quickly. The tip of the pencil tore the paper. He sat on his hands and counted to ten to calm himself. When Father Aucoin entered the kitchen he was finishing his ninety-first line.

The priest ran his finger over the neat rows of lines and said, "I hope you've learned your lesson, Daniel."

The boy said, "Yes."

"Very well, you can go to bed now."

The boy went to bed and dreamed of Élodie Cormier and the thought that one day he would run away from the presbytery. He would run to some place far.

On Sunday, the fishermen asked if Father Aucoin would pray to keep the ice of the lobster grounds, but the priest said he could not do it anymore. He said it was too hard.

The sea ice used to freeze into a spectacular, rough white blanket against the cliffs that stretched as far as the eye could see. The sunlight was brilliant and the harbour itself would freeze over entirely making the connection between the land and ocean seamless. It's been a long time since I've seen ice strong enough to skate on in the harbour or ice piled up against the shore. The winters are not cold enough, and without the shore ice, the winter storms tear great gouges out of the cliffs, changing the shoreline from winter to winter.

Nonetheless, the little harbour is as beautiful as ever, the mountains cradling it safely from the sea. Without the fish plant, it's become pristine. You can eat the mussels imbedded in the shore, look down into the clear blue-green water that shimmers like a jewel, the eel grass waving below. Lobsters and crabs moving about like small underwater machines. Fingerling fish flitting about like motes of sunlight in the clear water. There's lots of life there yet. It works for humans too.

We swim in the harbour now. It's less trouble than going to the beach and just as much fun. The grandchildren like to play push-off on the paddleboard, their voices rocketing around the contained space up to the houses on the hillside. It feels like home to me even though my own grandfather could never have imagined children swimming in the old harbour when it was awash in fish guts from the plant and the detritus from the encrusted hulls of many busy boats.

"You can't go home" is an old saying, and for a long time I did feel that way. I think this must have been part of the reason for the tears from the man sitting on the steps at the Doryman. I'm guessing he was overwhelmed with this sudden, visceral understanding that no matter how warm his memories of family and place were, too much time had passed. The village had moved on and so had he. I certainly felt this way for a long time after Grandfather's farm was sold. What was the easiest place to be in the world suddenly became the hardest for the family. We no longer had a familiar place to rest our heads, and the village itself was changing at light speed.

In cities change is expected. Older buildings are constantly being demolished, new ones being built. Each year, thousands of new residents arrive and they bring new ideas and different ways of being in the world. The city is in constant evolution, that is part of the urban magic, but the changes in Grand Étang have been just as profound and harder to integrate. Part of the reason that I had no idea how to respond to the questions from the French academics was because I did not understand these changes.

It's hard to believe but 65 percent of the residents of North Inverness are now seasonal. When I was a youngster, the village was entirely local. You would never meet anyone that wasn't a neighbour or you weren't related to. All this has changed. Some villages along the coast, like the much photographed Margaree Harbour, have hardly a single four-season household left in the village. The village wakes up in the spring and goes to sleep in the autumn.

The Mi-Carême Centre celebrates a way of life that many remember but that no longer exists. Our village has changed in so many ways. I see it every time I drive by Grandfather's old farm. What was his front field by the sea where we used to grow hay and potatoes, that had a spring bubbling with cold, clear water for the cows in the night pasture, now has five seasonal summer homes on it, and the spring has been capped so that the water can be pumped to the houses. Somehow, we have to figure out how to live, not with the poverty of the past but with some of its amazing resilience. Living better with the sea, as GAMS is trying to do, and relearning how to use the land, as Russell Daigle is doing, are ways to start.

CHAPTER 22

Burying Mother

*A baby needs no country
but a mother's arms,
and I had mine.
She carried me
into the vast, dark shed,
into the new world
with nothing to recommend it
but her own beating heart.*
—for Katherine Emma Oliver on her eightieth birthday

My mother was a practising Anglican and remained faithful to her childhood religion all her life, but she had no sense of the superiority of her own faith. She saw it as just one of many, but it was hers. Her idea of a pleasant afternoon, when she was travelling, was to find a church where someone was practising the organ. There she would sit and listen as long as the organist played. When she first went to my father's village, she discovered the priest could play the organ and she went faithfully to the church to listen to him practise. I seem to have developed the same habit. Mother understood complexity, and one of the many things she did for me was to help me understand it also. Although a faithful practising Anglican, she did not believe that she was going to heaven.

As we talked to the priest to arrange Mother's funeral, it didn't seem to be the right time to be exposing this peculiarity of my mother's belief system, but for some reason I felt impelled to do it. Like my mother I can be stubborn, and it seems to me she would not want to be buried under false pretences. The priest looked straight at me. He did not seem to be affronted, and I pushed on. I explained that I did not mean she was not a faithful Anglican. She was. She was christened in St. Paul's in Hammersmith, London, and wherever she had lived she searched out the local Anglican church to attend each Sunday. Nonetheless, it didn't feel right for me to pass my mother off as a believer in the manner that you are supposed to be if you're a member of the church.

I was sure of this because I had asked her straight up. She had responded calmly and very clearly. She believed people came together in churches for the comfort of community, good music, and because everyone was afraid of dying. For her, the church was a way of holding a candle against the dark. She figured being Anglican had been dictated by the circumstances of her birth. The Olivers and Reddings had always been Anglican, and she saw no reason to change this. Although as she once explained to me, if she had had the chance to choose a religion before she came into the world, she would have chosen to be a Buddhist. Buddhism seemed to her to be the healthiest of all the religions, but I don't tell the priest this either.

In her final years, her opinions became ever more direct and succinct. She stopped having the patience for anything extra. This was partly because her hearing was weak and she was forced to search out the centrality of any conversation and partly because she was no longer interested in parsing the fine points of any discussion. She didn't have the time for equivocation. She went straight for the jugular and left the carcass of the conversation for others to render. In her last years, she retreated into books and lived a good deal between the covers, floating in those small harbours as she had when she had been an only child in her parents' home.

"Who will be speaking?" asks the priest.

"Her grandson Julian will," I say, confident of this because Julian is an actor and writer used to delivering eloquent text under stress. "He will start with two poems, one by Wordsworth, 'I wandered lonely as a cloud' and one by A. A. Milne, called 'Disobedience.'"

"'Disobedience'? I'm not sure I know that."

"My mother used to read the poems of A. A. Milne to us as children, and she did the same for her grandchildren," I say and repeat the refrain from "Disobedience," finding the words lodged where they always have been. "James James Morrison Morrison Weatherby George Duprey took great care of his mother, though he was only three. James James said to his mother, 'Mother,' he said, said he, 'you must never go down to the end of town without consulting me.'"

The priest looks at me a bit mystified.

I explain: "The poem ends with the mother going down to the end of the town without consulting her son, 'James James Morrison Morrison Weatherby George Duprey.' And she never returns."

To this moment, I have been resolutely under control. Suddenly, I can't seem to put a harness on the emotions and memories that polite social intercourse requires. I fall silent and focus hard on not weeping. Fortunately, the priest is organized, calm, and reassuring and allows the moment to float away. "It's important that someone give a thumbnail sketch of your mother's life, because not everyone will know her. Others will want to be reminded. Is there someone who can do this?"

My sister Lydia shakes her head.

My sister Anna says, "I'm not sure, maybe."

The priest looks at me.

My mother was not supposed to die. She thought of any type of aging as very bad form, not something anyone sensible should ever contemplate. At sixty, she looked as majestically feminine as Sophia Loren did at the same age. At seventy-six she got a facelift. At eighty-seven she looked, well, eighty-seven, and she cannot forgive anyone for this, for her spirit had remained as lively as it was when she was a girl.

"About seven minutes is how long you should speak, that should be enough to get everything out that you want," says the priest.

I nod again, but the idea that I can reduce my mother's life to seven minutes seems slightly crazy. My parents were like a jazz tune. They improvised and invented themselves as they went along. Both broke religious barriers, class barriers, national barriers, language barriers just by being who they were. Mother had little idea of what Canada might be like and little support for marrying my father. She had been dating a perfectly acceptable English boy and neither of her parents understood why she would want to move to "the colonies."

In 1946, people didn't know that much about other parts of the planet. Nor was it easy leaving all she had ever known and loved, because the other side of the ocean wasn't a commute. It meant forever. Mother would say later, "I felt a sense of betrayal at leaving Britain. Everything was still rationed. We had been through so much and to leave just as the war had ended, it didn't feel right."

"Is your father still alive?" asks the priest.

"He has Alzheimer's."

There is a silence.

My sister Lydia says, "He is still lucid. He knows Mum has died."

In 1946, Pier 21 was the principal entry point for all newcomers to eastern Canada, and mother's ship docked at that famous pier. Pier 21 is an enormous hangar, dwarfing the individual, and Dad must have gazed up at the railings of the ship from the busy dock with some anxiety, searching for the face of his bride and the baby he had never seen.

Mother was there, leaning over the railing, looking for the tall, slim young man she had married, but he was no longer in an airman's uniform. She found him but dressed as a student, wearing a university sweater and stylish grey slacks, standing beside someone she didn't recognize. It was one of his brothers, Philias, still in his RCAF uniform. The separation had been long and they must have greeted each other a little shyly before driving together to Antigonish where Dad had begun his studies for a Bachelor of Arts degree.

"Will your father come to the funeral?" asks the priest.

It is difficult to imagine that arrival for my mother. Canada was still raw, scarcely out of the egg. Halifax was the largest city in Nova Scotia, but to her London eyes it would have seemed scarcely more than a town. In a couple of minutes, they would have been through it and on the way to the college in Antigonish. They travelled on a narrow two-lane road with nothing much at the edges but fields and trees. The villages they passed through would not have seemed like villages, just a scruffy collection of clapboard houses scattered at the edge of the road. The car windows would have been open and to her English experience, the summer heat tropical. Everywhere people would have noticed her accent. Some people thought she must be Dutch because the liberation of the Netherlands had been a good deal in the news.

The main street of Antigonish had two restaurants, and the university was no more than a few brick buildings at the edge of the town. It was very Catholic. Many of the professors at the university were priests. The Catholic church, St. Ninian's, was the largest building in town.

At the edge of town, there was a small Anglican church with the same name as her mother's London church, St. Paul's.

It had about a hundred members and was built in the cottage, steeply pitched roof tradition of rural England. Here she found some familiar horizons. The young curate was a handsome and sympathetic young Nova Scotian named Leonard Hatfield. By good fortune, Mother had stumbled on one of Nova Scotia's great parish priests who immediately and sensitively understood her sense of displacement. They became friends and that friendship would endure all of their lives.

The vulnerability of these young war brides was tremendous. One of the young women Mother met on the boat and became friends with was also joining her husband in Antigonish. She had two tiny tots with her. Her friend would be greeted not by a happy husband but by the news that her wartime love was seeking an annulment of their marriage in order to marry a first-year student. How you annul a marriage when there is a wife with two children in tow puzzles me, but he got his annulment and married the student in a grand celebratory affair at St. Ninian's. Mother's shipboard friend returned to England with the children. She never saw or heard of her again.

On Dad's side of the equation, no one in anyone's memory had married someone who hadn't been Catholic and Acadian. A Mi'kmaw wife from Eskasoni would have fit more easily into the family, sharing the same religion, music, and Nova Scotia history. Mother was as exotic as an Amazonian wildflower to her new in-laws, and they were equally alarming to her. There was nothing about their lives that she did not find surprising. She was the only child of a very prim and proper English family who supervised their use of language rigidly, dressed to a very strict code, and behaved carefully, which you had to do to survive in a country where everyone knew their place and there was a place for everyone—and not an inch more.

Suddenly, Mother was parachuted into a village on an island in the middle of nowhere where socializing was not meticulously choreographed and finding her place was a challenge for everyone. On her first Sunday in the village Uncle Philias went to early Mass so there would be someone in the house with her and the baby when the entire family went off to high Mass. Thoughtfully, Grandfather turned on the radio so she could listen to the Salvation Army Sunday service. The Salvation Army was Protestant, so he figured this would be acceptable to his new daughter-in-law as all Protestants were, well, Protestant.

A kitchen full of Acadians is conversational anarchy. Everyone talks at once. The best storyteller wins centre stage, but there are always lots of adjacent stages. No holds are barred. Bad language is ecclesiastical, not scatological. A fart was a fart and even women were unafraid to say these words—in public. Mother's first visit to her husband's village was one long cultural shock to the sensibilities of her youth.

Before she met my father, my mother's love interest was David Tomlinson. At the time, he was a Spitfire pilot and a dashing one. After the war, he got into a spot of trouble flying his plane under the arches of London bridge just for the hell of it. David became an actor, playing for both stage and screen. Whenever my parents went to London, mother would check to see if David was in a play and go to see him if he was. The role he would become best known for in North America was Mr. Banks, in the Disney film *Mary Poppins*.

When my daughter Emma saw the film with her grandmother and was told the actor playing Mr. Banks was an old boyfriend, someone she might have married, Emma, never shy about asking difficult questions, immediately inquired, "Why hadn't you?" He seemed acceptable.

Mother replied, "Nothing much happened when I kissed him."

Emma's reply, like her grandmother's, was very practical. "Well, it's probably a good thing then. You have to kiss them for a long time."

The priest is looking at me. It occurs to me that he is waiting for me to say something. I can't think of what I should say. I'm feeling numb, as if my body has been injected with some kind of stun drug. Nothing seems to work.

I walk home alone, searching in the human story for some comfort, as I often do. Burying our loved ones with ceremony marks the very beginning of humans being humans. It is when we begin to find graves with humans still arrayed in their finest clothes with their cherished possessions around them that we know we have found people that were like ourselves. No one has ever really understood either birth or death, but we have always done our best to honour the passage. This is part of how we are human.

A funeral is a strange thing. The entire focus is on one person, someone who can't be there to appreciate it, and this gives it an unbearable poignancy. Katherine Oliver's last party was no different. The service and the church brought her presence alive, and I felt her life as if she was sitting with us. She would be dressed in a smart spring coat of a bright hue, perhaps red, and she would be wearing a hat that made a statement. When I sat down beside her she would turn to me and smile, pleased to see me in church.

We held Mother's funeral at St. Bartholomew's, a little Anglican church on McKay Street in the shadow of the Governor General's residence. In spite of its location, there is nothing grand about it. St. Bart's is built in the same cottage style as her first Canadian church, St. Paul's in Antigonish. It is a warm and very simple, peak-roofed building. The service was resolutely English. We sang some of her favourite songs from her youth, closing with "There'll be bluebirds over the white cliffs of Dover—just you wait and see."

My colleagues from city council attended en masse, which was a fine and welcome sight. Mother's grandson Julian gave a wonderful speech. I'm not really conscious of what I said.

Her youngest daughter, Anna, was able to speak and wore a grand hat in her mother's memory.

Dad and I walked to the gravesite together. He did not lean on me but stood tall and secure in himself. A small, fierce breeze sprang up and pulled at our dark blue suits, pushing at us as we walked across the rough ground. It seemed as if Mother was saying goodbye. In spite of his memory problems, Dad was entirely aware he had lost his beloved. Tears streamed down his face. I reached out to support him as we crossed the rough ground, but he wanted no help. He said, "I'm a lucky man."

CHAPTER 23

Ronald Caplan, Cape Breton's Magazine, *and "Philibert the Sheep"*

> *Ron: Have you ever been in love?*
> *Marguerite: Well, of course I was in love. But you know what I think? I think love is one of the greatest mysteries on earth. It's like sleep. Did you ever stop and think of sleep? You lie down in bed and you're not sleeping. All of a sudden you are asleep. Can you explain it? Well, it's just like love.*
> —Interview from *Cape Breton's Magazine*

Ron Caplan is about six feet five inches with the shoulders and build of a football player. He would have made an inviting target for the Viet Cong. Fortunately, they never had a chance to practise on his shoulder blades. He grew up in Pittsburg, Pennsylvania, and arrived in Cape Breton just as everyone I knew was busy leaving. My cousin Roland à Gerard Doucet was on his way to New Orleans to learn how to play the guitar like the Cajuns did. Cousin Roger à Calixte Doucet had decamped for the American west and was learning how to be a computer guy. I was headed for the University of Toronto. None of us could imagine staying. Ron could.

A big part of the reason he could was that although he was only thirty, Ron came to Cape Breton with an impressive bundle of unique experiences. He was a little older than we were. He wasn't just starting out in life. He had already had a reasonable crack at it. He had been a VISTA volunteer in the US, Volunteers in Service to America, the domestic peace corps that was analogous to the Company of Young Canadians. Through VISTA, Ron volunteered and worked for a year to support the famous grape workers' strike in Delano led by Cesar Chavez. Then he went on to the Artists' Workshop in Detroit and did some small press mimeo publishing, eventually returning to Pittsburgh where he produced several books for Frontier Press of West Newbury, Massachusetts. There he met his wife; they married and had their first daughter.

When I learned about Ron's history prior to arriving in Cape Breton, suddenly I understood why he had been able to see and do what no one else could. Telling the stories of people's lives had been a big part of the War on Poverty efforts by VISTA. The formation of the Farm Workers Union and the strike were all recounted in Eugene Nelson's book *Huelga: The first hundred days* (*huelga* is Spanish for strike), and it is still available. The volunteers had discovered storytelling was crucial to getting wider public support for a fairer deal for farm workers.

One day, Ron and his young family left Pittsburg, following a friend who had already left for Cape Breton. He got into a ramshackle car and pointed it north, not really sure where Cape Breton was or what he would find when he got there. Ron wasn't alone. This search for meaning to life defined by yourself, not the expectations of the previous generation, was at the heart of much of the sixties unrest.

The best impulse of our generation was about wanting to rethink why we were on the planet and what we were supposed to do while we were here. It wasn't a trivial impulse, although sometimes its expression was. Nonetheless it led to many fine things. Ron's arrival on Cape Breton Island was one of them.

Ron stopped driving when he ran out of road in North Sydney where the sea meets the highway and Newfoundland is seven hours away. Not wanting to spend the money on the ferry, he kept following the road north around the coastline of the island. He stopped at Wreck Cove.

At Wreck Cove, the mountains plunge straight down to the ocean and there is nothing between the houses and Europe but the Atlantic. On my side of the island, the west side, there is a plateau and more room to live. There the sun rises behind the mountains and sets behind the sea. If I could see beyond the ocean's horizon from my front door, past the curve of the earth, I would see the Magdalen Islands, then the St. Lawrence, Quebec, Montreal, Toronto, all the way to Vancouver.

At Wreck Cove, on the east side, there is no plateau between the mountains and the sea. It's more rugged. Ron found himself standing in the field of what was a mountain farm looking at a worn, wooden house built in 1835. The house was solid but no one wanted it. It was built straight out of the Highland diaspora. It's the same kind of house that the seven-foot-nine Cape Breton giant Angus MacAskill grew up in just down the road.

It wasn't the most convenient location or house, but Ron didn't see inconvenience. He saw the romance of the fine stone fireplace in the centre of the house, tall ceilings, views of the ocean, and the tiny, easy-to-heat rooms. This was a place where he could live.

Wreck Cove isn't the centre of any known universe, and I would have thought being from the benign climate and multitudes of Pennsylvania, Ron would have been appalled by how remote and poor it was; instead he was entranced. More importantly he figured out a way to make a living that would surprise everyone.

His idea came from just listening to his neighbours in Wreck Cove. He began to record their stories and take photographs of the people he met. They were the stories of ordinary people, doing ordinary things, farming, fishing, hooking rugs, dancing, but there was nothing that Ron did, heard, or saw that he did not find interesting. Then he did something no one expected. He started publishing the photographs and stories he was recording in an odd-looking magazine that he brazenly called *Cape Breton's Magazine*.

Cape Breton's Magazine didn't look like anything anyone had ever seen before. It was the size of a newspaper. Inside, the stories were printed on rough newsprint in simple black and white. There was no colour to it at all, and like a newspaper, *Cape Breton's Magazine* had advertisements for everything from Rent-a-Car franchises to Sydney Ship Supply to Stone's Drugstore. If someone was doing business in Cape Breton, sooner or later they ended up advertising in *Cape Breton's Magazine*, but unlike a newspaper, the articles were bound together under a stiff cardboard cover, and it had no daily news. If there was a war going on somewhere it wouldn't appear in the pages of *Cape Breton's Magazine*. Ron left that to others.

From the beginning, *Cape Breton's Magazine* made a splash. When it began appearing in gas stops and stores it was impossible to miss. If nothing else, *Cape Breton's Magazine* took up a lot of real estate. The size allowed Ron to print generous stories and large-format photographs. Physically, opening the magazine felt like dropping into another world.

The content was also something no one had ever seen or heard before outside of the privacy of their own kitchen. A series of stories that I remember well were interviews with Marguerite Gallant from Chéticamp. She was a wonderful storyteller with a thoughtful, original take on the world, somewhere between magical and gravely philosophical, and always eccentric. Ron recognized her importance and made

Marguerite the featured story of one issue with a large photograph of her on the front cover. In that photograph, Marguerite is sitting in a child's wagon, her wild white hair pinned loosely about her head. She is smiling wickedly for the camera and wearing dark-rimmed glasses. She definitely looked the part of modern witch-woman, but it was also possible to imagine her as a younger woman when she had been beautiful with thick, dark, glossy hair, harmonious features, and bright, sparkling eyes. She was the kind of woman you would have thought would have been married at least a couple of times, but she never had, and about that part of her life she remained resolutely private.

I have read many issues of *Cape Breton's Magazine* and was always impressed by my own blindness. I hadn't been able to see what Ron had seen. I had taken what was around me largely for granted. It never occurred to me to wonder about village storytellers like Marguerite Gallant, Loubie Chiasson, or Marcellin Hache, or where their stories came from or why.

It took *Cape Breton's Magazine* for me to grasp that they were the last of a storytelling tradition that went right back to the Middle Ages. All three used an archaic form of French that Molière would have found perfectly correct. What is now thought of as the literary tense, the simple past, they used in ordinary conversation. It is conjugated entirely differently than any other tense, and unless you grow up with it, it is hard to use.

No one replaced these storytellers when they died. The tradition died with them because the culture changed. People no longer stayed up all night with the corpse laid out at home as if the person has just decided to take a long sleep. This expression of love and grief doesn't happen anymore. The corpse goes to a funeral home and there is a polite reception there where people stand up, shake hands, and sign a book. Today, no one would think of sitting up all night to accompany the departed on their last voyage or inviting a storyteller to lighten the long night and the grief.

People listened to storytellers at wakes not just to be entertained but to confront their own fears of mortality, of loss and the mysteries of eternity. In their arsenal, the storytellers had myths, stories of the devil, despair, courage, hope, laughter. With the magic of the storyteller's art, people didn't feel so overwhelmed by the reality of the recent death, for the story always walked that delicate line between the imagined and the real.

Storytellers were able to tell tales of the devil and hell in ways that allowed you to peer over the precipice. Just as a Mad Max film today can evoke an end-of-the-world scenario that can frighten the audience but not so terribly that life after the film cannot go on. Storytellers did the same thing. After the wake, people could go home and carry on doing all the ordinary things life requires—sleep, prepare meals, wash the dishes—having confronted their worst fears.

It was in *Cape Breton's Magazine* that I first read an interview with Père Anselme Chiasson, the famous Capuchin priest from Chéticamp who collected hundreds of stories and songs from storytellers. And through *Cape Breton's Magazine* that I very gradually began to understand the complexity and importance of storytelling. Storytelling has never really changed since Homer recounted the complications of Paris and Helen's love affair and the moral gymnastics of the Trojan War. The simple telling of stories by a talented raconteur did all the things that the film industry does today but with only one voice made by one human being, and in this way was more magical than any multi-million-dollar film could be.

When Ron interviewed Marguerite, she was an old woman and no longer beautiful. She was living in a two-bedroom cabin by herself on the little isthmus between the village and Chéticamp Island. Her cabin was jammed with old stuff. Her odd collection spilled out of her house into a shed beside it. Everyone in Chéticamp agreed that Marguerite was an unusual woman who could tell stories and sing old songs, but no one had ever thought she was important enough to appear in a magazine, which is curious because people talked about her all the time. "Like Marguerite Gallant" was an expression people had for having original thoughts and not bothering about the community measure.

Some of her songs Ron recorded in French. Her bright, feisty, independent spirit comes across clearly in all the interviews. She wasn't intimidated by Ron or his magazine. Her curt comment on making breakfast for him when he spent the night at her place was: "I've never cooked breakfast for a man and I'm not about to start now." Ron smiled, came downstairs, and prepared his own.

Marguerite Gallant was wearing purple long before that phrase was coined to describe an independent older woman. Ron had the imagination to understand Marguerite's life and that her little cabin told its own version of island history.

A collection of teacups, old household equipment, books, paintings are given meaning by the collector. It is through the collector's knowledge and affection for the physical objects that the collection is given life. After Marguerite departed the planet, Ron suggested that the inside of her cabin be sprayed and sealed with several coats of clear Varathane and left as a single piece of art.

It was a brilliant suggestion and would have created a museum all on its own, but it wasn't to be. A small representation of her collection of glass, beach finds, plates, and things that had special meaning to her was kept and reorganized into a small, anemic copy in the village museum. Unfortunately, when the locale and the mind behind her collection disappeared so did much of its charm and beauty. If people had followed Ron's advice and left intact the objects as she had placed them in her little house, a whiff of her intelligence and poetry would have survived.

What happened to Marguerite's collection is standard fare. When the collector dies, so does the collection. On the death of the collector, personal collections are always dissembled from the greatest to the most humble. When Charles Ephrussi died, his brilliant Paris collection of Impressionist art disappeared into museums and private homes all over the world. Samuel Pepys's book collection is one of the very few private libraries to have survived the collector's death. His books can still be found in a room dedicated to them at Magdalen College at Oxford University. To walk around that sunny room and just gaze at the titles on the bookshelves is to get a sense of the man and his age that can be achieved no other way.

Marguerite's house is now a summer beach residence. A few oddments from her collection remain in Les Trois Pignons, the village museum in Chéticamp, and her memory was honoured by naming the road in front of the cabin Chemin Marguerite Gallant.

Three times a year, *Cape Breton's Magazine* came out with stories no one else had thought were worth publishing—interviews with traditional fiddlers, step dancers, soldiers, and sailors. Just people: "All as true as I'm sitting here." In the process, Ron compiled a unique history of a place and time written in the sweat of people's daily lives, not by national or world events. To go fishing for mackerel or herring in the fall for recreation is a pleasant experience, to need those fish to survive the winter is another thing entirely.

There's not a lot of comfy times in *Cape Breton's Magazine*. Life is raw. Not much more than a child herself, Marguerite was sent to a large household in Terre Noire to help the woman of the house raise her own large family. Marguerite worked there for years without a cent of payment. All she received was food, a bed, and a considerate mistress. *Anne of Green Gables* is an elegant, charming survival story of an orphan with no place to go and no hope but that someone would adopt her. It was not an unfamiliar story. There were children like Anne in every village. Marguerite Gallant was one.

Stories from the coal mines and steel mills, Mi'kmaw, Acadian, and Scots history are all recorded in the broadsheet pages of *Cape Breton's Magazine* in the matter-of-fact tone of people recalling the weather. There's a Mi'kmaw story of "A man who married a beaver" by Chief Nicholas Jerome, poems by the famous Mi'kmaw poet Rita Joe, a Gaelic story of the Milky Way. As in life itself, the prosaic is mixed with the magical. From the prosaic side comes a story of the last decades of Cape Breton's streetcars. Like everything else in Cape Breton, the Sydney and Glace Bay streetcars have a unique history that managed to survive the tough times of the Depression.

When the American owners of the streetcars pulled out in 1931, the drivers cobbled together two hundred dollars each for a down payment and began to run them themselves. Co-operatively owned, the streetcars ran successfully until 1947, when the older drivers wanted to cash in their original investment, their two hundred dollars having morphed by then into the grand sum of $216,000. The younger drivers didn't have the resources to buy out the older ones, and as happened everywhere else, the streetcars were then sold to rubber tire interests, the system decommissioned, and the rail lines torn up.

There is a vintage photograph in the magazine of the last tram to run down Commercial Street in Sydney. The front of the tram is decorated to look like a human face with a tear coming out of one eye. On the side of the tram hangs a large banner with the message: "Goodbye, my friends. Goodbye."

Ron gives the last word on Sydney's streetcars to Dougald Blue, a tram driver and later a bus driver: "In 1947, they started taking the tram cars off…but you know, I loved the old streetcars. I never liked the buses."

Whenever I read library copies of *Cape Breton's Magazine*, they feel like old friends, and I find myself turning the pages oblivious of time and place. When I put them down, they make me wonder why so much of Canadian history by "professional" historians feels so lifeless. There's so much more to life than politics and Parliament Hill. People do fall foolishly, unreasonably in love, sometimes for the better, sometimes not. People endure through terrible times with dignity and joy, and suffer terrible things that they don't understand. In *Cape Breton's Magazine*, the history of the island comes alive in the hands of the people who made it.

Ron also started an island publishing company called Breton Books, specializing in Cape Breton writers and Cape Breton subjects. Under the Breton imprint, he has published many wonderful books. My favourite is still *The Woman from Away* by Tessie Gillis. Her stories about her young life on a remote mountain farm have an aching charm and a clean, easy style that feels as natural as the sun shining. Her stories stick, which is the thing all writers wish for in their work.

Over the years, many writers have responded to Ron's requests for stories and are grateful that they have. A version of "The Gaelic Ship," which appears in this book, was first published in one of Breton Books's short story collections.

To get Breton Books out into Island stores, Ron built beautiful little wooden display cases for them. You can still find these attractive wood bookcases in stores all over the island. Ron is now in his seventies and is still publishing. He has been awarded an Order of Canada medal. When I congratulated him, he shrugged, smiled, and simply said: "It's really Cape Breton's medal."

I don't quite agree. It is *about* Cape Breton, but the magazine is Ron's.

"Philibert the Sheep" is a story I thought Ron might like.

PHILIBERT THE SHEEP

The ewe disappeared the day that Philibert got falling down drunk. Daniel searched for her from one end of the field to the other. She wasn't there. She wasn't hiding in the shade of the red currant bushes. She wasn't hiding in the woodlot. He'd been in every corner and crevice of the barn. He'd searched the fenceline. There was no mark, no break that one pregnant ewe could have passed through.

"Then where is she?" asked Father Aucoin looking up from his desk annoyed. "She has to be in the field. Look again."

"Perhaps she fell over the cliff," said Daniel. "It happens sometimes."

"No, I don't think so," said the priest thinking about this. "She's there somewhere."

Daniel went back to the field and began to walk in an aimless way back and forth across it. The cows and sheep began to trail after him. They made a curious picture, the boy walking in a desultory way, the little flock fanned out behind him.

Philibert arrived at the front door of the presbytery playing his harmonica. He had the inclination to play long, tuneless dirges when he was drunk. He sat down with a clunk on the presbytery stairs and waited. It didn't take long. His cousin emerged.

"I'd like to make a confession," announced Philibert without looking directly at the priest.

"Confessions are held on Tuesday and Thursday in the church, not on the presbytery stairs," said Father Aucoin, already exercising the virtue of patience.

"But that will be too late. By Tuesday, I may be a hardened sinner. I need to confess now when I am contrite and defeated. No, Tuesday will definitely be too late." Philibert shook his head with great exaggeration.

"Philibert, you have been defeated and contrite before."

"It's not entirely my fault. People take advantage of me. I'm easily led."

"That may be entirely possible, but I advise you to take yourself home."

"I don't want to go home. My wife will make me sleep in the barn."

"A wise woman."

"It's humiliating to sleep in the barn. The neighbours will talk."

"If you don't want them to talk, don't drink."

"My wife treats me like a stray dog."

"So she should. If it were up to me, I'd put a collar on you and keep you chained up in the front yard."

"I don't understand. You're a priest. You're supposed to be solicitous to us poor sinners."

Philibert lay back on the porch and the entire sky began to revolve in a rather discouraging way. He sat up and then stood up and vomited vigorously. The entire contents of his overburdened stomach liberated themselves onto Father Aucoin's small flower bed.

"What a waste," said Philibert and sat down shakily on the porch stairs.

"Go down to the barnyard and wash yourself off in the horse trough," said the priest. "That's if the horse will let you."

Philibert wagged his finger at the priest. "See? You're disgusted with me. I can tell. I'm not. Not in the slightest. That's the trouble with you, cousin, you don't understand evil. It always surprises you. It never surprises me. On the contrary, what I find amazing is not that I am presently wretchedly drunk, but that I am so often stone cold sober. This is what I find discouraging. It takes a great deal of effort to get this drunk. All I can think is that the devil must have a very weak grip on me."

"Shall I send for Zabine to come and get you?"

"Oh no," said Philibert, his pale face becoming paler.

"What are you going to do?"

"Can I sleep in your barn? No one will know if I sleep there, and then I can go home in the morning."

"I don't let smokers sleep in the barn. It's too dangerous."

"I don't have any cigarettes. Not a one."

"Empty your pockets."

Philibert emptied his pockets. One yellow, battered package of cigarette tobacco emerged, one package of papers, one small box of all-weather matches, fifteen cents, and one pocket watch.

"I thought you said you didn't have any cigarettes left?"

"I don't, not one made."

"You are not only a drunk, Philibert. You are a liar and a corrupting moral influence."

"You're right. I've seen better days, but just for tonight can I sleep in your barn? I promise I will be gone in the morning. I will be silent. No one but you will know I've been there."

"The boy will know. He does the barn chores."

"Daniel won't say anything. I know the lad."

"Why in heaven's name should I protect you? Go home, Philibert. Face your wife."

"It's not entirely my fault," said Philibert.

"Did someone force the rum down your throat?"

"It's not entirely my fault that I'm not like you, cousin. It's not my fault that at ten years old you knew you were going to be a priest."

"I didn't."

"Oh yes you did. I remember, and don't you deny it. Your father asked us at the dinner table what we were going to be when we grew up and you piped, 'I'm going to be a priest.' You said that at ten years old."

"I said it, Philibert, because he wanted some sort of an answer and it seemed like a reasonable thing to say."

"You didn't want to be a priest?"

"Not at ten."

"You just said it."

"I just said it."

"I always thought you were born wanting to be a priest."

"No."

"Well you are now."

"Yes."

"Where are you going?" called Philibert after the priest.

"I'm going to look for the boy. He's disappeared again."

Philibert nodded vaguely and just stood at the presbytery porch, holding onto the bannister. The priest stopped and came back. He picked up his cousin's tobacco and matches.

"Go to sleep in the barn, Philibert."

Philibert nodded as if he had been expecting this all along and began to walk shakily toward the barnyard. He asked the horse if it would be alright to use the water trough. The horse did not seem to mind. Then he knelt down at the trough and washed his face for a long time. The water felt wonderfully clean and fresh, better than the whiskey.

Philibert climbed into the mow and bedded down comfortably in the loose hay. The world still revolved, but a little more slowly now. He dreamed that he was rich. He owned a great number of things, although he was not sure what, except it was a good deal. There were blueberries and cream and fresh, strong tea. There was a Scottish girl who smiled at him. Yes, he was rich, so rich he did not have a worry in the world.

Daniel had found the ewe. She had dropped her two little lambs in the depths of some prickly red current bushes, right beside a fox hole. The fox had butchered one already, and the ewe was standing with a dazed expression on her face making futile little trots sometimes in the direction of the fox, sometimes in the direction of the remaining lamb.

The dead lamb was severed into pieces. By the time the boy found it, there was nothing left but little bloody pieces of bone. The fox had cracked the skull open and was carefully licking out the brains. It was a large dog fox with a flaming tail as long as its entire body. The ewe began to bleat feebly. It was as if there was something caught in her throat. She made a strangled sound. The remaining newborn lamb, unaware of any danger, kept walking unsteadily toward the sheep's udder, but she ignored him, turning always to face the fox.

The fox nosed the remains of the dead lamb and then stood up, stretching comfortably from forelegs to hips. Then he began to walk toward the second lamb, which was now standing alone and trembling, aware now that something was wrong but unable to understand what. The mother began to trot back and forth with bulging, vacant eyes. The fox stopped to watch her for a moment and then turned his attention back toward the lamb. He was like a cat with a particularly pleasing mouse. He wanted the lamb to run, but the little creature was too unsteady. He still carried the bloody marks from the birth.

Daniel came pushing through the bush and stumbled onto the scene. The fox looked up, uncertain for a moment about what to do. The ewe finally found her voice and began to bleat energetically. Daniel clapped his hands together making a short, sharp sound and then dove toward the lamb, sweeping the little creature up into his arms. The fox's lips curled back over his fangs and he was gone.

When the priest arrived, the boy was trying to get the lamb to suckle at the teat of the mother, but she would have nothing of it. She kept pawing stupidly at the remains of her first-born and ignoring the second.

"You're going to get that lamb killed," said the priest. "She's going to kick him. What's the matter with her?"

"A fox killed the first one. She's frightened."

"I'll hold her and you introduce the young one to dinner." The priest straddled the sheep, pinning the animal between his knees. She stood still for a second and then began to kick and buck like a wild bronco. Now that the fox was gone and the danger past, her little brain had decided to engage with great and terrified fury. The priest was thrown to the ground and the ewe went bleating and bucking across the field to join the rest of the flock.

"This is not my day," said Father Aucoin, prying himself up to his elbows.

"What are we going to do with the lamb?" asked the boy, who was afraid the shivering little creature would die.

"We'll take him to the house and get Mrs. Cross to make a bottle up for him." The priest stood up and dusted himself off.

"Can we give him a name?" asked Daniel, feeling the lamb's heart beating against his own.

"It's not normal to name something you are going to eat," said the priest, thinking about this.

"We could keep him as a ram. We have no ram."

"We could," said the priest in an absent-minded way as he was trying to remember what he was annoyed about and could not. "What would you like to call him?" he asked, thinking of the problem of the name instead.

The boy considered this and did not reply immediately.

"How about a prophet?" asked the priest, looking at the little lamb. "We could call him Amos. Amos was interested in justice and this little creature has suffered some rough justice."

The boy shook his head. "No," he replied and then the name came to him. "I'd like to call him Philibert."

"Philibert the sheep?" said the priest, and Father Aucoin began to laugh. He laughed and laughed until tears sprang from his eyes and his sides were sore.

Daniel had never seen the priest laugh like this before and he began to grow alarmed.

"Is there anything wrong?"

"Nothing at all. Nothing at all," replied the priest, still gasping. "I just love the name, Philibert the sheep," and he started to laugh all over again.

The bell sounded from the church spire and the priest finally remembered what he had come to get the boy for. "The Angelus! We'll be late for the Angelus!" He hitched up his soutane and began to run across the hummocky pasture toward the church. The boy followed along carrying Philibert the lamb.

CHAPTER 24

St. Maximin la Sainte-Baume

Shaped by God to shape the city.
—Inscription outside St. Paul's Anglican Church,
Hammersmith, London, founded 1630

St. Paul's was my mother's parish church. I attended it with my grandmother when we visited my Oliver grandparents. It sits right in the middle of Hammersmith circle. It is a lovely building that was renewing itself last time I visited with the addition of a sunny meeting hall. The new meeting hall was to be used for a day care. The old walls were still covered with the bright paintings of children. I have always liked churches; the cement of a church is hope. There is something profoundly moving just sitting in a grand and tranquil place that has been built in the hope it will help us find some connection to the mystery of eternity. It may be a vain hope but it is a genuine one and has accompanied human beings for as long as humans have been human. I have felt the same emotion in the great caves of Europe where paleolithic wall paintings still exist. Like my mother, whenever I am near a church or any place built for a conversation with the divine, I like to pay my respects in a grateful and humble way.

I think I would have felt the same way in a pagan temple. The old Greek gods are much trivialized. They should not be.

In inventing the gods, the Greeks began to invent modern man. The gods were part of a complex, changing, and a profoundly devout conversation. It was much like the Christian conversation that is filled with sound and fury, contradictory ideas, and impossible ideals, but in one essential way the polytheistic pagan world differed from the monotheistic. Monotheism attempted to freeze that conversation in a series of prescriptions that left little room for individual thought. Monotheism required a belief in one God, which was followed by a set of prescriptions or religious laws that determined whether or not you qualified as a believer.

This was the principal difference between monotheism and polytheism. Polytheists don't trust that any single god, including the most powerful, Zeus, could encompass the entire truth. On this matter, I am a polytheist. Nonetheless, churches are excellent places to think these long thoughts, and the world would be poorer without them. The impulse to build a temple, a mosque, church, or synagogue all comes from the same spiritual place. In this way, they are all conjoined.

The priest in Grand Étang in his homily last Sunday said, "It doesn't matter to God if one is baptized or not." When I heard him say this I could not believe it. I expected some sort of revolution in the pews. Nothing happened. Not a word of protest. Does the Pope know what his priests are preaching? It wasn't so long ago that people used to risk death to have a baby baptized for fear of losing the newborn without their ticket to heaven. I was staggered to hear this from the pulpit. This is a change so fundamental that I could scarcely believe my Catholic ears, for it takes away the tribalism of the religion for which Catholics are famous.

When the children were young, Patty and I expatriated the family to the south of France where we rented a cottage from Madame Bonneaud and lived there for a year in an earthly splendour that was beyond anything we had ever imagined.

The cottage looked over the ancient valley of the river Arc, which the Consul Marius had marched down two thousand years ago to fight the Teutons. The valley was filled with history and the sweet smell of thyme, lavender, and grapes. Above us were blue skies of such clarity that it was possible to imagine the effect it had on the Dutch painter Van Gogh.

My daughter Emma says I liked France so much because it was like one long weekend for me. She was right. I was left alone to mind the cottage while the children and Patty went to school. During the day, my principal job was to listen to the radio and take care of Zola, a village kitten we had adopted.

Sometimes I would bicycle along the old National 8 toward the village of Saint Maximin. Provençal legend has it Saint Maximin was one of the men who brought Christianity to the south of France. The legend says he was also a friend of Mary Magdalene who had retired to a grotto high on nearby mountain called la Sainte-Baume.

When Mary Magdalene's final moments came, friends carried her down from her grotto on the mountain to receive the last rites from her friend Maximin. She didn't quite make it to the church and received the final rites from her friend beside the road. Today there is a little Roman monument at the side of the road that marks the place where Mary Magdalene died. There is something about its simplicity that is quite moving and in a way convincing at least in the context of it standing there.

There is both sacred and unchained violence in the valley of the Arc. On the violence side, legend has it that so many died in the victory of General Marius, the river Arc was coloured red for weeks. To celebrate his crushing victory against the Cimbri and the Teutons, his soldiers built a cairn beside the road in the village of Pourrières, which means stink or rotten.

La Sainte-Baume mountain has no violence directly associated with it. It's a very pleasant walk in the dappled shade of its cool and magnificent forest. The Grotto of Mary Magdalene itself was much more comfortable than I imagined. It has a generous stone platform in front of the cave and several spacious rooms in the mountain behind the broad patio. The cave's front deck overlooks the long trail that winds gracefully up the mountain through tall trees. It is said Mary Magdalene spent part of each day on the actual mountaintop, which has a view all the way to the Mediterranean. The legend is that she watched for Christ's return from there. The cave has been kept continuously as a place of worship all the way back to the third century. When I was there the altar in the cave was being decorated with white linen and candles in preparation for a church service.

It is not a sure thing Mary Magdalene ever lived in the grotto, for there are several towns around the Mediterranean that claim her presence after the Crucifixion. Nonetheless, I found that her legend in Provence was comprehensive and idiosyncratic enough in its many details to make me think it might have been possible.

It was easy to imagine a medieval French king making his pilgrimage on horseback up the mountain, confident he was getting some credits for heaven, the jingle of the horse's harness and the quiet chatter of his retainers as they rode comfortably through the forest along the broad path. The king's trip was not singular. Millions of other visitors have made this same pilgrimage to the grotto site.

According to the legend, Mary Magdalene arrived in Provence at St. Marie de la Mer farther west, with other refugees from the Crucifixion. From there, she made her way east before settling in the security of the remote vastness of la Sainte-Baume. The little column that marks her death at the side of the road is unmistakably Roman. Roman stone has an unmistakable soft grey colour, broad cuts, and the stone surfaces are weathered by time. It's impossible not to recognize it as Roman. It looks like nothing that came after.

The bicycle ride from Rousset to St. Maximin would take a good hour or more, depending on the direction of the wind. On the way back, it was not an easy trip either, as the village of St. Maximin was at the bottom of a steep valley. From the plateau high above the village, the roof of the grand basilica commemorating St. Maximin and its associated royal convent looked like a mother hen with the much smaller red-tiled roofs of ordinary houses clustered like chicks around it.

Standing right outside, St. Maximin, the basilica, didn't seem very grand. Its walls were dull and featureless like the tall sides of an old warehouse, but inside it was like sitting in an old-growth forest. The pale winter sunlight would descend in columns from the high clerestory windows, bringing shafts of light streaming down from the roofline to light the shadows. The lines of stone columns supporting the roof were gigantic, disappearing into the sky above while shafts of faint winter sunlight lit their columns. The inside of the church was filled with power and wonder. It was an easy place to just sit and wonder.

To walk in an elevated frame of mind from the light and shadows glowing in the great church to the village cafe on a winter day felt like a whiff of the eternal. In the cafe, I would sit quietly by myself sipping on hot coffee and milk, not far from a large, roaring fire. The flames crackled, filling the cafe with pungent scents of grapevine roots and cheering heat while the smoke rose in the chimney toward heaven. It was sitting in front of the fire in a cafe at St. Maximin where I first conceived of writing stories about St. Joseph de la Mer.

They began with the sound of the voice of an old man sitting on the other side of the fire from me. He was telling a story to some friends. The heat from the fire and the warm drink had made me sleepy and I was scarcely awake, but his melodious voice began to penetrate my hazy condition. Slowly, I realized although he was speaking with a very different accent, in a different place, he was telling a story that I had heard told before but in Cape Breton.

I could scarcely see the man through the haze of the cafe heat and smoke, but his words were clear and soothing. It was as if this storyteller had become every storyteller who had ever told a tale, from Homer to Marguerite Gallant. For stories have always been the way people have put order in the chaos of creation. They are like candles that illuminate a cave wall and help protect us from mindless fear of eternity. It was all here in this cafe and had been around me all my life. I just hadn't seen it.

The south of France is a long way from Cape Breton, but at that moment it didn't seem so. It seemed as close as my own breath, and suddenly stories of St. Joseph de la Mer began to roll off my pen as if they had been waiting to be let out the door.

CHAPTER 25

The World Acadian Congress, Barbara LeBlanc, and "The Scholarship"

A quarter of a million people are descending on New Brunswick for the Retrouvailles. Everyone from great literary stars like Antonine Maillet and great athletes like Jean Beliveau to women like the Doucet cousins travelling from Montreal and Ottawa whom I met at the border. We are like salmon swimming up a river impelled by a force we scarcely understand.
—from my book *Notes from Exile: On Being Acadian* (McClelland & Stewart, 2000)

In 1988, Acadians living in Edmonton, Alberta, had the extraordinary idea to try and hold a worldwide reunion of descendants of the 1755 deportation. People were to be invited to come to New Brunswick for a reunion, which they called *les Retrouvailles* (to find ourselves again). It would be a vast celebration with eating, singing, dancing, talking, and generally trying to figure out what had happened to their long-lost relatives 250 years ago. It took almost ten years to organize but in 1994, it happened. The big question was, would anyone come? The deportation was a long time ago, and it had scattered people from the Falkland Islands to Africa, South America, Europe, Louisiana, as well as all down the eastern seaboard of the United States. The answer was swift. They did. I was one of them. So was Barbara LeBlanc.

Barbara had good reason to come. She was the director of Grand-Pré National Historic Site, just outside of Wolfville, Nova Scotia. The land had originally been assembled by a Nova Scotian Acadian but was now owned and maintained by Parks Canada. It is a small but quite beautiful site, with a chapel built in memory of the Acadians who were deported from Grand-Pré.

In spite of her job and very Acadian name, Barbara didn't grow up with any profound feeling of being Acadian. Like me, she grew up in an English-speaking milieu (for Barbara it was New Waterford, Cape Breton) and at a young age refused to speak French with her parents for it seemed more like a parental imposition than a real language. When we talked at the Retrouvailles I thought I might never see her again, but to my delight I have discovered she now lives in Terre Noire, just down the road from Grand Étang.

Barbara is now a professor at Université Saint-Anne, a little French Acadian university located at Pointe de l'Église (Church Point) on the Bay of Fundy, but she teaches students from their St. Joseph du Moine campus on Cape Breton Island. (Saint-Anne has four satellite campuses distributed around Nova Scotia.) Now, it is possible for students from British Columbia to Newfoundland to sit down in front of their screens, dial Barbara up, and participate in her courses, no matter where they are or she is. It's something that would have been science fiction when I was boy. To teach or be a student, there was no choice but to physically move to a place that had a university campus.

It's a curious thing to live in the deep country far from any grand centre. Like stones on the beach, the houses all look roughly the same, but when you get closer you realize that they are as different as the people inside. Barbara lives in Terre Noire because it allows her to take care of her ninety-six-year-old mother, Josephine, in her own home.

In the Acadian community, Barbara is famous for all kinds of reasons. Not only was she the first female director of Parks Canada's Grand-Pré National Historic Site, she has a doctorate in Ethnology and has created a Nova Scotian school guide for teaching traditional dance and song, as well as writing many academic articles and several books. The one I have enjoyed best is titled *Postcards from Acadie* in which Barbara traces not just the long and interesting history of Grand-Pré as a national historic site, but also reflects on how myth and reality around the Acadian story connect and disconnect. It is in *Postcards from Acadie* that I found the story of how Canadian Pacific used Longfellow's vision of *Évangéline* to entice Canadians to travel east.

When Barbara and I first met, we sat at a picnic table somewhere in Moncton and just talked and talked, which is what the first Retrouvailles was all about. When I listened to Barbara, I didn't feel like an odd combination of English and Acadian. I felt normal and this was a wonderful moment. Here is a small piece from that day's conversation.

Barbara: "After university, I went to see what Europe was all about. I had a wonderful time, especially in Italy. I fell in love with the countryside and the language. I was only supposed to stay for the summer months and then come home and find a job, but I didn't want to come home. It would have been like finding the perfect cup of cappuccino and taking only one sip, so I stayed."

Me: "How long?"

Barbara: "About ten years, mostly working in the theatre."

Me: "Did you find it hard to learn Italian?"

Barbara: "I lived and worked in the language. After a couple of years, people didn't know I wasn't a native speaker."

Me: "What brought you home?"

Barbara: "One day, we were sitting in a trattoria, and the people I was with were talking about their roots, the towns that they were from, their traditions and so on, of which they were very proud, and I realized with a kind of shock that I had my own roots, my own language, my own traditions. The more I thought about it, the more I wanted to come home."

Me: "You make it sound easy."

Barbara: "It wasn't. Ten years away from your own country is a long time. Making the decision to come home was easy, but actually living the experience through was another thing entirely. When I actually got home, I felt very confused. I hadn't spoken French since I was a child and had forgotten it long ago. All I could recall were a few phrases. My parents were happy to see me home but didn't know what I was about either. I was always asking questions. Why did we leave Chéticamp? What was the Tintamarre? Why did Mother always make pâté at Christmas?

"My father didn't want to feel as if he was being examined all the time. He would say, 'Why all the questions?' It wasn't just me who was confused, so were my parents. They had spent a lot of time when I was a child trying to teach me about my Acadian heritage and language, and I had spent an equal amount of time resisting it to the point that I wouldn't even speak French to them. Now suddenly I come home and the shoe is on the other foot. It was me who was pestering them to speak French and to teach me all the things that I had been so anxious to dump.

"The first winter home, I decided to go to Mexico. I told myself it was to learn Spanish, but in retrospect I think it was to find some neutral ground. Some place that wasn't Canada, wasn't Europe, and wasn't the US. Some place where I could sort my confusions out. It worked. I came home again, but this time with a plan. I went back to university where I studied Acadian history, Acadian folklore, and I relearned French in a systematic way. Five years later I had a Ph.D. from Laval University and was working at Grand-Pré. In a very small nutshell that is it."

Barbara smiled again as if daring me to take her seriously. I can't help smiling back. "I still don't really know why you left the land of pasta to come home," I say.

"Maybe some things aren't entirely explainable. Why are you here? Why aren't you back in Ottawa doing whatever you do in Ottawa?"

I had no answer so I keep quiet.

"I think I know," Barbara continued. "It's called connections and community. I see it all the time. During the summer, we get thousands of tourists at Grand-Pré. Mostly they want to see the place Évangéline came from. It's a bit like tourists going to Prince Edward Island to see the house where Lucy Maud Montgomery lived. The church at Grand-Pré has the same feel as the Anne of Green Gables house. It's an ornament from the past hanging around in the present, but I'm not sure the Grand-Pré church has much to do with anything. Unlike Montgomery's house, it didn't even exist when Grand-Pré was Évangéline's home. Being director there is a bit like being an usher at a wedding that's been cancelled."

"Then why stay?"

"Because cancelled weddings still have guests, and the guests are interesting. I've noticed, for example, that the kids with Acadian names have less interest in where Évangéline might or might not have lived. They are more interested in trying to make sense out of Acadian history in a personal way. These kids—many of them speak French only haltingly—all feel this connection; they realize that their families ended up in Boston or Montreal or wherever not just by accident but because of this one central event to which not just Évangéline but they are connected. For them, *Évangéline* isn't just poem. There is an Évangéline and a Gabriel story somewhere in their own family history. When I realized this, I started writing about Acadian history myself, but from the perspective of a young person."

Barbara stops for a moment and we watch the big CBC trucks rolling up with the equipment for the gala opening of the academic conference that evening. This is the event Prime Minister Chrétien, UN Secretary General Boutros Boutros-Ghali, and other luminaries would be attending. We watch them curiously.

I met many other Acadians at the Retrouvailles. The Cajuns from Louisiana had a brilliant impact, bringing great food, music, dance, and a manner of speaking French that felt like home. There was David LeGallant who would become the publisher of the international magazine *Veritas Acadie*, but for me it was the meeting with Barbara LeBlanc that became the key metaphor for what the first World Congress of Acadians was all about. Nor was it as simple as it appeared on cheery television sound bites.

At ground level, many things were happening. One of the most important was thousands of encounters between individuals and families as people sought out genealogical connections, shared history, and to simply celebrate what it meant to be Acadian. For eighteen days, under the temporary tent of the Retrouvailles, a magical Acadian city emerged. One that brought together people from all over the world to share ideas, literature, dance, music, history, food, love, and curiosity. At an international level, it was an attempt to understand what Acadie was today and what it could be in the future. The UN Secretary General saw the Acadians as a beacon for how one might be a proud Kurd in Turkey, a proud Shi'a in Syria, and a proud Yazidi in Iraq without challenging the nation-state structure. He appreciated the possibilities and difficulties of what the Acadians were attempting to do with the Retrouvailles.

Barbara LeBlanc was skeptical of the speeches and their effect. "The speeches that we will hear tonight will be forgotten almost as soon as the cameras stop grinding, but the connections between people that are happening now, between you and me, between people from the States, from Ontario, from Quebec…they will endure. And from them something may come."

Four more Retrouvailles were held at five-year intervals. The second was in Louisiana, the third in Nova Scotia. They were both wonderful and for a time it looked like Boutros Boutros-Ghali's hopes would be realized and the Acadian community would find new ways to define itself as a people across borders but without impinging on national ambitions; but it wasn't to be. The fourth and fifth Retrouvailles returned to New Brunswick where it dissolved into the familiar outline of a maritime summer festival. The organizers seemed to have forgotten that the idea for the Retrouvailles had come from the Acadian diaspora in Alberta, not New Brunswick, and had been about finding new ways to express the community across borders but without any political territory.

No Acadian Estates General emerged or any other innovative, international institutional changes that could have provided new ways of integrating the Acadians of the diaspora with the Louisiana and Baie de Chaleurs communities. The foment and excitement of the first World Acadian Congresses gradually eroded as the grand assembly melted into a summer New Brunswick tourist experience.

In 2004 Barbara's father died. He had built a lovely house for his retirement in Terre Noire, just down the road from Grand Étang where I live in the summer. When he died, Barbara was teaching at Université Saint-Anne on the Bay of Fundy.

The main campus of the university is about as far away from Terre Noire as it is possible to be and still be in Nova Scotia. It's near the extreme southwest end, while Terre Noire is at the north end of Cape Breton. A journey of about eight hours by car separates the two communities with no air, bus, or train connections. In her eighties at the time, Barbara's mother, Josephine, didn't drive.

Barbara requested to be relocated to the campus building in St. Joseph du Moine, which is a village between Terre Noire and Grand Étang and only about a ten-minute drive from her mother's home. Like so many other things in Barbara's life it was a first. She was the first university professor to come to this campus, which had been focused exclusively on college-level courses.

When we talked in Moncton, we did so across a picnic table. In Terre Noire, we sat on her front steps.

"How have you found teaching over the internet?"

"It was a big jump but well worth it. It's made me realize technology is the pencil of the twenty-first century. When my students become teachers themselves, they will have to be comfortable using it for both research and how to teach, because it is changing how we learn.

"One of the courses I teach is called Museums in Schools. What it does is link student teachers with the exhibits held in museums. With the internet, you don't have to go to Ottawa or the Mi-Carême Centre to check out a museum. You can do it virtually and you can do it creatively with a pre-visit, a visit, and then a post-visit; that's how I've taught this course, in units of three. The student's imagination becomes the limit of the museum visit. I've seen many amazing student responses—all via the internet."

"Barbara, you're coming up to retirement yourself. Any thoughts on your own career and the future of a little village like Terre Noire or Grand Étang?"

"It will be a change for sure. I've been an ethnologist all my life before I even knew what the word meant. Ethnology is the study of people, their culture, and their values. As a young woman, I went to Europe because I wanted to learn more about people and how they lived, and when I returned I did so for the same reason. I wanted to find out more about my own culture and heritage, and that decision triggered everything else.

"Teaching has given me a chance to share that knowledge with others. My dance book, the work at Grand-Pré, my website Acadian Explorations—they are all about sharing with others. When you learn about a people, you're learning about all people, because we're all linked. We sing in every culture. We all tell stories. We dance. In learning about another culture, we're learning about ourselves, because we all share in this common humanity."

"What about life in the village here? How do you see the future?"

"Now you're asking me to crystal ball it. Who knows? But I see four distinct groups that are coming together to change things. There are the people who never left. Call them the year-rounders. Then there are the seasonal residents who come to enjoy summer. There are the people who were originally from here and have come back to live out their last act. The fourth group are young families who have decided to raise their children here, which thankfully we're seeing more of. The four groups are all very different, but they all pay taxes, go to the stores, and participate in the community. They all help. People tell me that the county as a whole is doing well."

"What does 'doing well' mean?"

"Port Hood, which is the county seat, collects enough taxes to plow the roads, collect the garbage, and so on. In the end, we all have to pay the bills," said Barbara, and she smiled.

"Can I ask what you are going to do when you retire?" I said.

"I have always been a collector of rings. I will be writing a column in the *Oran*, a local paper, talking about rings and the ties that bind. What about you?"

"I guess I'm one of those people who've come back to live out their last act."

"That sounds a little grim."

I take what Barbara says seriously, but am not sure my situation is grim at all. To write some stories, to watch the sun set beyond the sea feels like I'm doing what I want to do. Living in the place where I want to live. Here is a story for Barbara.

THE SCHOLARSHIP

One day Philibert came to see his cousin, the priest. They were not often on the best of terms, for Philibert was often in some kind of trouble. The last was a Chandeleur party that he and his wife Zabine gave. They say that it was the best Chandeleur ever held. There was more food and more people and more dancing than anyone had ever seen. Some danced right up to the 10:30 Mass on Sunday, which became another "scandal" that Father Aucoin laid at Philibert's door, although it was really Zabine who had organized the party.

Zabine had four daughters and no sons. The three older daughters were like Philibert, lots of trouble. They had their own minds made up about everything from the youngest age, and they all married young. Marie-Claire married a fisherman and that turned out very well. He was lively and so was she. Marie-Louise married a soldier and that turned out very well also. Marie-Jo married a sailor in Halifax and that didn't take. She came home with a baby and helped her mother who also had another one of her own, another girl, at forty-eight. So they were mothers together, which seemed to work out. Marie-Jo made fun of her mother for having a baby at such a late stage, and Zabine made fun of her daughter for having a baby too soon.

Philibert had another cousin on his father's side, Marcel Boudreau, who had a family of all boys, and with Philibert's being all girls and the two families living not far from each other the two fitted together, until Marie, Marcel's wife died. Then it all changed. Marcel went into a deep hole from which he never really emerged. His boys were older than Philibert's girls and suddenly less inclined to simple friendships, and at the same time Philibert's girls also lost interest in their childhood connections. The youngest Boudreau boy, Daniel, disappeared entirely from view. Except for Philibert, no one paid him much attention, but Philibert did. He noticed when the boy began to fail in school, and he would fret about the boy he always called "Marie's youngest."

One day, Philibert went to the church presbytery and knocked on the door with a great banging, determined to see the priest who was usually not keen on seeing his cousin. Mrs. Cross answered. She looked at him suspiciously. "Yes," was all she said, for she didn't want to be impolite and being impolite with Philibert came easily to her.

Philibert breathed deeply. "I would like to see Father Aucoin."

"He's not available right now," said Mrs. Cross. She could have said, "He's teaching right now," which was obvious because they both could hear Élodie Cormier taking her piano lesson with Father Aucoin. But "he's not available" sounded more important, and Mrs. Cross felt you had to be clear with someone like Philibert.

Philibert said simply, "That's fine. I want an official appointment."

Mrs. Cross blinked. "An official appointment?" Excepting the bishop, she'd never really heard of such a thing. Father Aucoin just met with people when they asked. There was never anything official about it, but Philibert had cleverly realized her weakness for the proper social address and she was flustered enough to reply only, "I'll see what I can do" and closed the door.

Philibert walked home.

At ten o'clock on Tuesday, which was Father Aucoin's quietest day, Philibert had his "official" meeting.

The priest was sitting behind his desk in the study, a pile of papers in front of him and books stacked in every direction. Philibert had never seen so many books, and he found their presence a little intimidating. "Have you read all of them?" he couldn't help asking, gesturing toward the piles of books.

"Some of them twice."

"Twice?"

"You didn't come here to talk about books, Philibert," said Father Aucoin, who was never interested in wasting time.

"No, I didn't, but then maybe I did," and he smiled in that disarming way that had made him so many friends.

"You're interested in books?"

"Not much, but I would like it if Daniel Boudreau was."

"Why?"

"Because I would like him to go to university."

The priest raised his eyebrows in pure astonishment. Daniel was a Boudreau. The Boudreaus were neighbours of Philibert's noisy brood of girls, for which the priest had a very low regard. If they stayed out of boy trouble, the priest figured that was already their principal accomplishment, but fortunately he kept this thought to himself.

"Daniel is smart. He learned how to read before he went to school. I know because I helped Marie teach him."

"Really," said the priest.

"We taught him the alphabet and that was all he needed. Once he could make the sounds out, he taught himself the rest."

"Didn't he fail last year?"

Lines appeared on Philibert's forehead and he inhaled deeply. "He did but it wasn't his fault. He failed because," and

Philibert paused here, "because I am a bad example. I've been a bad example for my own girls and I have been for Marie's youngest. They see me promenading around with only grade 8 to my name and think they don't need to go to school."

The priest tried not to smile. Philibert lived in a house that did not have a scrap of paint on the outside and not much more on the inside. Everyone knew that Philibert, for all his fine talk, was poor. "Daniel needs a better example than he can get with me."

"What about his father?"

"His father is away a good deal working in the woods. His older brothers are supposed to take care of him, but they are too busy," said Philibert, stubbornly soldiering on with the reason that had brought him to the presbytery for an official meeting.

"For once we agree," said the priest smiling.

Philibert nodded as if they had both already reached some kind of entente. "I was hoping he could come here next year and work for you. You could give him a good example."

Father Aucoin did not respond. He was astonished. The priest leaned back in his chair and picked up a book. He did so to cover his confusion. It was the last thing in the world he had been expecting. "No, I don't think so," he said finally, quite sure that this was the only response possible.

"Why not? Daniel is a good boy, but he needs a little direction."

There was another long silence and Father Aucoin thought of all the deserving boys who might live next year at the presbytery, and then he thought of Daniel and it struck him as ridiculous, but again he kept this thought to himself. Instead he said, "I'll write to Father LeBlanc in Chéticamp. Sometimes he takes boys that I recommend to him."

Philibert shook his head. He knew the priest was going to suggest this and he replied with a voice that Father Aucoin didn't usually hear. It was very clear and very determined.

"If you take Daniel in the fall, I will provide a university scholarship—all the fees will be paid—for any worthy boy the parish chooses."

The priest put down the book he was holding and was even more astonished than he was before. "What lies are you telling now, Philibert?"

Philibert had been expecting this and passed his Credit Union savings book directly to the priest, who was forced to take it. Father Aucoin opened the little blue book gingerly as if it might bite him. To his surprise the withdrawals were far outnumbered by the deposits.

"But where did you get all this money? From matchmaking?"

"From matchmaking. From doing taxes. From buying and selling property. I receive a fee for all of that work."

"You buy and sell property?"

"I hear about a house or a piece of land for sale and then think of someone who might be interested in it. It's not that different from matchmaking. It's just matching property to the person."

"And people give you money for this?"

"They do and sometimes if the deal is particularly good, I buy and then sell the land myself."

The priest looked at the little blue book again. "But you're rich." And the priest's face was quite white, for he was not sure that the money had been acquired honestly.

"I don't know if I am rich, but I have enough money to pay for a scholarship, which is not a bad way to spend some money."

"No, it isn't," agreed the priest, nodding but still feeling baffled by this strange turn of events.

"No one needs to know the money comes from me. I would prefer that they didn't. You can set the scholarship selection up anyway that you want. Maybe one of those committees you're so fond of. I don't care. I will sign the cheque, that is all. All I want is to see...," and there was slight tick in his voice when he said it, "is that Marie's youngest has a chance to work at the presbytery with you."

The priest ran his fingers through his hair, which he only bothered to do when he was feeling considerable pressure. "Philibert, the boy will get no favours. He will have to do as Mrs. Cross tells him, split wood for the stove, pull weeds in the garden, assist me with early morning Mass and high Mass on Sunday, learn to read music, and do his homework without fail. It's not easy. Do you really think Daniel Boudreau is prepared to do all this?"

"We will find out," said Philibert grimly.

"I don't need to find out. I need to have a boy who will succeed. Failing won't be good for the boy or the reputation of the presbytery."

Now it was Philibert's turn to look pale. "Daniel will have no choice because his father and I will tell him before he goes that he can't come home until the year's up."

"You've talked this over with Marcel?" asked the priest surprised at the care with which Philibert seemed to have organized his proposal.

"I have."

There was another silence. This one stretched on for so long that Philibert began to think the priest had fallen asleep. His eyelids were almost shut and his chin sunk toward his chest. Finally, he looked up and said, "And how long would this scholarship last?"

"Four years," said Philibert.

"Would it be for boys and girls?"

"Set it up any way that you want."

"What happens if Daniel comes home after two weeks?"

This time the silence was all on Philibert's side of the desk. Finally he said, "A deal is a deal."

The news went round the parish like a gunshot. Marcel Boudreau's son had been chosen to be the next *domestique du prêtre*.

No one could quite believe it, least of all Daniel. He went directly to his father and said, "I won't go."

"You're going," said Marcel.

Daniel said, "I won't go," and he ran out of the house to Philibert and Zabine's.

It did no good. Philibert just shook his head and just said, "You're going."

The boy could not believe his ears. "Father Aucoin is a tyrant. Everyone knows that. I'll be working from sunrise to sunset every day of the week."

"For which you will receive payment. It's not much, but it will be something."

"I'll have no holidays. Sundays will be the worse day of all. I'll have two Masses before other boys are even out of bed. It's not fair."

"I promised you would go for one year."

"You spoke to him?"

"I did."

Daniel threw a fit. He fell on the floor and pounded his fists so loud that the drumming could be heard outside the house. He yelled. He screamed. He tore buttons off his shirt. Philibert's daughters tried to console him, then tried to intercede on his behalf with their parents, but the older generation—Marcel, Philibert, and Zabine—were all of one mind. Daniel was going to the presbytery.

If sullen had a face, it was the face of Daniel Boudreau when his father and Philibert dropped him off at the presbytery. Philibert was too tired from the fighting to even go in with him. He just knocked on the door and Mrs. Cross appeared and Marcel said very gravely, "Here is my son Daniel."

The two men shuffled the boy in front of them so he could not run. The boy stood there, his feet growing roots in the gravel, his fist clutching a small suitcase. The presbytery loomed above him. It was much bigger than his own little home. It had a big veranda that circled the front half of the house and an attic floor as well as a second.

The priest was working in his study when the boy went to see him. He was writing something very fast, so fast that the pen whirled, dancing across the page with such small letters that the boy did not know how anyone could read it.

"Will I be able to go home for Christmas?" asked the boy.

"It's not normally the practice because of the weather and the distance, but you are from our parish, so I don't see why not. You don't have far to go."

"After midnight Mass for the *réveillon*?"

"Yes, that would be fine."

The boy nodded.

"Mrs. Cross will give you a list of your house chores, and I will need you to serve Mass with me at the first Mass of the day. It is the Mass the old people like to attend and we cannot disappoint them. It is very quiet. I don't think you'll find it hard."

"I do not want to take piano lessons," said the boy, his face looking pinched.

The priest nodded and then said, "Do you hear that?"

"Someone practising," said Daniel, his face stubborn.

"It's a girl and one day she will be a fine pianist. When she started she knew less than you do now, or at least that's how Philibert tells it—which may be false, now that I think of it. But why do you want fail before you start?"

The boy did not respond.

"Do you know why you're here, Daniel?"

"Because my father spoke to you."

"No."

The priest did not say anything more, and the boy just sat there until the silence grew heavy.

"Why?" asked the boy. "Why am I here? I don't understand."

"Because you learned how to read before you went to school. All the boys who have stayed here have been different each from the other, but they all learned to read before they went to school. They all had that in common."

"My mother taught me," said the boy, his face now flushed and angry. "It's not my fault she taught me."

"It's not just that she taught you. You learned."

The priest stood and moved to the piano in the other room. The boy followed. "See that dot with the little flag? That's this," and he tapped out the sound. "Listen again. There's the sound. That's the dot and flag. Make the sound."

The boy did.

"What dot and flag represents that sound?"

The boy pointed to the correct note.

"You just read music," said the priest. "See? It's not hard. If you can read words, you can read sounds." And he dismissed the boy so that he could continue his lesson with Élodie Cormier.

The boy was not sure what he hated most—the priest, Mrs. Cross, or school, or the house, which excepting the kitchen was large and cold. He hated it all. At school, the teacher made him sit at the front instead of the back with his friends. He had to sit at the front and answer questions. The only thing he looked forward to was seeing his family at church on Sunday, but it was not like he had hoped. He had time only to steal a few glances in their direction, that was all.

One day before the snow fell, Mrs. Cross decided it was time to put the garden away for the winter, and he was obliged to follow her around pulling plants and shovelling dirt and listening to his friends who were putting up the boards for the hockey rink with their fathers. It was then that he decided he could not stand it any longer. He would go to Inverness and get a job as a coal boy driving the pit ponies. At least then he would earn some real money. And he quietly packed up his suitcase and let himself out of the side door and began to walk toward Inverness.

He walked fast and it wasn't long before he had left the village and saw the sign for Terre Noire, which was the next village. Then he heard the familiar clip-clopping of the priest's old horse behind him. He stopped.

"Where are you going, Daniel?" asked the priest as he pulled up beside him.

"To Inverness. I'm going to hire on as a coal boy and drive the pit ponies."

There was a silence and then the priest said, "Is life at the presbytery that bad?"

"Yes," was all the boy said.

There was another silence.

"What is the worst thing that you can think of?"

"Pulling weeds with Mrs. Cross."

"All the boys do garden work with Mrs. Cross. You have young backs."

"I have one afternoon off. One afternoon!" the boy repeated, and his voice vibrated. "And I spent it pulling weeds with Mrs. Cross. I don't think a job in the mines will be as bad, and I will get paid more."

"What if someone else was to pull the weeds with Mrs. Cross?"

"Who?"

"I will pull the weeds with Mrs. Cross."

"Why you? Why not the hired man?"

"The world is a big place." The priest stopped the horse and the boy stopped walking also. "You have scarcely started walking but already we are out of our little village, headed toward Inverness, and Inverness is only at the very end of the rail line. One day, you will get on the train and who knows where you will go? Perhaps Halifax, perhaps Boston, maybe you will go to university like your brother. Who knows?"

The boy looked up, astonished to hear the priest talking to him as if they were equals.

"Our little village is no more than a thumbprint on the sand, that is how big the world is, and the world is nothing in God's universe. My part of that thumbprint is the presbytery, but in the presbytery I am the boss and if the boss wishes to pull weeds with Mrs. Cross, then he pulls weeds, that's just the way it is. And if you choose to run away, I guess that's also just the way it is. I don't think God will mind." He nodded at the boy and said nothing more.

The boy stood at the side of the road, trying to understand what the priest had said. In the end, he could not make up his mind, but he climbed into the buggy to sit beside the priest. The priest slowly wheeled the horse around and they began to clip-clop homewards. Neither said anything.

At the presbytery, there was a message waiting for the priest. A baby girl had been born to the Burns family on the mountain. The parents wanted the girl baptized but were afraid to come to the church because the baby was coughing and feverish. The priest went into the house and got his thickest coat out and threw a blanket in the trunk, for the wind was turning bitter.

Mrs. Cross said quietly, "I think the boy should go too. It's safer with two, should anything happen."

The priest shook his head, but the boy began putting on his coat.

By the time the priest and the boy began the long climb up the mountain, the wind had become so fierce, the horse was forced to walk, and suddenly the horse stopped and tried to turn homewards, but the priest would not let him. When they crested the edge of the plateau to take the mountain road, the trees whipped and groaned about them. The wind slashed at the trees, pushing them so hard it was as if they were being torn from their roots. Suddenly a tree snapped with an explosion so loud it sounded like a canon had gone off beside them, and the horse bolted straight across the road into the rock face of the cliff. The horse went down on both knees as if it had been shot, and for a moment the boy thought he was dead. Then just as suddenly he heaved himself to his knees and then to his feet. Both forelegs began to tremble violently. One knee was cut and bleeding.

There was no relief in standing in the middle of the road with the wind howling and bending the trees like grass, but the horse would no longer move. He was frozen, just standing still, his legs shaking, his eyes wide and rolling in white terror.

The priest took the horse by the bridle and said to the boy, "We can't stay here, we must walk, otherwise the horse will die from fright."

The boy felt his own heart hammering and wondered if that was possible.

"You take one side like this, we must keep the horse's head sheltered between us."

The boy did as he was told and this is the way they proceeded, the priest on one side of the horse's head holding the bridle, shielding the horse from the sight of the violently swaying trees, which terrified the animal, and he on the other. Afterwards, he would sometimes wonder why they had not just turned back, but again he said nothing. He followed the priest as he turned up the mountain road, and they began to struggle up it until the boy could not remember how long they had been walking. All he thought about was putting one foot after the other.

At the beginning the horse limped and flinched from the wind in a way that frightened the boy because he did not think they were strong enough to hold the horse if he decided to bolt as he had before, but slowly the horse stopped shivering and settled down, lowering his head into the wind between the two of them, and in this way they pushed on silently as if their silence could somehow compensate for the roar of the storm.

When they arrived at the house, it was past midnight. Near the door, they could hear the baby crying. "Good," said the priest, "she is still alive. Can you put the horse in the barn?"

The boy nodded and they separated.

When the boy woke in the morning from a sleep so deep it felt as if he had been dead, the storm had passed. He wondered if the baby had died when he was sleeping, for he could not hear a sound but the crackle of the fire in the kitchen stove. The parents and the priest's eyes were sunken and their faces hollow. The baby was breathing with a strange, soft gurgle, but her fever had diminished and her breathing seemed easier.

When he went to the barn to fetch the horse the sun was glinting off the new snow sending thousands of shimmering lights back up to the sky, which was pale blue and so clear it looked as if you could fall off the mountain into it. He put some more liniment on the horse's torn knee and fashioned a bandage from some clean rags the man had given him. On the way back to the presbytery, the priest fell asleep and the boy took the reins.

CHAPTER 26

Father DeCoste Goes to Heaven

> *The death of Reverend J. A. DeCoste calls for more than a passing notice. The writer knew him as a college chum and can testify to the ability and character that made him an outstanding figure among his fellows. He had universal talent. He took early to Math and the Classics. He went further in his knowledge of Greek than any student of his time. French Acadian as he was, he surpassed everybody by taking the coveted prize in the difficult Shakespearian examinations.*
> —Moses Coady writing in the 1950s
> (J. A. DeCoste is the priest upon whom
> Father Aucoin of St. Joseph de la Mer is based.)

Stuck in the fly-leaf of my father's war diary, I found a one-page, typewritten letter. The page is still white. The print impressions from the typewriter hammers are still clear and dark. It looks like it's just been typed. It is a letter from Joseph Aloysius DeCoste, the parish priest of Grand Étang. The letter is filled with unalloyed happiness that the war has ended and the boys are coming home. Father DeCoste is sure the next generation will do better than ever and that the village will prosper. He is eager to see the young Doucet boy again. The boys will come home and they will make a difference.

Father DeCoste belonged to that extraordinary generation of Maritime clergy who were great social activists as well as devoted priests. Catholic priests like Jimmy Tompkins and Moses Coady, Protestant clergy like Sammy Prince and Leonard Hatfield coached and loved and sometimes bullied their parishioners to form credit unions, set up fishing co-operatives, libraries, and later pushed governments to build schools and low-cost housing. They wanted to change the world so that it was better for all. Today, they would be at the forefront of the Occupy movement.

The most accomplished of that extraordinary generation of Maritime priests would be hard to pick. I have my favourites. The tall, handsome, and graceful Anglican Leonard Hatfield, who welcomed my mother to Antigonish would be at the top of my list. So would the shorter and more intense Father DeCoste, who shepherded many village boys and girls through their school studies toward a successful provincial matriculation. If there is indeed such a thing as a saint, it's hard to see how both wouldn't qualify.

The best known of that extraordinary cohort was Moses Coady. Coady was a six-foot-four-inch giant with a boom of a voice and the wild grit that comes with the Highland Scot. He was born and grew up in a village just down the road from Grand Étang on the Scottish side of Margaree Harbour bridge. As it did for DeCoste and Hatfield, Nova Scotia remained Coady's home; nonetheless his life played out on a wider stage. He earned a doctorate in Rome and later wrote *Master of Their Own Destiny*, which became a handbook for local economic justice based in the co-operative movement.

Coady dedicated his life and talents to preach and teach a more humane form of capitalism, one where the profits were controlled by the community and stayed in the community.

He preached at United Nations conferences, church basements, and taught at the adult education outreach service of St. Francis Xavier University, a service that now bears his name: the Coady International Institute.

Teachers from "The Coady" have helped spread the idea of co-operative community enterprise and microcredit all the way to Asia, where it has taken strong root in distant places like Bangladesh. A Bangladesh proponent of community microcredit was recently recognized with a Nobel prize.

Joseph DeCoste lived on a much smaller stage, where his days were filled with music and preaching, praying and community projects. During the Depression, DeCoste's brother, a doctor in Boston, gave him some money with the strict instructions it was to be used to buy a car. The money was to not be used for anything else.

Father DeCoste decided the graveyard needed a fence around it and organized a large work party, using up all his car money to pay the wages of the men who built the fence. He wrote apologizing to his brother, explaining, "How can I spend money on myself when so many of my parishioners have so little?"

Suddenly without ever knowing why, he could not do what he used to do with ease—play the organ, lead the liturgy, tutor students, garden. It all crumbled in his hands. In the middle of Mass, he stopped and simply said, "I'm sorry. I can't do this anymore." He faced his own end with a calm serenity, but there was such sadness in the community that some people suggested they approach the bishop to talk about canonization. Father DeCoste got wind of this and became greatly agitated. He insisted that no such thing ever be done. He died without a penny at the age of sixty-seven.

Dr. Coady lived longer than his school chum but ended his days without the comfort of a peaceful state of mind. He was not optimistic for the future of co-operative capitalism.

He feared his life's work had been for naught and that all would be washed away in a coming tidal wave of consumerism and corporate gigantism.

It is curious. Father DeCoste spent his whole life being nothing more than a parish priest in a remote village. He had no ambitions except the welfare of his parish. In fact, he was careful to make sure he was not appointed to anything important, not even the board of a village co-operative. Moses Coady was famous. He was not.

It's hard to argue against Moses Coady's disappointment, because as usual he was right. The world was turning toward the consumer model of society we have today. "Can you get it cheaper?" is today's constant refrain. And as he predicted, the vibrant Atlantic co-op movement has suffered a long slow decline, with much of it today being swallowed up by the Sobey's supply chain.

There are always beginnings and endings. Our sun is in middle age. It is about halfway on its own cycle from birth to death. It began about 4.6 billion years ago, and 4.6 billion years on it will expand into a giant red star and then explode, streaming star dust out into our galaxy. That energy will then begin to coalesce to begin life again somewhere. We are all stardust. Our own smallness is unimaginable in this immense cycle of life. The sun, so crucial to every moment of our existence, is only one star among millions of others in our own small galaxy, and our galaxy is only one in millions of others.

The universe is filled with confusing spirals, circles, ellipses. Life isn't a train track. It's more like the confusing, intersecting, overlapping ellipses that a child's spinning top makes on the floor as it spins. Each revolution of the child's spinning top carves a circle or ellipse on the floor, each one slightly different from the last. If our spinning planet left vapour trails in the sky behind it as it turns through space and around the sun, it would leave marks similar to those the child's spinning top makes on the floor.

Dr. Coady's life pushed his generation microscopically in a direction it would not have gone otherwise. But the line his life left on the floor is easily confused with other intersecting lines that other spinning tops have made with their own lives. He correctly anticipated the coming age of corporate greed would derail his own ambitions, but in the spinning top model of change, all this greed is just another tiny blip. Wall Street towers are products of a conquest philosophy just as Assyrian temples were products of Assyrian conquest philosophies. Nor is there much difference between the motivations of Assyrian kings and Wall Street masters of the universe, except it's not likely Wall Street will endure as long as Assyria.

The thing is, there are no masters of the universe. Life is a collective adventure. We don't go through it alone. We need and depend on others, and others need and depend on us. It is in the changing nature of that dependency that hope can be found, and the nature of our relations with others is driven by philosophy, not money.

Philosophy is more important than Assyrian kings or Wall Street billionaires. Philosophy imagined the atom before it was seen, conceived of cave paintings before they were painted, has organized the rule of law, the life of cities, written poems. Philosophy matters.

I suspect that's why Father DeCoste died so easily. His life was about faith, compassion, and hope in its rawest, most elemental form, teacher to student, person to person. When the village Co-op needed money to get started, he cashed in his life insurance policy and funded the start himself. Father DeCoste was on the side of the only revolution that can assure continuity for our species—people caring about each other.

As far as science can tell there are at least two implacable forces in the universe: gravity, which tethers us safely to our planet, and the counter forces that protect us from gravity's crush and allow physical life. Zoroaster, an Iranian sage, was the first modern prophet who preached a dualist world.

We see this same fundamental conflict today expressed in popular films like *Star Wars* and books like the Harry Potter series. The language and images are different, but the essential division remains the same. The powers of Yoda and Obi-Wan Kenobi are about compassion, creativity, and hope. The powers of Lord Voldemort and Darth Vader are about control and cruel compression.

Father DeCoste died long before *Star Wars* or Harry Potter ever appeared on the horizon, but he would have been in Harry Potter's camp, for he was firmly allied on the side of love, compassion, and creativity. In that vision of the universe, he was going to heaven after doing all he could do to create it here. His expectations of heaven were thus entirely aligned with his life.

CHAPTER 27

On Hope

*We are born old and young
at the same time.
We are born with great loves
and great pains
that we grow into like an acorn
grows into an oak tree,
like God grows into the universe.*

For twelve years I began my community newspaper columns with a poem like the one above. City politics are often tough stuff. At best, people want more than you can deliver and often get less than they should, so news in the city councillor's community newspaper column is never quite what you would want. A poem was my way of beginning with hope.

Hope is what makes us human. It is as natural to the human spirit as appetite is to the body. It has sustained human beings in the most execrable conditions—in prison, in slavery, in war, in illness—and in the most exalted of religious and political ambitions. It is a multitudinous, complex engagement. Hope is in the mother's watchful eye. It is in children when they trudge off to school to learn. It is in citizens when they think and talk about whom they would like to represent them in Parliament and at city hall. Hope infuses the athlete when she strains to finish faster, further. Hope catches the artist when he picks up his paintbrush. It is in the scientist when she contemplates the same problem that she thought about yesterday and the week before, the month before, the year before, yet still looking forward to finding a solution.

Nonetheless, the corroding reality of the twenty-first century is that any sustained reflection on the impending catastrophe of climate change cannot help but damage this natural ebullience of the human spirit, simply because of the speed and comprehensiveness of this great peril advancing toward us.

Three days is not much time. In a crisis, three days is how much food cities have on hand to feed their populace. For me, three days is a metaphor for how much time humanity has to start thinking and acting differently. Yet we behave as if we have decades to change our ways. The more that I have written and thought about cities and this climate threat, the more it has forced me to reflect on hope, because hope is the foundation of continuity for all of us. Without it, life is not possible. We must have hope. As my old buddy Jack Layton said so succinctly in his final letter to Canadians, "Hope is better than despair."

So where can we find hope in these times?

Life is the great astonishment. Each of us is connected to at least four billion years of evolution. In each of us, there resides a small part of the long history of our planet, and in each of us lie the many amazing possibilities for the future. I have tried to respect that heritage and think of the future by working in very simple, practical ways for more sustainable cities. In this belief, I have tried to express the destiny of my own soul and feel a connection to friends and neighbours.

A bright age ahead is not only possible. It is attainable. Right now, Germany produces 50 percent of its energy from renewable sources. If we had the same amount of renewable energy from sun, wind, and water in Canada, we could power the entire country in a sustainable way.

As my old mentor Jane Jacobs predicted, a bright age ahead or a dark age ahead are both possible, but it's up to us. It's always been up to us. Human society is not like a lake or a mountain. We humans are the authors of our villages and cities. We create them and un-create them. Succeed or don't with them.

When I look around our little village, I see myself surrounded by hope. The Mi-Carême Centre, the GAMS Cooperative marine research station, Russell Daigle's garden—these are all about people who have not given up, who in their elder years continue to work for a fairer, more secure, more exciting world. They inspire me.

CHAPTER 28

A Safe Harbour

In the end, our safe harbour is the planet. The place where we most belong and the place we need the most. This is what I feel every time I walk outside and see the night sky arcing above. I have built my house on the edge of the sea in my father's village because it is the place where I feel most part of that larger safe harbour. I would say this to the French academics if I met them again.

I would also talk about Russ Daigle and Monique Aucoin, Barbara LeBlanc, Ron Caplan, and Gretchen Noyes-Hull. They are magical and wonderful, which shouldn't surprise for there is much magic and wonder in the world. Water is magical. All of our science hasn't been able to figure out where it comes from or why or how its molecules form and reform. In the Old Testament water preceded the arrival of God. God needed water to make life. Water is as mysterious as the idea of God. Love is another mystery. We will die for those we love and yet sometimes people commit horrible crimes in the name of that same emotion. We are surrounded with mysteries. The best sparkle and laugh and fill us with curious joy. Many of them we invent ourselves.

I belong to the very last school generation to be educated when Latin still played an important role in the syllabus. Not long ago, this was considered entirely normal. My father studied Latin all the way to the university level and could sight-read Virgil, and not so long ago we heard the Mass declaimed in Latin as it had been for two thousand years, repeating the words faithfully ourselves.

I remember the morning my own Latin education began as clearly as if it were yesterday. I was in grade 5 in St. John's, Newfoundland, when my first ink-stained Latin grammar arrived on my desk. I opened the innocuous little book and peered into the tables of long, complicated declensions of Latin verbs and thought with excitement, "Ah, finally, I've grown up," my thought being that anyone could read English but only the educated could read Latin.

Today, I can barely remember enough to read a Roman gravestone, but what I haven't forgotten are the little pictures that appeared as illustrations at the start of each chapter in my high school grammar. The illustrations were just simple black-and-white sketches of ordinary Roman life: market scenes; a baker at work; a sketch of Pulia and her brother Marcus playing a board game; another of Pulia being read to by her mother as they sat comfortably beside an impluvium (a small indoor pool). There is nothing of this complex, urban life left today but ruins. Even the language is gone, but from the moment I opened that grade 5 Latin grammar I began to understand that life was malleable, that everything I took for granted could change. The world of Pulia and Marcus, which was once as confident and encompassing as our own, had entirely disappeared.

Nor does it need centuries to change. I have watched the city of Ottawa change from a small city of tight little neighbourhoods built around streetcar lines to a vast sprawl of six-lane roads, malls, and tract housing. Geographically, it is now the largest city in Canada. The moment that vast change began is printed in my memory as clearly as the day I opened my first Latin grammar.

In the autumn of 1960, my Ottawa classroom overlooked the city's principal crosstown rail line, which as I sat in the class was being torn up and replaced with an east/west expressway. This project would transform the city forever, changing it from a streetcar- and pedestrian-based series of neighbourhoods to a car-based universe. In the same year, the city began to build the crosstown expressway; it began to rip up three hundred kilometres of streetcar lines and convert entirely to buses. No one had any idea of the significance of these events, the environmental and sustainability disasters. It was considered progress.

The electric streetcars had been powered by hydro power from the river. This power was as sustainable as the earth turning. The buses and expressways would depend entirely on the internal combustion engines powered by oil imported from thousands of miles away. I'm a grandfather and lived these changes so they seem self-evident, but some of the changes since my boyhood are subtle enough that they are hard to describe to anyone. But they are as important as the loss of the city streetcar systems across North America. Jane Jacobs describes these changes in the character of society in her last book, *Dark Age Ahead*. I see the same things she does but would explain them with a simple Maritime story.

When I was a boy, Robert Stanfield, the Progressive Conservative premier of Nova Scotia and later the federal Progressive Conservative leader, would visit my grandfather's house during his provincial election campaigns. It was a smart move because Grandfather had ten children and was known as a pillar of the parish. Grandfather would greet him at the door with a smile and say straight up, "I'm not sure I'm worth your time, Mr. Stanfield. I'm a Liberal."

And Mr. Stanfield would reply, "Mr. Doucet, you let me decide what's worth my time." Then both men laughed and shared a cup of tea together, which is the Cape Breton way of welcoming guests. Mr. Stanfield didn't speak enough French to converse easily, and they soon switched to English. Nonetheless, he was respectful of the Acadian community and had taken the time to learn about the history of even a little village like Grand Étang.

He knew that my grandfather's uncle, Moses Doucet, had been a Progressive Conservative MPP and joked with Grandfather that it was time Inverness County had another one, which wasn't a welcome thought for Grandfather, who was a dyed-in-the-wool Liberal. As family patriarch, he preferred to think it was not possible for any Doucet to vote any way but his way. Nonetheless, Mr. Stanfield's welcome was genuine, and to Grandfather's chagrin some of his sons did switch their vote to support Mr. Stanfield's side of the house. This was a scandal that endured for many years.

What strikes me now is not my grandfather's chagrin at his sons deciding to vote for Mr. Stanfield. It is the civility of the story. Elections are always fiercely fought, but there was a respect for the other side that seems to have entirely disappeared from the public discourse. The very quality of patriotism seems to have melted into something harsher, nastier.

Canada now has a beautiful flag, which all politicians love to be photographed standing near, but no matter how beautiful, a flag is only a shorthand symbol for a nation's character. It is the stories that we hear from our families and the stories we create with our own lives that give the flag's red-and-white metaphor its meaning. My father's generation didn't even have a national flag, but their idea of the nation was deeply rooted and expressed clearly in the conduct of their own lives.

For the boys that went off to the Second World War, Canada was simply a grander version of the town or city neighbourhood where they had grown up. Whether it was the Beaches in Toronto, the North End in Winnipeg, or Grand Étang in Nova Scotia, being Canadian meant you said what you meant and meant what you said, took elections seriously, and were considerate of your neighbours. Those were basement values and when the boys came home from the war, they set about electing governments that would create public services that people needed. As soldiers they had had public health care and they didn't see why others shouldn't have it. No one should be bankrupted because they had the misfortune to be ill.

Their generation invented co-op housing for those on limited incomes. There was a vast expansion of national parks, new public universities were built, and public broadcasting was expanded. French immersion schools were invented and went from coast to coast; the English part of Canada especially became much more accomplished linguistically. The differences between the rich and poor flattened. People shared more. Between 1946 and 1975, all the core institutional elements that have come to be thought of as modern Canada were created or greatly expanded.

This was the context of my youth. This was the context of my national safe harbour.

All governments like to commemorate battles fought by Canadian soldiers, but equally important was what they accomplished after the war—a compassionate, responsive, civil nation that was a reflection of their own communities and lives. At university, Fern was part of a veteran's study group that helped those veterans succeed who were having trouble navigating a subject. University wasn't about dividing winners from losers. It was about learning new things to take everyone forward. They did not want anyone left behind.

After 1975, successive governments have steadily cut away at all these government programs and policies. Not surprisingly, wealth has steadily concentrated into what is now called the 1 percent. Not surprisingly, people no longer have the same confidence in public purpose, because it doesn't benefit all equally.

You cannot see the values my parents had. They are as inscrutable as the atom, but like the movements of invisible particles they have great power. Those values helped create the culture, economy, and the compassionate philosophy upon which a fine, modern nation was built. To remember all this is to have hope, for what you can remember, you can keep.

Epilogue

When I awake in the morning, lobster fishermen are setting their traps. They buzz about on the surface of the water just a few metres off my shore, busy dropping their traps in favourite spots; they will return again in the afternoon to pull them. The curious and very tasty lobster is still bountiful, and throughout the spring harvest season the little harbour is alive with fishermen with their boats and trucks coming for the lobster from all over the island. I never tire of seeing the fishing boats skid about on the ocean surface like large water bugs chasing members of the lobster tribe.

There is something reassuring about all this. During the last great glacial period, small groups of hominids survived living in caves along the South African and Mediterranean coasts. Midden heaps have been found around their cave entrances, piled high with mussel shells. Shellfish have helped our species survive for a long time. They still do.

If I could do the interview with the French academics again, I would not stumble. I would say, "I have built a house in hayfield out of love—love for many things, for my family, my country—and hope for the future, believing that the future must have some roots in the past."

I would also count my blessings in an old-fashioned way. It is a great thing to have your family in good health and good spirits, which Patty, our children, and grandchildren all are.

Felix understands. He said this summer, "When I'm grown up I'm going to bring my children. No! My grandchildren!" Felix is only ten and already has a wicked sense of humour, but if he ever does bring his grandchildren it will be for the same reasons I built the house, and how can that be foolish?

To look forward with hope is a wonderful thing and that's what I am doing now. I will take another crack at running for mayor, I will not give up. And no matter what, my house by the sea will stand as a testament to that.

Clive Doucet
Grand Étang, Nova Scotia